The Clock of Vipassana Has Struck

The Clock of Vipassana Has Struck

The Teachings and Writings of Sayagyi U Ba Khin
with Commentary by S.N. Goenka

Compiled and edited by Pierluigi Confalonieri

VIPASSANA RESEARCH PUBLICATIONS
P.O. BOX 15926
SEATTLE, WASHINGTON, 98115
WWW.VRPA.COM

First published in Italy in 1993 by Ubaldini Editore, Rome, entitled *Il Tempo della Meditazione Vipassana é Arrivato.*

First United States Edition 1999

ISBN 0-9649484-6-X

Library of Congress Catalog Number 99-67273

Publisher's Catloging-in-Publication Data
(provided by Quality Books, Inc.)

Ba Khin, U., 1889-1971
    The clock of Vipassana has struck : the teachings
and writings of Sayagyi U Ba Khin / with
commentary by S.N. Goenka ; compiled and edited
by Pierluigi Confalonieri. — 1st United States ed.
    p. cm.
    Includes bibliographical references.
    LCCN: 99-67273
    ISBN: 0-9649484-6-X

    1. Vipaśyanā (Buddhism) 2. Meditation—
Buddhism. 3. Buddhism—Doctrines. 4. Ba Khin,
U., 1889-1971. I. Goenka, S.N. 1924-
II. Confalonieri, Pierluigi. III. Title

BQ5630.V5B3 1999   294.3'443
          QBI99-1544

Dedication

I dedicate this collection to the teacher S.N. Goenka, living testimony of love, compassion and dedication to spreading the universal truths of the Dhamma through teaching the technique of Vipassana meditation in the tradition of Sayagyi U Ba Khin. To him goes the merit of having inspired in me—with his enthusiasm and great feeling of gratitude toward his teacher Sayagyi U Ba Khin—the wish to develop this quality of gratefulness myself and to make this great human being known to others. As a man and as a teacher, U Ba Khin made an immense contribution to the dissemination of the technique of Vipassana meditation, the essence of the Buddha's teachings. The merit of S.N. Goenka lies not only in having related to us numerous episodes from the life of his teacher Sayagyi U Ba Khin and having explained his teachings in a simple and comprehensible manner, accompanying us throughout this book with answers and clarifications, but above all for continuing to spread throughout the world the seed of actual practice that U Ba Khin has planted.

Pierluigi Confalonieri, Editor

Contents

PART THREE
The Practice of Meditation

Publisher's Preface

The Clock of Vipassana Has Struck first appeared in Italian, entitled *Il Tempo della Meditazione Vipassana é Arrivato*. It was published in Italy in 1993 by Ubaldini Editore, Rome. Pierluigi Confalonieri, who compiled and edited the material, is a longtime student of Vipassana who was appointed assistant teacher by S.N. Goenka in 1994. He is also the translator and author of two other books on Vipassana. *L'Arte di Vivere* (Biblioteca Universale Rizzoli, 1990) is the Italian translation of the *Art of Living*, by William Hart; and *La Saggezza che Libera* (Arnoldo Mondadori Editore, 1995) focuses on some of the important *suttas* of the Buddha.

The writings and discourses of Sayagyi U Ba Khin were originally all in English, as was the interview with Goenkaji that Mr. Confalonieri conducted for this book. So with this edition of *The Clock of Vipassana Has Struck* we are returning the majority of the text to the original language, and translating to English the portions written by Mr. Confalonieri.

During U Ba Khin's lifetime his country, Myanmar, was known as Burma. Throughout this book, in historical material from articles published before the name change, the nation is referred to as Burma. At times the adjective form "Burmese" will also be used to refer to the language and the people of Myanmar.

Acknowledgments

The material in this compilation is primarily derived from the *Sayagyi U Ba Khin Journal*, a commemorative edition produced by the Vipassana Research Institute (VRI) in 1994. We are grateful for all the work done by so many people in writing, editing, proofreading and publishing that incomparable source. Additional material is from the *Vipassana Journal*, 1983; selected questions and answers from various interviews given by S.N. Goenka; and other articles published by VRI.

The editor also gratefully acknowledges the inspiration derived from: William Hart, *The Art of Living* (Harper San Francisco, 1987); Amadeo Solé-Leris, *Tranquillity and Insight* (BPS, 1992); Eric Lerner, *Journey of Insight Meditation* (Schocken Books, 1977); and the interview by Stephan Bodian that appeared in the Yoga Journal (Sept./Oct. 1988, No. 88).

The publishers of this English edition wish to thank Dr. Winston King for permission to use his reminiscence from *A Thousand Lives Away: Buddhism in Contemporary Burma* (Asian Humanities Press, 1964) and to gratefully acknowledge the organization and editing done by Shoshana Alexander and the translation work done by Eleanora Angelini.

Editor's Preface

My approach is essentially practical, not theoretical. Vipassana meditation is so subtle and delicate that the less you talk about it, the more you can obtain good results.

—Sayagyi U Ba Khin

Nearly three decades have elapsed since the death of the great meditation teacher, Sayagyi[†] U Ba Khin, from Myanmar (formerly Burma). U Ba Khin, whose life spanned the first seventy years of this century, was one of the outstanding figures of his time. His accomplishments, in two usually incompatible fields, were singular: he was a master meditation student and teacher as well as a government official of tireless devotion and impeccable conduct. His service to the country of Myanmar was noteworthy, but his example to the citizens of the world is no less remarkable; for in a time of increasingly complex global crises, his life demonstrates a simple, powerful truth—that an individual of pure mind exerts a positive, corrective influence on society. U Ba Khin's career was that of an ideal householder, combining unwavering dedication to Dhamma (the truth, the teaching) with unwearying commitment to public service.

Before he died on January 19, 1971, U Ba Khin was able to realize one of his most cherished dreams. He saw the ancient meditation technique of Vipassana, which had been preserved in his country for over two thousand years, returned to India, its land of origin. It was returned to its birthplace by U Ba Khin's devoted student,

---

[†]*Sayagyi* is a title in the Burmese language, meaning "respected teacher."

S.N. Goenka. For the past two millennia, the sublime practice of Vipassana—the heart of the teaching of the Buddha—had been the province of only a small number of meditator monks and house-holders in a few Asian countries. Today, thousands of seekers have had the opportunity to receive the teaching and experience its benefits. These people come from scores of different countries, Eastern and Western, representing all religions, creeds, castes and communities.

Because of the pressing demands on his time, Sayagyi confined his teaching to a relatively small number of students who came to his meditation center in Yangon (formerly known as Rangoon). Now, in 1999, there are over fifty international centers—twenty-five in India, the remainder in fifteen other countries—which offer the technique of Vipassana taught by Sayagyi U Ba Khin, and carried on by his student, S.N. Goenka. (See the list of contact addresses at the end of this book.) In his teaching S.N. Goenka has always placed primary emphasis on the actual practice of Dhamma—what is called, in Pāli, the language of the Buddha, *patipatti*. It is only through practice that one can have the direct experience which will take one to the final goal of freedom from all suffering. In this approach, Goenkaji follows the example of his teacher, who always insisted that Dhamma must be applied if it is to have real meaning.

However, there is another important aspect of Dhamma: *pariyatti*—understanding at the theoretical, intellectual level. This is helpful to inspire one to undertake the actual practice of meditation, and to elucidate questions that may arise while one is practicing. Unfortunately, the amount of material in English which can provide a suitable theoretical foundation for a student of Vipassana has not kept pace with the growth in the availability of the practice of Dhamma. This collection of historical and theoretical research has been compiled to respond to this need and to shed light on various aspects of Vipassana meditation.

The Clock of Vipassana Has Struck is a tribute to Sayagyi U Ba Khin and, indeed, its contents are an outgrowth of his life's work. This collection is offered primarily to inspire the practice of

Dhamma, for those who have taken courses as well as those who have no experience in Vipassana meditation. It should not, however, be used as a teaching manual for the technique. Attending a ten-day course under the careful guidance of a qualified, authorized teacher is essential to properly establish oneself in the practice of Vipassana. Those who feel inspired by reading this book to try the technique of Vipassana as taught by S.N. Goenka in the tradition of Sayagyi U Ba Khin can refer to the list of Vipassana centers at the end.

All of the work of Sayagyi and Goenkaji, all the present worldwide Dhamma activity, has only one purpose: to help people find the way out of suffering. The technique which provides this path was lost in India, and unknown in most of the rest of the world for many centuries. It is now available once again. Sayagyi believed in the ancient prophecy that 2,500 years after the time of the Buddha, Dhamma would arise anew and spread around the world. This belief is being verified. As he used to say, "The clock of Vipassana has struck."

Since the practice of Vipassana meditation is the essence of the Buddha's teachings and the most important contribution of U Ba Khin, with this collection we wish to accomplish two goals:

1) To describe the life and personality of U Ba Khin, as a man and as a teacher of meditation, by narrating episodes of his life and reminiscences from people who met him and to underline the importance of his contribution to the dissemination of this technique.

2) To delineate the essential characteristics of the practice of this technique of meditation by presenting U Ba Khin's writings, along with commentaries thereon.

The first part of the book recounts the most important details and some significant episodes from U Ba Khin's life, as narrated primarily by S.N. Goenka, his disciple, and the Vipassana Research Institute (located adjacent to Dhammagiri, the meditation center in Igatpuri, India).

The second part of the book introduces Sayagyi's writings and includes an important section of questions and answers with S.N. Goenka, explaining the essential principles of the technique taught by him and his teacher.

The third part describes in detail how Vipassana meditation courses are organized, outlines how the technique is taught and gives information about where it is possible to learn it.

The book ends with a simple glossary of the most important *Pāli* words related to the practice of Vipassana.

A Note on the Use of Pāli

Pāli is the language in which the Buddha taught and in which his teachings (the Dhamma) have been preserved. As with Sanskrit and Latin, Pāli is not a contemporary spoken language but a so-called "dead language" that has been preserved and used as a monastic language, studied in the countries of the oldest *theravāda*[†] tradition, serving in this way to translate and explain a tradition that is still alive.

Pāli is unique in many ways. One of the meanings of the word *pāli* is "line" or "norm," and in this sense it is applicable to the language of the canonical or "normative" texts. Other basic meanings of the word *pāli* are: "series" or "sacred text." These definitions refer directly to the "lines" of verse and the "series" of texts of various lengths that make up the canonical text of the Pāli literature. Another meaning is "that which protects or preserves." Pāli preserves the words of the enlightened person, Gotama the Buddha. According to tradition, by expressing the sublime teaching which allows beings to be liberated from the rounds of suffering, Pāli also protects the people; it preserves the invaluable treasure of the Buddha's own words. Adherence to the language of the Buddha

---

[†] *theravāda*: literally, "teaching of the elders." The teachings of the Buddha as they have been preserved in the countries of South and Southeast Asia (Myanmar, Laos, Cambodia, Sri Lanka, Thailand), generally recognized as the oldest, most direct transmission of the Buddha's teaching extant today.

has been a profoundly significant part of the living tradition of teachings transmitted from generation to generation.

The question arises: if the Dhamma is universal, if it is the law of universal nature, non-sectarian and relevant to people from different nationalities and backgrounds, why then is Pāli used to transmit the teachings? The answer lies in the nature of language itself and of this particular language.

No language, no matter how rich it may be, can adequately convey the sophisticated, complete technical terminology with which the Buddha expressed himself in describing the different experiences of meditation. There are no equivalents for these concepts in other languages; words that attempt to be equivalents will only be approximations.

For example, the word "Dhamma" is a term which encompasses a wide spectrum and depth of meaning. It means the truth, the teaching, the law of nature. It also refers to the characteristics, or nature, of everything manifest in the world; hence it means "phenomenon," and "object of mind." To attempt to render such a term into an equivalent would not do justice to the depth of its meaning. The same is true of many words used by the Buddha to explain extremely subtle concepts.

For this reason in this book we convey the most important concepts of the teachings in their original language, explaining them by the context in which they are used. The glossary at the end of the book provides further assistance. At times we have translated the Pāli words with expressions that emphasize their meaning in light of the actual experience of meditation. The Pāli words spoken by the Buddha were always derived exclusively from the truth that he had realized by direct experience through meditation.

S.N. Goenka paying respects to his teacher, Sayagyi U Ba Khin. This photograph was taken in the 1960s, prior to Mr. Goenka's departure from Myanmar.

Introduction

Gratitude to Sayagyi

—S.N. Goenka
January 19, 1981

Most Revered Dhamma Teacher!

It is now ten years since you passed away, but your inspirational presence is still being felt. My heart fills with gratitude towards you, my magnanimous teacher, who most compassionately, most lovingly and affectionately bestowed upon me this invaluable Dhamma-jewel. If I had not received this Dhamma-jewel, what would my plight have been? I would have wasted this life in the pursuit of earning and hoarding wealth, and in the rat race for status. You nurtured the seed of Dhamma within me. If you had not, then I would have been content to remain bound in sectarian fetters, mistaking them for ornaments. I would have passed my life taking pride in the experiences of others rather than my own. Where would I have obtained this real and direct experience of the truth? I would have contented myself with the mental projections of imagination. Where would I have had this *yathābhuta ñāṇadassana* (wisdom of the direct experience of the truth as it is)? I would have wasted my life taking intellectual knowledge as true wisdom. I would have squandered this invaluable human life by performing rites, rituals and recitations, and in getting conditioned by non-experiential, sectarian philosophies. My peerless Dhamma teacher! You have made my human life truly successful and worthwhile by bestowing the gift of this unrivalled, incomparable Dhamma upon me.

Verily, unrivalled and incomparable is the practice of Dhamma. How easy! How clear! How scientific! How beneficial! Leading from bondage to freedom, from delusions and mirages to the reality, from the apparent truth to the ultimate truth—may this invaluable jewel remain in its unblemished purity!

I solemnly make these meritorious resolutions on this auspicious day, the anniversary of your demise:

May I not commit the monumental sin of adulterating the teaching. May this invaluable technique remain in its flawless purity. May its practice open the door of deathlessness and salvation for one and all. Fulfilling these resolutions is the only way to respect, honor and revere you.

Sayagyi U Ba Khin: A Shining Star of Dhamma

—S.N. Goenka

Sayagyi U Ba Khin was one of the foremost teachers of Vipassana of our time—a source of inspiration to many, including myself. One of his unique contributions was that he gave much attention to foreigners and non-Buddhists in his teaching. Sayagyi's predecessors were Saya Thetgyi and Ledi Sayadaw. The other disciples of these teachers who were teaching Vipassana in this tradition used only the Burmese language for the most part and so had only Burmese students. Sayagyi, however, spoke fluent English and was able to explain Dhamma in English in a way that Buddhists and non-Buddhists, Burmese and non-Burmese alike could grasp and appreciate.

Sayagyi's way was not the way of scholars. Every word that he spoke came from his own experience. Therefore his teachings have the life of experience within them, and this is why every word said by him was very powerful and encouraging to his students. He wrote little, and he spoke little, but still, many students were benefited by his teaching. He was engaged in government responsibilities until the age of sixty-seven and had very little time to spare for the teaching of Dhamma. Therefore, he took a vow:

"May only ripened people with very good *pāramīs* (virtues) from the past come to me to take Dhamma, and may these people later take the torch of Dhamma, and spread it 'round the world."

He used to recite a Pāli verse:

> By virtue of this meritorious action
>   may I not come into contact with the ignorant.
> May I encounter only wise, saintly people
>   until I attain *nibbāna.*

Sayagyi could not work with the masses; he was working to serve a few individuals for whom he could spare more time. One time when he came to my home, I was chanting and at the end I recited this verse. Sayagyi smilingly admonished me, saying, "These words are not for you! You are to give seeds of Dhamma to a very large number of people. If you take this vow, how will Dhamma spread? This vow is for me because I have little time, and I am just on the border of 2,500 years after the Buddha when Dhamma has to start spreading. You are getting Dhamma at the time when the new era has started. So you have to work vigorously. You have to spread the seeds of Dhamma to large numbers of people. So don't recite this!"

Besides being an ideal government executive with outstanding ability and integrity, he was a very human teacher of the noble path. He taught with immeasurable love and compassion in spite of his insistence on strict discipline. He gave equally compassionate attention to the ex-president of Burma (Myanmar) and a peasant, to a judge of the Supreme Court and a criminal. Such was U Ba Khin, a jewel amongst men. Such was my noble teacher who taught me the art of a sane life.

He has chosen me to plant seeds of Dhamma around the world. Comparing my capacity with his, I feel very humble. And this makes me all the more confident that it is Dhamma that is working—not simply some individual. I have been chosen by my teacher as a vehicle for the Dhamma. And by helping to carry out his mission, I receive the benefits of developing my own *pāramīs*. With this understanding, I continue to work. And in the same way, you of the next generation have the responsibility—the wonderful opportunity—of carrying on the work.

It is his mission. It is Dhamma's work. He will keep on shining as a brilliant star in the galaxy of teachers from Buddha to the present and into the future. Sayagyi was looking forward to the second *sāsana* (era of the Buddha's teaching), when the Dhamma would help people throughout the world. May his wishes be fulfilled.

May more and more suffering people around the world come into contact with Dhamma, especially now, when throughout the world there is so much misery, so much conflict, so many tensions. May more and more people come into contact with Vipassana.

PART ONE

Sayagyi U Ba Khin:
The Man and the Teacher

Chapter One

The Life of Sayagyi U Ba Khin: The Man and the Teacher

A person like Sayagyi will never die. You may not see him, but his teachings live on.
— Ven. Webu Sayadaw

Sayagyi U Ba Khin was born in Yangon, the capital of Myanmar on March 6, 1899. He was the younger of two children in a family of modest means living in a working class district. Myanmar was ruled by Britain at the time, as it was until after the Second World War. Learning English was therefore very important. In fact, job advancement depended upon having a good speaking knowledge of English.

Fortunately, an elderly man from a nearby factory assisted U Ba Khin in entering the Methodist Middle School at the age of eight. He proved to be a gifted student. He had the ability to commit his lessons to memory, learning his English grammar book by heart from cover to cover. He was first in every class and earned a middle school scholarship. A Burmese teacher helped him gain entrance to St. Paul's Institution, where every year he was again at the head of his high school class. In March of 1917, he passed the final high school examination, winning a gold medal as well as a college scholarship. But family pressures forced him to discontinue his formal education to start earning money.

His first job was with a Burmese newspaper called "The Sun," but after some time he began working as an accounts clerk in the office of the Accountant General of Burma. Few other Burmese were employed in this office since most of the civil servants in Myanmar at the time were British or Indian. In 1926 Sayagyi passed the Accounts Service examination, given by the provincial government of India. In 1937, when Myanmar was separated from India, he was appointed the first Special Office Superintendent.

Sayagyi's government service continued for another twenty-six years. He became Accountant General on January 4, 1948, the day Myanmar gained independence from the British. For the next two decades, he was employed in various capacities in the government, most of the time holding two or more posts, each equivalent to the head of a department. At one time he served for three years as head of three separate departments simultaneously and, on another occasion, as head of four departments for about one year. When he was appointed as the chairman of the State Agricultural Marketing Board in 1956, the Myanmar government conferred on him the title of "Thray Sithu," a high honorary title. Only the last four years of Sayagyi's life were devoted exclusively to teaching meditation. The rest of the time he combined his skill in meditation with his devotion to government service and, as a married householder with five daughters and one son, to his responsibilities to his family.

It was on January 1, 1937, that Sayagyi tried meditation for the first time. A student of Saya Thetgyi—a wealthy farmer and meditation teacher—was visiting U Ba Khin and explained *ānāpāna* meditation to him. When Sayagyi tried it, he experienced good concentration, which impressed him so much that he resolved to complete a full course. Accordingly, he applied for a ten-day leave of absence, and only one week after trying *ānāpāna*, he was on his way to Saya Thetgyi's center at Pyawbwegyi. That someone so responsible as U Ba Khin would leave his headquarters on such short notice is testimony to his determination to learn Vipassana.

Because of his highly demanding government duties, Sayagyi was only able to teach a small number of students. In 1950 he founded the Vipassana Association of the Accountant General's Office where lay people, mainly employees of that office, could learn Vipassana. Many of his Burmese students were connected with his government work. In 1952, the International Meditation Center (I.M.C.) was opened in Yangon, two miles north of the famous Shwedagon pagoda. Here many Burmese and foreign students had the good fortune to receive instruction in the Dhamma from Sayagyi. Sayagyi's students from abroad were small in number but diverse, including leading Western Buddhists, academics, and members of the diplomatic community in Yangon. Many Indian students were introduced by Goenkaji. From time to time Sayagyi was invited to address foreign audiences in Myanmar on the subject of Dhamma.

Teaching the growing number of students coming from many parts of the world, Sayagyi was convinced that the time had arrived for the teachings of the Buddha to be spread beyond their traditional area of influence. He was aware of the material well-being and the technological expertise of other countries, but he was also aware of the ignorance regarding the mind in those countries and the enormous suffering resulting from that lack of knowledge. He realized that it was time for the Buddha's teaching to reach the residents those areas. Out of love and compassion, Sayagyi wanted to travel abroad to spread this technique. Although Myanmar's policies made it virtually impossible for him to leave, his determination remained. Before his death he named a number of teachers from various countries who could go in his place to take Vipassana out into the world. Sayagyi knew that the teachings would spread beyond Myamar and Asia, and that not only the theory but the practice of the Buddha's teachings would take root around the world.

Sayagyi was active in the planning for the Sixth Buddhist Council known as Chaṭṭha Saṅgāyana (Sixth Recitation) which was held in 1954-56 in Yangon. In 1950 Sayagyi was a founding member of two organizations which later merged to become the Union of Burma Buddha Sāsana Council (U.B.S.C.), the main planning body for the Great Council. He served as an executive member of the U.B.S.C. and as chairman of the committee for *paṭipatti* (practice of meditation). Sayagyi also served as honorary auditor of the Council and was therefore responsible for maintaining the accounts for all *dāna* (donation) receipts and expenditures.

An extensive building project was undertaken for the Sixth Buddhist Council. Spread over 170 acres, it consisted of housing, kitchen and dining areas, a hospital, library, museum, four hostels and administrative buildings. The focal point of the entire enterprise was the Mahā Pāsāṇaguhā (Great Cave), a massive hall where approximately three thousand monks from Myanmar, Sri Lanka, Thailand, India, Cambodia and Laos gathered to recite, authenticate, edit and publish the *Tipiṭaka* (Buddhist scriptures). Working in groups, the monks prepared the Pāli texts for publication, comparing the Burmese, Sri Lankan, Thai, and Cambodian editions and the Roman-script edition of the Pali Text Society in London.

Sayagyi remained active with the U.B.S.C. in various capacities until 1967. In this way he combined his responsibilities and talents as a layman and government official with his strong Dhamma volition to spread the teaching of Buddha. In addition to the prominent public service he gave to that cause, he continued to teach Vipassana regularly at his center. Some of the Westerners who came to the Sixth Council were referred to Sayagyi for instruction in meditation since at that time there was no other teacher of Vipassana who was fluent in English.

Sayagyi finally retired from his outstanding career in government service in 1967. From that time, until his death in 1971, he stayed at his meditation center, I.M.C., teaching Vipassana.

Some Episodes from the Life of Sayagyi U Ba Khin

—narrated by S.N. Goenka

In Wartime, as in Peacetime, a Man of Integrity

During the month of February, 1942, the invading Japanese Imperial Army had occupied Yangon and was advancing toward Mandalay, a city in central Myanmar. The Japanese Air Force started an aerial bombardment of the city, in which the railway station was destroyed.

At this time Sayagyi was stationed in Mandalay as Accounts Officer of the railways, with responsibility for whatever funds were kept in cash. After the bombardment was over, he went to the ruined station, searched through the debris, and found still intact the iron safe in which the cash was kept. Having the key with him, he opened the safe and removed the cash contents—a substantial sum of money.

Now what to do with this money? U Ba Khin was at a loss. The British authorities had already fled in retreat from the fast-approaching Japanese. Mandalay at that moment was a "no man's land" between the two armies—a city without any government. It would have been very easy for Sayagyi to take the money for himself, without anyone's being the wiser. After all, what right did the defeated, fleeing British colonial government have to this money? It could be construed as a patriotic action to deprive them of it. Moreover, Sayagyi had great need of money at that time, since his young daughter was seriously ill, and his expenses were therefore unusually heavy, severely taxing his means. U Ba Khin, however, could not even conceive of misappropriating government funds for his own use. It was his duty, he decided, to hand over the cash to his superior officers even though they were fleeing from the country.

From Mandalay the British had fled helter-skelter in every direction. The railway officers had retreated first to Maymyo, in hopes of making their way from there to Nationalist China and thence by plane to India. Sayagyi did not know whether he would be able to catch up with them in their flight. Nevertheless, he had to make the attempt. He hired a jeep taxi and made the three-hour journey to Maymyo. On his arrival, he found that the British were still in that city. He sought out his superior officer and handed over the cash to him, breathing a sigh of relief at having been able to discharge his duty.

Only then did Sayagyi ask, "And now, sir, may I receive my salary for this month, and my travelling expenses to here?" This was U Ba Khin, a man of perfect integrity, of incorruptible morality, of Dhamma.

Dhamma Transforms a Government Department

By introducing the practice of Vipassana meditation to the officers and staff of the Burmese Accountant General's office, Sayagyi U Ba Khin had brought about remarkable improvements in that government department. The Prime Minister at that time, U Nu, was an honest man and wished the entire administration of the country to be similarly freed from corruption and inefficiency. One of the most important government offices, the State Agricultural Marketing Board, was in poor shape. This organization was responsible for purchasing paddy (a type of rice)—as well as other produce—from the farmers, and arranging for milling the rice and exporting the bulk of it.

In colonial times, the entire rice export business had been in the hands of British and Indian traders. After Myanmar's independence, the Board had taken over this function. Most of its officers and staff had little prior experience. Although the margin of profit in the trade was huge, somehow the Board suffered a chronic deficit.

There was no proper system of accounting; inefficiency and corruption were rampant. The Board officials, in collusion with the rice millers and foreign buyers, were embezzling huge amounts of money from the state. Additionally, great losses occurred due to poor storage practices and inefficient loading and transport.

The Prime Minister set up a committee of inquiry headed by Sayagyi to thoroughly investigate the affairs of the Board. The report of this committee unflinchingly exposed the entire net of corruption and inefficiency. Determined to take strong action—even though it meant overriding the opposition of traders and some of the politicians of his own party who were involved in the corruption—the Prime Minister requested U Ba Khin to take the post of Deputy Chairman of the Board. Sayagyi, however, was hesitant to undertake the responsibility of reforming the Board unless he could have clear authority to undertake any necessary measures. Understanding the problem, the Prime Minister instead appointed Sayagyi to chairmanship of the Marketing Board, a cabinet-level position normally held by the Minister of Commerce. It was generally known that this position afforded great political leverage—and now it was being given to an honest civil servant!

When the intended appointment was announced, the officers of the department became nervous that the man who had exposed their malpractices and inefficiencies was now to become their superior. They declared that they would go on strike if the appointment was confirmed. The Prime Minister replied that he would not reconsider, since he knew that only U Ba Khin could undertake the job. In retaliation, the officers carried out their threat. So it was that Sayagyi took up his appointment in an office where the executive staff was striking while the clerical and blue collar workers continued to work as usual.

Sayagyi remained firm despite the unreasonable demands of the strikers. He continued the work of administration with just the clerical staff. After several weeks, the strikers, realizing that Sayagyi was not going to submit to their pressure, capitulated unconditionally and returned to their posts.

Having established his authority, Sayagyi now began, with great love and compassion, to change the entire atmosphere of the Board and its workings. Many of the officers actually joined courses of Vipassana under his guidance. In the two years that Sayagyi held the Chairmanship, the Board attained record levels in export and profit; efficiency in minimizing losses reached an all-time high.

It was common practice for the officers and even the Chairman of the Marketing Board to amass fortunes in various illegal ways during their terms of office. But U Ba Khin could never indulge in such practices. To forestall attempts to influence him, he refused to meet any traders or millers except on official business, and then only in his office and not his residence.

On one occasion, a certain merchant had submitted to the Board a bid to supply a huge quantity of burlap bags. According to the usual custom, this man was prepared to supplement his bid with a private "contribution" to an important Board member. Wanting to assure his success, he decided to approach the Chairman himself. He arrived at Sayagyi's house, carrying with him a substantial sum of money as an offer. During the course of their conversation, when the first hint of bribery arose, Sayagyi was visibly shocked and did not hide his contempt for such proceedings. Caught in the act, the businessman hastened to emphasize that the money was not for Sayagyi himself but rather for his meditation center. Making it clear that the meditation center never accepted donations from non-meditators, Sayagyi ordered him out of the house, and told him he should be thankful that the police were not called into this.

As a matter of fact, unbeknownst to the merchant, his bid—the lowest one submitted—had already been accepted by the Board. Since all official requirements for this transaction had already been met, a bribe could be harmlessly accepted without interfering with the interests of the state. In such circumstances, it would be commonplace for an official to just accept the gratuity "in the flow of the tide" (as such a situation was popularly referred to). Sayagyi might have easily accrued these material benefits, but doing so would have been totally against the moral integrity of such a Dhamma person.

In fact, to thoroughly discourage any attempt to influence him, Sayagyi let it be known that he would not accept even small personal gifts, despite the common practice of such exchanges. Once on his birthday, a subordinate left a gift at Sayagyi's house when he was not at home: a silk *longyi*, a wraparound sarong typically worn by both men and women. The next day Sayagyi brought the present to the office. At the end of the working day, he called a staff meeting. To the mortification of the staff member who had left it for him, Sayagyi berated him publicly for so blatantly disregarding his explicit orders. He then put the *longyi* up for auction and gave the proceeds to the staff welfare fund. On another occasion, he took similar action on being given a basket of fruit, so careful was he not to allow anyone to try to influence him by bribes whether large or small.

Such was U Ba Khin—a man of principles so strong that nothing could cause him to waver. His determination to establish an example of how an honest official works brought him up against many of the practices common at the time in the administration. Yet for him the perfection of morality and his commitment to Dhamma were surpassed by no other consideration.

Soft as a Rose Petal, Hard as a Diamond

A saintly person, who is full of love and compassion, has a heart that is soft, like the petal of a rose. But when it comes to his duty, he becomes hard like a diamond. Both of these qualities manifested in Sayagyi's life from time to time. A few of the many incidents illustrating this are included here.

When Myanmar attained independence from Britain in 1948, the newly-formed national government faced an immediate crisis. Throughout the country, followers of different ideologies were challenging the government: some were communists, some socialists, some provincial secessionist groups. The insurgents had no scarcity of arms and ammunition, because during the Second World

War both the Japanese and the Allies had freely distributed arms and ammunition to attract the Burmese youth to their fold. The rebels started fighting on so many fronts that it became impossible for the newly-formed national army to handle the crisis. Soon the insurgents gained the upper hand, but with their different causes and slogans, a chaotic situation prevailed throughout the country. Each different group with its own unique cause occupied and ruled a different territory.

A time came when the federal government of Myanmar was in fact only the government of the city of Yangon. Soon even this nucleus of control was imperiled when one group of rebels started knocking at the door of the city, occupying a village ten to twelve miles away. There was no rule of law anywhere in the country; the continued existence of the federal government was hanging in the balance. If the government of Yangon fell, the Union of Myanmar would disintegrate into competing factions. The government was distressed, the army was distressed—but what could be done? There seemed to be no way out.

Sayagyi was deeply devoted to his country, and wished peace, harmony and prosperity for Myanmar, but what could he do? His only strength was in the Dhamma. So at times he would go to the residence of the Prime Minister and practice *mettā* (meditation of goodwill and compassion for all). At other times in his own home, he would generate deep *mettā* for the security of his country. In a situation such as this, Sayagyi's heart was very soft, like the petal of a rose.

But it could also become hard as a diamond. It so happened that during the same crisis, the government appealed to a neighboring country for assistance. This friendly country agreed to come to Myanmar's aid, but whatever items were to be given had to be transported by air, and the government of Myanmar did not have adequate air transport. The airplanes required for the purpose would have to be procured outside the country. To succeed in this plan, the government made a hurried decision which did not fall within the framework of the country's laws.

At that time U Ba Khin was the Accountant General, and he declared the decision to be illegal. The government was now in a dilemma. The Prime Minister knew very well that Sayagyi would not compromise where principles were concerned. (Sayagyi always asserted: "I get my pay for one purpose only—to see that not a single penny of government funds should be used in a way which is contrary to the law. I am paid for this!") The Prime Minister had great respect for Sayagyi's integrity, his adherence to duty. But the situation was very delicate. He therefore called Sayagyi for a private discussion, and told him: "We have to bring these provisions, and we must make an expenditure for the air transportation. Now, tell us how to do this in a legal way." Sayagyi found a suitable solution, and the government followed his advice to save itself from using a wrong means for a right action.

The crisis continued until eventually the rebel groups, one after the other, were overpowered by the national army and defeated in most of the country, except for the remote mountainous areas. The government then started giving more importance to social programs for the improvement of the country. Thanks to the diligence of the community of monks, there was a high rate of basic literacy throughout most of Myanmar, except for some of the hill tribes; but higher education was lacking. The Prime Minister took it upon himself to address this situation. In a large public gathering, he announced a strategy to implement adult education throughout the country, and he authorized a large sum of money for this purpose to be given immediately to the ministry concerned.

Sayagyi was fully sympathetic to the virtues of the plan, but he determined that the amount specified did not fit into any portion of the national budget. He therefore objected. The Prime Minister was placed in a very embarrassing situation, but U Ba Khin's objection was valid: according to law, the announced amount could not be directed to its proposed purpose.

Sayagyi's judgment was accepted, but the program had already been announced, so something had to be done. The Prime Minister called the officers of the Rangoon Racing Club and requested their cooperation in helping to implement the adult education program. He suggested that they sponsor a special horse race with high entry fees; whatever money earned would be given as a donation to the noble cause. Who could refuse the Prime Minister's request? The Racing Club agreed. All went according to plan, and they earned a huge amount on the special race.

Once again, a large public meeting was organized, and with great pomp and ceremony, a check for a large amount was presented to the Prime Minister by the officials of the Racing Club. The Prime Minister, in turn, handed the check over to the minister concerned.

After this event, however, the case came before Sayagyi, and again he raised objections. The Prime Minister was in a quandary. It was, after all, a question of his prestige. Why was Sayagyi now stopping the payment of the check? This was not the government's money; what right did he have to stop it? Sayagyi pointed out that the income from the race included tax for the government. If the government tax was taken out, the rest could go towards supporting the adult education program. The Prime Minister was speechless, but he smiled and accepted U Ba Khin's decision.

Just as Sayagyi was fearless in disposing his official responsibilities, so he was free from favoritism. The following incident is one amongst many incidents illustrating this trait.

In the Accountant General's department, one of the junior clerks was also one of Sayagyi's Vipassana students. This man was very humble, ever willing to lend a helping hand. He was always very happy to serve Sayagyi, and Sayagyi had great paternal love for him. Even paternal love, however, could not become an obstacle to Sayagyi in fulfilling his appointed duty.

It happened that at the end of the year it was time for staff promotions. At the top of the list prepared by the staff was the name of this junior assistant. Because he had the greatest seniority in the department, he was next in line for rightful promotion. If Sayagyi had wanted, he could easily have recommended this promotion, but he did not do so. For him, promotion should not depend only on seniority. It should also take into consideration one's ability to work efficiently. The assistant, who had many other good qualities, was unfortunately lacking in this area. Sayagyi called him and lovingly explained that if he was able to pass a certain accountancy examination, he would get the promotion. The disciple accepted the advice of his teacher, and it took him two years to study and pass the examination. It was only then that Sayagyi granted the promotion.

There are very few people who are free from fear or favor, or who have a love which is paternal yet detached. Sayagyi had all these qualities. Soft as a rose petal, hard as a diamond. I feel fortunate to have learned Dhamma from such a teacher. I pay my respects, remembering these shining qualities of his.

Memories of U Ba Khin from Some of His Students

Modern Interpretation of the Teaching of the Buddha
—by U Ko Lay,
former Vice Chancellor of Mandalay University

Sayagyi's understanding of Dhamma, as taught by the Buddha, was profound and penetrating; his approach to it modern and scientific. His was not mere conventional acceptance of the teaching of the Buddha; his was a wholehearted embrace of Dhamma with firm conviction and faith as a result of personal realization through actual practice.

Sayagyi learned Vipassana meditation at the feet of the great meditation master Saya Thetgyi. When he reached a certain stage of proficiency, Saya Thetgyi felt certain that his student U Ba Khin was destined to play the role of the torchbearer after he had passed away. But it was only in 1941, after Sayagyi had met and paid homage to Webu Sayadaw, believed by many to be an *arahant* (a liberated being), that he finally decided to help people find the path laid down by the Buddha. In his technique, U Ba Khin did not make the slightest deviation from the Buddha's teaching but, after ceaseless practical research and experimentation, he developed instructions of his own, more suited to the demands of modern times.

He felt the need of a course of instructions particularly for householders, rather than strictly for monks and recluses who had given up worldly life. A discipline for monks could not be ideally suitable for laymen. The Vipassana Research Association, initiated by Sayagyi while he was the Accountant General of Burma, undertook research and experiments in Vipassana meditation. Results and findings from these studies carried out in a special shrine room at the Accountant General's office enabled Sayagyi to present the Buddha's Dhamma to laymen in a systematic, scientific manner, thus appealing to the modern mind. His regimen of Vipassana exercises encompasses completely the three requisites laid down by the Buddha (namely *sīla*, *samādhi* and *paññā*), but is so streamlined and disciplined that satisfactory results could be expected within a short period.

Foreign intellectuals and organizations first became acquainted with Sayagyi in 1952 when he gave a series of lectures to a religious study group composed of members of a special technical and economic mission from America. Rendered in booklet form, the lectures soon found their way to various Burmese embassies abroad and Buddhist organizations the world over. (see Chapter Six: "What Buddhism Is")

Sayagyi made a few more expositions of the life and teachings of the Buddha, but mere interpretation of the Dhamma had never been his main object. He applied himself solely to the task of helping sincere workers to experience a state of purity of mind and realize the truth of suffering, resulting in "the peace within" through practicing Vipassana meditation. He achieved astounding results with the presentation he developed to explain the technique. To his last breath Sayagyi remained a preceptor rather than a preacher of Vipassana meditation.

Human Qualities of the Teacher

—by Mrs. Vimala Goenka,
sister-in-law of S.N. Goenka

I once considered Sayagyi U Ba Khin an old, dry and uninteresting person who taught something which was fit only for aged people who had little interest and activity in the things the outside world offered. I regarded him with awe and fear, for I had heard much about his outbursts of anger. I visited him at the center with the elders of my family very seldom, and only when I had to. All these feelings evaporated, one by one, when I stayed with him for ten days and learned meditation under his guidance.

I found Sayagyi to be a very affectionate person. He was like a father to me. I could freely discuss with him any problem that faced me, and be sure not only of a sympathetic ear but also of good advice. All his anger which was talked about was only surface-deep; the core was filled with unbounded love. It was as though a hard crust had formed upon a liquid material. The hard crust was neces- sary—rather, very important for the work he was doing.

It was this hardness which enabled him to maintain strict disci- pline at the center. Sometimes people took undue advantage of his loving nature and neglected the purpose for which they were there. They would walk around the place and talk with other students, thus wasting not only their own time, but disturbing others as well. Sayagyi's hard nature was required to set them on the right track. Even when he got angry, it was loving anger. He wanted his stu- dents to learn as much as possible in the short time available. He felt such negligent students were wasting a precious opportunity which might never come again, an opportunity of which every sec- ond was so precious.

Sayagyi was very generous. He wanted to teach all he knew. He was so keen upon giving away his knowledge and experience that he made untiring efforts to teach a student. He gave freely. It was only the student's capacity to absorb his instructions which was the limiting factor.

Sayagyi was very patient in his teaching too. If a person found difficulty in understanding the process, he would explain thoroughly with examples and illustrations. But he never believed in too much talking. He loved practical work and was of the opinion that experience in the training itself will take care of all the theoretical doubts. Discussing only theories will not land us anywhere. The practical aspect was most important. How right he was! Not only in Dhamma but even in our day-to-day affairs, practical work gives better results than mere discussion.

Sayagyi himself had a great zeal for work. He held six or seven highly important executive posts in the government with grave responsibilities and also conducted the classes of meditation in his free time. In fact he had no free time at all! He was always busy. He had such a large capacity for work at an age when other people think of resting and leading a quiet life. He found peace and calmness in his work.

Even with so much work to do he devoted some time to gardening. It was his favorite hobby. He loved to grow flowers and plants. The center had such a pleasing, colorful look with all the greenery around. The beauty and peace Sayagyi created at the center will always linger in my heart. He taught a rare thing which is of great value to old and young alike. He was a great teacher and a very affectionate man indeed.

Qualities of the Man

—by Dr. Om Prakash,
former consulting physician, United Nations Organization, Myanmar;
Vipassana teacher appointed by S.N. Goenka

His was a fine personality: majestic, sober, noble and impressive. He always bore a faint smile and the look of a calm, satisfied mind. When with him, you felt as if he cared for you and loved you more than anybody else. His attention, love, *mettā* was the same for all, big or small, rich or poor; in return he did not want anything but sincerity of purpose and a truthful nature.

U Ba Khin tolerated all religions. He never criticized or ridiculed any faith or belief. But he preached Buddhism, as he understood it, and he understood it well above many others. He never asserted anything, never forced any idea on you. He followed what he preached or taught and left it to you to think over and accept his view, in part or in full as you wished.

He did not smoke or take alcohol or any narcotics. He took tea and coffee in moderation; liked milk, ovaltine, etc., especially towards the later part of his life. His love of "life" was extreme. He

Sayagyi sitting in the garden at the International Meditation Center

would not allow even mosquitoes to be killed at the center. Even the use of pesticides and insecticides was prohibited there.

He had a great aesthetic and artistic sense, loved flowers very much, and took special care about getting rare varieties. He had a beautiful collection of flowering plants, which were all over the garden around the pagoda. He knew all his plants well and would talk about them at length with the center's visitors.

Sayagyi had a good sense of humor and was witty. He was fond of making little jokes, and laughing, laughing very loudly. Just as he would shout loudly, he would laugh loudly!

He kept himself well-informed about world politics and the modern advances in science and technology, and was a regular listener to radio and a reader of foreign periodicals. He was especially fond of Life and Time magazines.

U Ba Khin had a great desire (a desire which was never fulfilled) to go abroad, especially to the U.S.A. He wanted to teach his method of meditation which he believed—and very correctly so—to be the easiest and most logical way to practice meditation. He had the means to go, had many invitations from foreign disciples, but some technical formalities in obtaining passports and so on always stood in his way. Excepting this one desire, he had all his desires and wishes in the world fulfilled. He led a full life.

Sayagyi bore disease and illness bravely and well, and was a very intelligent and cooperative patient. He never took a pessimistic view of life; he was always optimistic and took a hopeful view. He took suffering and disease as a result of past karma and said it is the lot of one born into the world. Even his last illness which came and took him away from us suddenly, he treated very lightly.

Sayagyi was a very pious and great soul; pure of mind and body, and loveable to everyone.

An Academic Assessment

—*by Winston L. King, Prof. of Religion, Vanderbilt University*

The center [I.M.C.] is actually the projection of the personal life and faith of its founder, U Ba Khin, who is its director and Gurugyi also. He is now a vigorous man, just over sixty, who in addition to the center work—where he spends all of his out-of-office hours during the courses—holds two major government responsibilities.

By any standards, U Ba Khin is a remarkable man. A man of limited education and orphaned at an early age, yet he worked his way up to the Accountant Generalship. He is the father of a family of eight. As a person, he is a fascinating combination of worldly wisdom and ingenuousness, inner quiet and outward good humor, efficiency and gentleness, relaxedness and full self-control. The sacred and the comic are not mutually exclusive in his version of Buddhism; and hearing him relate the canonical Buddha stories with contemporary asides and frequent salvoes of throaty "heh, heh, heh's," is a memorable experience.

...Because of his ability to achieve both detachment and one-pointed attention, he believes that his intuitional and productive powers are so increased that he functions far more effectively as a government servant than most men. Whether he is a kind of genius who makes his "system" work or whether he represents an important new type in Burmese Buddhism—the lay teacher who combines meditation and active work in a successful synthesis—is not yet clear in my mind.

—*excerpted from* A Thousand Lives Away: Buddhism
in Contemporary Burma, *written ca. 1960*

Questions and Answers

Most of the questions and answers at the end of each chapter are taken from an exclusive interview with S.N. Goenka in 1991, on the occasion of the 20th anniversary of Sayagyi's death. We have also drawn on articles and other sources to explain the technique and its benefits and to elucidate the personality and the teachings of U Ba Khin and the value of Vipassana meditation.—Ed.

Q: Did U Ba Khin call himself a Buddhist? How could he call the teaching universal without giving it a sectarian connotation?

S.N. Goenka: U Ba Khin was Buddhist by birth and felt quite proud and satisfied to say so, but it was very clear in his teaching that his intention was not to convert people from one organized religion to another organized religion. My own experience is an example: he never pressed me to become a Buddhist. Sayagyi's way of teaching always remained nonsectarian. The teaching of the Buddha is so universal that people from different sects and communities can follow it and experience its benefits.

For Sayagyi the essence of Buddhism was Dhamma, the universal law of nature, and a true Buddhist was one who practiced Dhamma, one who lived according to this universal law. He was interested in helping people to establish themselves in *sīla* (morality), in *samādhi* (concentration), and in *paññā* (wisdom); to show people how to convert themselves from misery to happiness. If someone who had undergone this conversion from impurity to purity then wished to call himself a Buddhist, Sayagyi was pleased; but the important point was the change which had come in the person's life, not merely the change in the name he called himself.

Sayagyi would even admonish enthusiasts who were eager to convert others to Buddhism, saying to them: "The only way to convert people is to become established oneself in Dhamma—in *sīla, samādhi, paññā*—and to help others similarly to get established. When you yourselves are not established in *sīla, samādhi, paññā*, what is the sense in your trying to convert others? You may call yourselves Buddhists but unless you practice *sīla, samādhi, paññā*, to me you are not Buddhists. But if someone practices *sīla, samādhi, paññā*, then even though he may not call himself a Buddhist, nevertheless he is a true follower of the teachings of the Buddha, whatever he may label himself.

One incident illustrating this nonsectarian attitude occurred when a staunch Christian came to take a course under Sayagyi. While the opening formalities were being explained, this man became frightened that he was being asked to convert from Christianity to Buddhism; and out of this groundless fear, he refused to take refuge in Buddha. "I can take refuge in Jesus Christ but not in Buddha," he said. "Very well," replied Sayagyi smilingly, "Take refuge in Jesus Christ—but with the understanding that you are actually taking refuge in the qualities of Christ, in order to develop these very qualities in yourself." In this way the person began to work; and by the end of the course he realized that his initial objection had been unnecessary, that his fears of conversion had been without cause.

Q: Why did U Ba Khin teach only a few very developed people, while you teach the same technique to all people no matter what their background?

SNG: Because Sayagyi was in an official position of responsibility at a time when the government of his country was inefficient and corrupt, the Prime Minister wanted him to make some improvements in the administration. That he could do by teaching Vipassana. But his dedication to government affairs continued until he was sixty-seven, so he didn't have time to give courses to the masses. He could teach only a few people. Because of that situation, he took a vow to teach only people with well-developed *pāramī* so that "I can give the seed of Dhamma to them and then they can later spread it around the world."

Q: Why do you call your teaching an "art of living"? And how can meditation be used as a tool for creating a better society?

SNG: The entire teaching of Buddha is an art of living. If one lives the life of *sīla,* of morality, this itself is an art of living. But living an ethical life while having many negative reactions in the mind also makes one unhappy. So controlling the mind and purifying the mind—*samādhi* and *paññā*—along with *sīla,* one lives a very peaceful and harmonious life. When one lives a life of negativity, one remains tense within and gives nothing but tension to others. When one is living a peaceful, harmonious life, one generates peace and harmony for others also. It is for this reason that Sayagyi used to call Buddha's teaching an art of living, as a way of life, a code of conduct.

In my own life before meeting Sayagyi, I found the tension was so horrible that I remained miserable, and I made others miserable. Coming onto the Path, I found that I was much relieved. I started living a better life, which was more beneficial for the members of my family, for my friends and for society. So if an individual remains full of negativity, society suffers. If an individual changes for the better, it has a good effect on society.

Q: Many episodes in Sayagyi's life demonstrate his commitment to his work in the government. Can you describe his feelings for social involvement and his attitudes toward his work?

SNG: Well, as a householder one must live a life of responsibility. As a monk one doesn't have this social responsibility because all the time is dedicated to meditation. But as a householder, as a lay person, one must take on that responsibility. Since he was a government servant, Sayagyi wanted to see the people under him working with integrity, discipline, honesty and with efficiency in their work so that they would give good results. By giving a great deal of his time to improving the public administration of his country, Sayagyi was serving society.

Q: Meditation has always been considered a withdrawal from society. Why did U Ba Khin give so much importance to the social aspect of meditation? In particular, for householders, do you think that our involvement in society, rather than isolation, can truly help the progress of our meditation?

SNG: To gain purity of mind and to gain the Dhamma energy, you withdraw from others and take your attention inside. But then that energy has to be used in an extroverted way. It is like someone making a long jump. You have to step back a little, then run and make the jump. In the same way, you withdraw inside yourself, and you get the energy you need, then you make a long jump into society to serve it. These two cannot be separated. Buddha left his householder's life for six years to gain Buddhahood, but once attained, he was involved in society for the next forty-five years, the remainder of his life, day and night. In the same way, anyone who develops in Dhamma does not run away from the responsibilities of society.

Q: How did U Ba Khin use Vipassana meditation to confront corruption?

SNG: Sayagyi's colleagues and subordinates who were involved in corrupt practices did so with minds full of greed and craving. When one begins practicing Vipassana meditation, greed begins to diminish. So these people, having begun to meditate, developed the will to refrain from illegally taking other people's money. Teaching this technique of meditation to his colleagues, U Ba Khin went to the root of the problem—craving in the mind.

Not everyone was corrupt, but still, many were inefficient. Because their minds were clouded, they were not capable of making decisions rapidly and effectively. With Vipassana, eliminating every kind of impurity, the mind becomes clearer, sharper, able to get to the root of any problem and respond effectively. So in this way their efficiency increased. Vipassana meditation was truly used to eradicate corruption and increase the efficiency of the administration. An important aspect of Sayagyi's personality that supported him in this endeavor was his absolute faithfulness to the truth, unwavering in face of pressure or temptation of any kind.

Q: Why did U Ba Khin continue to work after he reached the age of retirement instead of devoting himself entirely to teaching?

SNG: As we have seen, as a householder, he faced his responsibilities. When Myanmar became independent, the efficiency of the Administration was very low and moral integrity was minimal in many government functionaries. His own example was a way to demonstrate how Vipassana meditation could help the administration. Just as it could help an individual, it could help the masses, the society, the government, the nation. So I think he made a very good decision, doing the best he could do, on the one hand teaching Vipassana and on the other demonstrating by his example its results on society.

Q: Can you describe any significant or important episodes from your first meeting with U Ba Khin?

SNG: A friend of mine, knowing that I suffered from strong and incurable migraine headaches, suggested that I participate in a meditation course taught by U Ba Khin. When I met him, the whole atmosphere was so peaceful, and he was quite happy when I told him I was coming to take a course. He inspired me by saying: "You are a Hindu and a leader of the Hindu community, so don't hesitate to come. I won't convert you to any other religion. You will just get a good way of life, you will get peace of mind."

But when I said that I was coming to relieve myself of migraines, Sayagyi—a very straightforward person—said: "No, then I won't take you. You are devaluing Dhamma. Dhamma is not for this purpose. It is to take you out of the misery of lifetime after lifetime. For so many world cycles you have been suffering in misery, and you will continue to suffer unless you learn how to come out of it. To make use of Vipassana for this ordinary physical pain is devaluing it." At the same time, very lovingly he said: "Your aim is to purify the mind. Then all the diseases which are psychosomatic will naturally get cured as a by-product. But the aim should not be to cure a particular disease. Otherwise you will get neither this nor that." That had a very great impact on my mind.

Q: From the experience of U Ba Khin and from the personal experience of both of you[†] as householders, what suggestions would you give to all people who live in society to help them make the best use of their lives and to live happily?

SNG: Vipassana serves exactly that purpose. For those who leave the householder's life to live as monks, there is nothing to do but meditate, day and night, and arrive at a stage where they can help others. But householders must meditate and also make use of this meditation in their daily life, to fulfill their responsibilities toward the members of their family, their community, their society and their country. In that way they help others. When householders take Vipassana meditation, they must do it not only for their own good but for the good of others also.

[†]S.N. Goenka and his wife of 57 years, Illaichidevi Goenka, who accompanies him when he teaches.

Chapter Two

Introduction to Vipassana Meditation

It is a common belief that a man whose power of concentration is good and who can secure a perfect balance of mind at will can achieve better results than a person who is not so developed. There are, therefore, definitely many advantages that accrue to a person who undergoes a successful course of training in meditation, whether he be a religious man, an administrator, a politician, a businessman or a student. A balanced mind is necessary to balance the unbalanced minds of others.
—Sayagyi U Ba Khin

Before going into the historical background of this technique and the importance that U Ba Khin's method and writings had in its dissemination, it necessary first to present the principal characteristics and goals of Vipassana meditation, not only for readers who are hearing about it for the first time, but also for meditators, who can take advantage of this occasion to deepen their understanding. The most appropriate way to provide this introduction is through two clear and brief discourses by the internationally known teacher S.N. Goenka, who has contributed greatly to the spread of this technique around the world. These talks emphasize two characteristics that were especially important to Sayagyi U Ba Khin: 1) the practicality and usefulness of the technique in helping people to come out of their suffering; and 2) the universality of the practice.

The Art of Living

The following is taken from a public talk given by S.N. Goenka in Berne, Switzerland, July 16, 1980.

Everyone seeks peace and harmony, because these are what we lack in our lives. From time to time we all experience agitation, irritation, disharmony, suffering; and when one suffers from agitation, one does not keep this misery limited to oneself. One keeps distributing it to others as well. The agitation permeates the atmosphere around the miserable person. Everyone who comes into contact with him also becomes irritated, agitated. Certainly this is not the proper way to live. One ought to live at peace with oneself, and at peace with all others. After all, a human being is a social being. He has to live in society—to live and deal with others. How are we to live peacefully? How are we to remain harmonious with ourselves, and to maintain peace and harmony around us, so that others can also live peacefully and harmoniously?

One is agitated. To come out of the agitation, one has to know the basic reason for it, the cause of the suffering. If one investigates the problem, it will become clear that whenever one starts generating any negativity or defilement in the mind, one is bound to become agitated. A negativity in the mind, a mental defilement or impurity, cannot exist with peace and harmony.

How does one start generating negativity? Again, by investigating, it becomes clear. I become very unhappy when I find someone behaving in a way that I don't like, when I find something happening that I don't like. Unwanted things happen and I create tension within myself. Wanted things do not happen, some obstacles come in the way, and again I create tension within myself; I start tying knots within myself. And throughout life, unwanted things keep on happening, wanted things may or may not happen, and this process of reaction, of tying knots—Gordian knots—makes the entire mental and physical structure so tense, so full of negativity, that life becomes miserable.

Now one way to solve the problem is to arrange that nothing unwanted happens in my life and that everything keeps on happening exactly as I desire. I must develop such power—or somebody else must have the power and must come to my aid at my request—so that unwanted things do not happen and that everything I want happens. But this is not possible. There is no one in the world whose desires are always fulfilled, in whose life everything happens according to his wishes, without anything unwanted happening. Things keep on occurring that are contrary to our desires and wishes. So the question arises, how am I not to react blindly in the face of these things which I don't like? How not to create tension? How to remain peaceful and harmonious?

In India as well as in other countries, wise, saintly persons of the past studied this problem—the problem of human suffering—and found a solution: if something unwanted happens and one starts to react by generating anger, fear or any negativity, then as soon as possible one should divert one's attention to something else. For example, get up, take a glass of water, start drinking—your anger will not multiply and you'll be coming out of anger. Or start counting: "One, two, three, four...." Or start repeating a word, or a phrase, or some mantra, perhaps the name of a deity or saintly person for whom you have devotion; the mind is diverted, and to some extent, you'll be out of the negativity, out of anger.

This solution was helpful: it worked. It still works. Practicing this, the mind feels free from agitation. In fact, however, the solution works only at the conscious level. Actually, by diverting the attention, one pushes the negativity deep into the unconscious, and on this level one continues to generate and multiply the same defilements. At the surface level there is a layer of peace and harmony, but in the depths of the mind there is a sleeping volcano of suppressed negativity which sooner or later will explode in violent eruption.

Other explorers of inner truth went still further in their search; and by experiencing the reality of mind and matter within themselves they recognized that diverting the attention is only running away from the problem. Escape is no solution: one must face the problem. Whenever a negativity arises in the mind, they advised, just observe it, face it. As soon as one starts observing any mental defilement, it beings to lose strength. Slowly it withers away and is uprooted.

A good solution: it avoids both extremes—suppression and free license. Keeping the negativity in the unconscious will not eradicate it; and allowing it to manifest in physical or vocal action will only create more problems. But if one just observes, then the defilement passes away, and one has eradicated that negativity, one is freed from the defilement.

This sounds wonderful, but is it really practical? For an average person, is it easy to face the defilement? When anger arises, it overpowers us so quickly that we don't even notice. Then, overpowered by anger, we commit certain actions physically or vocally which are harmful to us and to others. Later, when the anger has passed, we start crying and repenting, begging pardon from this or that person or from God: "Oh, I made a mistake, please excuse me!" But the next time we are in a similar situation, we again react in the same way. All that repenting does not help at all.

The difficulty is that I am not aware when a defilement starts. It begins deep in the unconscious level of the mind, and by the time it reaches the conscious level, it has gained so much strength that it overwhelms me, and I cannot observe it.

So I must keep a private secretary with me, so that whenever anger starts, he says, "Look master, anger is starting!" Since I cannot know when this anger will start, I must have three private secretaries for three shifts, around the clock! Suppose I can afford that, and the anger starts to arise. At once my secretary tells me,

"Oh, master, look—anger has started!" The first thing I will do is slap and abuse him: "You fool! Do you think you are paid to teach me?" I am so overpowered by anger that no good advice will help.

But suppose wisdom prevails, and I do not slap him. Instead I say, "Thank you very much. Now I must sit down and observe my anger." Yet is it possible? As soon as I close my eyes and try to observe the anger, immediately the object of anger comes into my mind—the person or the incident. Then I am not observing the anger itself. I am merely observing the external stimulus of the emotion. This will only serve to multiply the anger; this is no solution. It is very difficult to observe any abstract negativity, abstract emotion, divorced from the external object which aroused it.

However, one who reached the ultimate truth found a real solution. He discovered that whenever any defilement arises in the mind, simultaneously two things start happening at the physical level. One is that the breath loses its normal rhythm. We start breathing hard whenever a negativity comes into the mind. This is easy to observe. At a subtler level, some kind of biochemical reaction starts within the body—some sensation. Every defilement will generate one sensation or another inside, in one part of the body or another.

This is a practical solution. An ordinary person cannot observe abstract defilements of the mind—abstract fear, anger or passion. But with proper training and practice, it is very easy to observe respiration and bodily sensations—both of which are directly related to the mental defilements. Respiration and sensation will help me in two ways. First, they will be like my private secretaries. As soon as a defilement starts in my mind, my breath will lose its normality; it will start shouting, "Look, something has gone wrong!" I cannot ignore my breath; I have to accept the warning. Similarly the sensations tell me that something has gone wrong. Then having been warned, I start observing my respiration, my sensation, and I find very quickly that the defilement passes away.

This mental-physical phenomenon is like a coin with two sides. On the one side are whatever thoughts or emotions are arising in the mind. On the other side are the respiration and sensations in the body. Any thought or emotion, any mental defilement, manifests itself in the breath and the sensation of that moment. Thus, by observing the respiration or the sensation, I am in fact observing the mental defilement. Instead of running away from the problem, I am facing reality as it is. Then I shall find that the defilement loses its strength: it can no longer overpower me as it did in the past. If I persist, the defilement eventually disappears altogether, and I remain peaceful and happy.

In this way, the technique of self-observation shows us reality in its two aspects, inner and outer. Previously, one always looked with open eyes, missing the inner truth. I always looked outside for the cause of my unhappiness; I always blamed and tried to change the reality outside. Being ignorant of the inner reality, I never understood that the cause of suffering lies within, in my own blind reactions toward pleasant and unpleasant sensations.

Now, with training, I can see the other side of the coin. I can be aware of my breathing and also of what is happening inside me. Whatever it is, breath or sensation, I learn just to observe it, without losing the balance of the mind. I stop reacting, stop multiplying my misery. Instead, I allow the defilement to manifest and pass away.

The more one practices this technique, the more quickly one will come out of negativity. Gradually the mind becomes freed of the defilements; it becomes pure. A pure mind is always full of love—selfless love for all others; full of compassion for the failings and sufferings of others; full of joy at their success and happiness; full of equanimity in the face of any situation.

When one reaches this stage, the entire pattern of one's life starts changing. It is no longer possible to do anything vocally or physically which will disturb the peace and happiness of others. Instead, the balanced mind not only becomes peaceful in itself, but it helps others also to become peaceful. The atmosphere surrounding such a person will become permeated with peace and harmony, and this will start affecting others too.

By learning to remain balanced in the face of everything one experiences inside, one develops detachment towards all that one encounters in external situations as well. However, this detachment is not escapism or indifference to the problems of the world. A Vipassana meditator becomes more sensitive to the sufferings of others and does his utmost to relieve their suffering in whatever way he can—not with any agitation but with a mind full of love, compassion and equanimity. He learns holy indifference—how to be fully committed, fully involved in helping others, while at the same time maintaining the balance of his mind. In this way he remains peaceful and happy, while working for the peace and happiness of others.

This is what the Buddha taught; an art of living. He never established nor taught any religion, any '-ism.' He never instructed his followers to practice any rites or rituals, any blind or empty formalities. Instead, he taught just to observe nature as it is, by observing reality inside. Out of ignorance, one keeps reacting in a way which is harmful to oneself and to others. But when wisdom arises—the wisdom of observing the reality as it is—one comes out of this habit of reaction. When one ceases to react blindly, then one is capable of real action—action proceeding from a balanced mind, a mind which sees and understands the truth. Such action can only be positive, creative, helpful to oneself and to others.

What is necessary then is to "know thyself"—advice which every wise person has given. One must know oneself not just at the intellectual level, the level of ideas and theories. Nor does this mean to know just at the emotional or devotional level, simply accepting blindly what one has heard or read. Such knowledge is not enough. Rather one must know reality at the actual level. One must experience directly the reality of this mental-physical phenomenon. This alone is what will help us to come out of defilements, out of suffering.

This direct experience of one's own reality, this technique of self-observation, is what is called "Vipassana" meditation. In the language of India in the time of the Buddha, *passana* meant seeing with open eyes, in the ordinary way; but Vipassana means to observe things as they really are, not just as they seem to be. Apparent truth has to be penetrated, until one reaches the ultimate truth of the entire mental and physical structure. When one experiences this truth, then one learns to stop reacting blindly, to stop creating defilements—and naturally the old defilements gradually are eradicated. One comes out of all the misery and experiences happiness.

There are three steps to the training which is given in a Vipassana meditation course. First, one must abstain from any action, physical or vocal, which disturbs the peace and harmony of others. One cannot work to liberate oneself from defilements in the mind while at the same time one continues to perform deeds of body and speech which only multiply those defilements. Therefore, a code of morality is the essential first step of the practice. One undertakes not to kill, not to steal, not to commit sexual misconduct, not to tell lies, and not to use intoxicants. By abstaining from such actions, one allows the mind to quiet down sufficiently so that it can proceed with the task at hand.

The next step is to develop some mastery over this wild mind, by training it to remain fixed on a single object: the breath. One tries to keep one's attention for as long as possible on the respiration. This is not a breathing exercise: one does not regulate the breath. Instead one observes natural respiration as it is, as it comes in, as it goes out. In this way one further calms the mind so that it is no longer overpowered by violent negativities. At the same time, one is concentrating the mind, making it sharp and penetrating, capable of the work of insight.

These first two steps of living a moral life and controlling the mind are very necessary and beneficial in themselves; but they will lead to self-repression, unless one takes the third step—purifying the mind of defilements by developing insight into one's own nature. This is Vipassana: experiencing one's own reality, by the systematic and dispassionate observation of the ever-changing mind-matter phenomenon manifesting itself as sensation within oneself. This is the culmination of the teaching of the Buddha: self-purification by self-observation.

This can be practiced by one and all. Everyone faces the problem of suffering. it is a universal disease which requires a universal remedy—not a sectarian one. When one suffers from anger, it is not a Buddhist anger, Hindu anger, or Christian anger. Anger is anger. When one become agitated as a result of this anger, this agitation is not Christian or Hindu or Buddhist. The malady is universal. The remedy must also be universal.

Vipassana is such a remedy. No one will object to a code of living which respects the peace and harmony of others. No one will object to developing control over the mind. No one will object to developing insight into one's own reality, by which it is possible to free the mind of negativities. Vipassana is a universal path.

Observing reality as it is by observing the truth inside—this is knowing oneself at the actual, experiential level. As one practices, one keeps coming out of the misery of defilements. From the gross, external, apparent truth, one penetrates to the ultimate truth of mind and matter. Then one transcends this and experiences a truth which is beyond mind and matter, beyond time and space, beyond the conditioned field of relativity: the truth of total liberation from all defilements, all impurities, all suffering. Whatever name one gives this ultimate truth is irrelevant; it is the final goal of everyone.

The Wisdom of Experience

—From a discourse given by S.N. Goenka
in Bangkok, Thailand, September, 1989.

Venerable representatives of the Buddhist community, friends: you have all assembled here to understand what Vipassana is and how it helps us in our day-to-day lives; how it helps us to come out of our misery, the misery of life and death. Everyone wants to come out of misery, to live a life of peace and harmony. We simply do not know how to do this. It was Siddhattha Gotama's enlightenment that made him realize the truth: where misery lies, how it starts, and how it can be eradicated.

There were many techniques of meditation prevailing in those days, as there are today. The Bodhisattva Gotama tried them all, but he was not satisfied, because he found that he was not fully liberated from misery. Then he started to do his own research. Through his personal experience he discovered this technique of Vipassana, which eradicated misery from his life and made him a fully enlightened person.

There are many techniques that give temporary relief. When you become miserable you divert your attention to something else. Then you feel that you have come out of your misery, but you are not totally relieved.

If something undesirable has happened in life, you become agitated. You cannot bear this misery and want to run away from it. You may go to a cinema or to a theater, or you may indulge in other sensual entertainment. You may go out drinking, and so on. All this is running away from misery. Escape is no solution to the problem—indeed the misery is multiplying.

In the Buddha's enlightenment he realized that one must face reality. Instead of running away from the problem, one must face it. He found that all the types of meditation existing in his day consisted of merely diverting the mind from the prevailing misery to another object. He found that when one practices this, actually only a small part of the mind is diverted. Deep inside one keeps reacting, one keeps generating *saṅkhāras* (reactions) of craving, aversion or delusion, and one keeps suffering at a deep level of the mind. The object of meditation should not be an imaginary object, it should be reality—reality as it is. One has to work with whatever reality has manifested itself now, whatever one experiences within the framework of one's own body.

In the practice of Vipassana one has to explore the reality within oneself—the material structure and the mental structure, the combination of which one keeps calling "I, me, mine." One generates a tremendous amount of attachment to this material and mental structure, and as a result becomes miserable. To practice the Buddha's path we must observe the truth of mind and matter. Their basic characteristics should be directly experienced by the meditator. This results in wisdom.

Wisdom can be of three types: wisdom gained by listening to others; wisdom that is gained by intellectual analysis; and wisdom developed from direct, personal experience. Before the Buddha, and even at the time of the Buddha, there were teachers who were teaching morality, were teaching concentration, and who were also talking about wisdom. But this wisdom was only received or intellectualized wisdom. It was not wisdom gained by personal experience. The Buddha found that one may play any number of intellectual or devotional games, but unless he experiences the truth himself and develops wisdom from his personal experience, he will not be liberated. Vipassana is personally experienced wisdom. One may listen to discourses or read scriptures. Or one may use the intellect and try to understand: "Yes, the Buddha's teaching is wonderful! This wisdom is wonderful!" But this is not direct experience of wisdom.

The entire field of mind and matter—the six senses and their respective objects—have the basic characteristics of *anicca* (impermanence), *dukkha* (suffering) and *anattā* (egolessness). The Buddha wanted us to experience this reality within ourselves. To explore the truth within the framework of the body, he designated two fields. One is the material structure: the corporeal structure, the physical structure. The other is the mental structure with four factors: consciousness; perception; the part of the mind that feels sensation; and the part of the mind that reacts. So to explore both fields he gave us *kāyānupassanā* (observation of the body) and *cittānupassanā* (observation of the mind).

How can you observe the body with direct experience unless you can feel it? There must be something happening in the body which you feel, which you realize. Then you can say, "Yes, I have practiced *kāyānupassanā*." One must feel the sensations on the body: this is *vedanānupassanā* (observation of body sensations).

The same is true for *cittānupassanā*. Unless something arises in the mind, you cannot directly experience it. Whatever arises in the mind is *dhamma* (mental content). Therefore *dhammānupassanā* (observation of the contents of the mind) is necessary for *cittānupassanā*.

This is how the Buddha divided these practices. *Kāyānupassanā* and *vedanānupassanā* pertain to the physical structure. *Cittānupassanā* and *dhammānupassanā* pertain to the mental structure. See from your personal experience how this mind and matter are related to each other. To believe that one understands mind and matter, without having directly experienced it, is delusion. It is only direct experience that will make us understand the reality about mind and matter. This is where Vipassana starts helping us.

In brief, understand how we practice Vipassana. We start with *ānāpāna*, awareness of respiration—natural respiration. We don't make it a breathing exercise or regulate the breath as they do in *prāṇāyāma*. We observe respiration at the entrance of the nostrils. If a meditator works continuously in a congenial atmosphere without any disturbance, within two or three days some subtle reality on this part of the body will start manifesting itself: some sensations—natural, normal body sensations. Maybe heat or cold, throbbing or pulsing or some other sensations. When one reaches the fourth or fifth day of practice, he or she will find that there are sensations throughout the body, from head to feet. One feels those sensations, and is asked not to react to them. One is instructed, "Just observe; observe objectively, without identifying yourself with the sensations."

When you work as the Buddha wanted you to work, by the time you reach the seventh day or the eighth day, you will move towards subtler and subtler reality. The Dhamma (natural law) will start helping you. You observe this structure that initially appears to be so solid, the entire physical structure at the level of sensation. Observing, observing you will reach the stage when you experience that the entire physical structure is nothing but subatomic particles: throughout the body, nothing but *kalāpas* (subatomic particles). And even these tiniest subatomic particles are not solid. They are mere vibration, just wavelets. The Buddha's words become clear by experience:

Sabbo pajjalito loko, sabbo loko pakampito.

The entire universe is nothing but combustion and vibration.

(Saṃyutta-nikāya I.5.7, Upacālā Sutta)

As you experience it yourself, your *kāyānupassanā*, your *vedanānupassanā*, will take you to the stage where you experience that the entire material world is nothing but vibration. Then it becomes very easy for you to practice *cittānupassanā* and *dhammānupassanā*.

The Buddha's teaching is to move from the gross, apparent truth to the subtlest, ultimate truth, from *oḷārika* to *sukhuma*. The apparent truth always creates illusion and confusion in the mind. By dividing and dissecting apparent reality, you will come to the ultimate reality. As you experience that the reality of matter is vibration, you also start experiencing the reality of the mind: *viññāṇa* (consciousness), *saññā* (perception), *vedanā* (sensation) and *saṅkhāra* (reaction). If you experience them properly with Vipassana, it will become clear how they work.

Suppose you have reached the stage where you are experiencing that the entire physical structure is just vibration. If a sound has come in contact with the ears you will notice that this sound is nothing but vibration. The first part of the mind—consciousness—has done its job: ear consciousness has recognized that something has happened at the ear sense door. Like a gong which, having been struck at one point, begins vibrating throughout its structure, so a contact with any of the senses begins a vibration which spreads throughout the body. At first this is merely a neutral vibration, neither pleasant nor unpleasant.

The perception recognizes and evaluates the sound: "It is a word—what word? Praise! Oh, wonderful, very good!" The resulting sensation, the vibration, will become very pleasant. In the same way, if the words are words of abuse, the vibration will become very unpleasant. The vibration changes according to the evaluation given by the perceiving part of the mind. Next the third part of the mind starts feeling the sensation: pleasant or unpleasant.

Then the fourth part of the mind—reaction—will start working: its job is to react. If a pleasant sensation arises, it will react with craving. If an unpleasant sensation arises, it will react with aversion. Pleasant sensation: "I like it. Very good! I want more, I want more!" Similarly, unpleasant sensation: "I dislike it. I don't want it." Generating craving and aversion is the part played by the fourth factor of the mind—reaction.

Understand that this process is going on constantly at one sense door or another. Every moment something or the other is happening at one of the sense doors. Every moment the respective consciousness cognizes; the perception recognizes; the feeling part of the mind feels; and the reacting part of the mind reacts, with either craving or aversion. This happens continuously in one's life.

At the apparent, surface level, it seems that we are reacting with either craving or aversion to the external stimulus. Actually this is not so. The Buddha found that we are reacting to our sensations. This discovery was the enlightenment of the Buddha. He said:

> *Saḷāyatana-paccayā phasso*
> *phassa-paccayā vedanā*
> *vedanā-paccayā taṇhā.*

With the base of the six senses, contact arises
with the base of contact, sensation arises
with the base of sensation, craving arises.

(Saṃyutta-nikāya II.1.1, Paṭiccasaumuppāda Sutta)

It became so clear to him: the six sense organs come in contact with objects outside. Because of the contact, a sensation starts in the body that, most of the time, is either pleasant or unpleasant. Then after a pleasant or unpleasant sensation arises, craving or aversion start—not before that. This realization was possible because the Buddha went deep inside and experienced it himself. He went to the root of the problem and discovered how to eradicate the cause of suffering at the root level.

Working at the intellectual level of the mind, we try to suppress craving and aversion; but deep inside, craving and aversion continue. We are constantly rolling in craving or aversion. We are not coming out of misery through suppression.

The Buddha discovered the way: whenever you experience any sensation, due to any reason, you simply observe it:

> *Samudaya dhammānupassī vā kāyasmiṃ viharati*
> *vaya dhammānupassī vā kāyasmiṃ viharati*
> *samudaya-vaya-dhammānupassī vā kāyasmiṃ viharati.*

He dwells observing the phenomenon of arising in the body.
He dwells observing the phenomenon of passing away in the body.

He dwells observing the phenomenon of arising-and-passing-away in the body.

(*Dīgha-nikāya II.9, Mahāsatipaṭṭhāna Sutta*)

Every sensation arises and passes away. Nothing is eternal. When
you practice Vipassana you start experiencing this. However unpleasant a sensation may be—look, it arises only to pass away.
However pleasant a sensation may be, it is just a vibration—arising-and-passing. Pleasant, unpleasant or neutral, the characteristic
of impermanence remains the same. You are now experiencing the
reality of *anicca*. You are not believing it because the Buddha said
so, or some scripture or tradition says so, or even because your
intellect says so. You accept the truth of *anicca* because you directly experience it. This is how your received wisdom and
intellectual understanding turn into personally experienced wisdom.

Only this experience of *anicca* will change the habit pattern of
the mind. Feeling sensation in the body and understanding that
everything is impermanent, you don't react with craving or aversion; you are equanimous. Practicing this continually changes the
habit of reacting at the deepest level. When you don't generate any
new conditioning of craving and aversion, old conditioning comes
on the surface and passes away. By observing reality as it is, you
become free from all your conditioning of craving and aversion.

Western psychologists refer to the "conscious mind." The Buddha called this part of the mind the *paritta citta* (a very small part of
the mind). There is a big barrier between the *paritta citta* and the
rest of the mind at deeper levels. The conscious mind does not
know what is happening in the unconscious or half-conscious. Vipassana breaks this barrier, taking you from the surface level of the
mind to the deepest level of the mind. The practice exposes the
anusaya kilesa (latent mental defilements) that are lying at the deepest level of the mind.

The so-called "unconscious" mind is not unconscious. It is always conscious of body sensations, and it keeps reacting to them.

If they are unpleasant, it reacts with aversion. If they are pleasant, it reacts with craving. This is the habit pattern, the behavior pattern, of the so-called unconscious at the depth of the mind.

Here is an example to explain how the so-called unconscious mind is reacting with craving and aversion. You are in deep sleep. A mosquito bites you and there is an unpleasant sensation. Your conscious mind does not know what has happened. The unconscious knows immediately that there is an unpleasant sensation, and it reacts with aversion. It drives away or kills the mosquito. But still there is an unpleasant sensation, so you scratch, though your conscious mind is in deep sleep. When you wake up, if somebody asks you how many mosquito bites you got during the night, you won't know. Your conscious mind was unaware but the unconscious knew, and it reacted.

Another example: Sitting for about half an hour, some pressure starts somewhere and the unconscious mind reacts: "There is a pressure. I don't like it!" You change your position. The unconscious mind is always in contact with the body sensations. You make a little movement, and then after some time you move again. Just watch somebody sitting for fifteen to twenty minutes. You will find that this person is fidgeting, shifting a little here, a little there. Of course, consciously he does not know what he is doing. This is because he is not aware of the sensations. He does not know that he is reacting with aversion to these sensations. This barrier is ignorance.

Vipassana breaks this ignorance. Then one starts understanding how sensations arise and how they give rise to craving or aversion. When there is a pleasant sensation, there is craving. When there is an unpleasant sensation, there is aversion, and whenever there is craving or aversion, there is misery.

If one does not break this behavior pattern, there will be continual craving or aversion. At the surface level you may say that you are practicing what the Buddha taught, but in fact, you are not practicing what the Buddha taught! You are practicing what the other teachers at the time of the Buddha taught. The Buddha taught how to go to the deepest level where suffering arises. Suffering arises because of one's reaction of craving or aversion. The source of craving and aversion must be found, and one must change one's behavior pattern at that level.

The Buddha taught us to observe suffering and the arising of suffering. Without observing these two we can never know the cessation of misery. Suffering arises with the sensations. If we react to sensations, then suffering arises. If we do not react we do not suffer from them. However unpleasant a sensation may be, if you don't react with aversion, you can smile with equanimity. You understand that this is all *anicca*, impermanence. The whole habit pattern of the mind changes at the deepest level.

Through the practice of Vipassana, people start to come out of all kinds of impurities of the mind—anger, passion, fear, ego, and so on. Within a few months or a few years the change in people becomes very evident. This is the benefit of Vipassana, here and now. In this very life you will get the benefit.

This is the land of Dhamma, a land of the teaching of the Buddha, a land where you have such a large Sangha. Make use of the teaching of the Buddha at the deepest level. Don't just remain at the surface level of the teaching of the Buddha. Go to the deepest level where your craving arises:

> *Vedanā paccayā taṇhā;*
> *vedanā-nirodhā taṇhā-nirodho;*
> *taṇhā-nirodhā dukkha-nirodho.*

Sensations give rise to craving.
If sensations cease, craving ceases.
When craving ceases, suffering ceases.

(paraphrasal of Paṭiccasamuppāda Sutta)

When one experiences the truth of *nibbāna*—a stage beyond the entire sensorium—all the six sense organs stop working. There can't be any contact with objects outside, so sensation ceases. At this stage there is freedom from all suffering.

First you must reach the stage where you can feel sensations. Only then can you change the habit pattern of your mind. Work on this technique, this process, at the very deepest level. If you work on the surface level of the mind you are only changing the conscious part of the mind, your intellect. You are not going to the root cause, the most unconscious level of the mind; you are not removing the *anusaya kilesa*—deep-rooted defilements of craving and aversion. They are like sleeping volcanoes that may erupt at any time. You continue to roll from birth to death; you are not coming out of misery.

Make use of this wonderful technique and come out of your misery, come out of the bondage and enjoy real peace, real harmony, real happiness.

Chapter Three

The History of Vipassana Meditation

It was after the sojourn of three months of the rainy season that the exhortation of the Buddha, "Move on, bhikkhus! Move on!" was first uttered. Let this be for our inspiration too. Let us purify our minds of defilements, be filled with compassion and, to the degree to which we have liberated ourselves to the best of our ability and capacity, may we also toil to serve humanity. If we are really benefited by practicing Dhamma, then we cannot remain merely content in our own good and happiness. We have also to work for the good and happiness of all. Let the objective of our lives be to direct all our labor to sharing Dhamma—that is, truth—resulting in happiness for more and more people.
—S.N. Goenka

Vipassana meditation is considered the essence of the Buddha's teaching. The fundamental principles of the technique have been delineated in various ways in his *suttas*, or discourses, collected in the Pāli canon, which is divided into three parts and is known as the *Tipiṭaka* (literally, "three baskets" or collections). It is undoubtedly a great good fortune that the monks have passed down to us in their original version all of the discourses of the Buddha, first orally and then in writing. But with time in some places the practice underwent modifications which sometimes completely

misrepresented what the Buddha had taught. Our deepest gratitude goes to those monks and teachers who maintained the
technique in its purity, passing it from teacher to student, to this
day.

A line of teachers who kept the practice intact is the one that
started in Myanmar in the distant past with the arrival from India
of the *arahant* monks Soṇa and Uttara. The most recent Burmese
teachers in this lineage are: the venerable Ledi Sayadaw, Saya Thetgyi and U Ba Khin. S.N. Goenka, born in Myanmar of Indian
heritage, was trained by Sayagyi U Ba Khin and has carried the
tradition from Myanmar, first back to India and then beyond.

In the distant past in order to have a "true practice" one was
required to renounce the world and live one's life within the walls
of a monastery or in the forest. To the lay person was left the observation of moral precepts, charity, and devotion in order to gain
merit for future lives in which they could finally begin work on the
path of liberation. However, as can be discerned from many of the
Buddha's discourses, a great number of lay people who received
the teaching of the practice in his time attained high levels of spiritual development. From this we can deduce that the Buddha himself
did not intend to exclude lay people from the practice of his teachings.

In the last few decades there has been renewed interest in Vipassana meditation, thanks to the work of numerous lay teachers
who have spread the teachings. This is true not only in countries
with a Theravāda monastic tradition, such as Myanmar, Sri Lanka,
Thailand, etc., but around the world. They have taken the practice
beyond the monasteries and, emphasizing the benefits of meditation in daily life, have helped develop a more popular attitude toward
it.

But how is one able to approach meditation without dedicating
one's life to silence and contemplation? And what role can the discipline of meditation play in the life of a householder?

According to the Pāli canon, the classic method of practice that was principally adopted by monks, required that they attain a certain degree of concentration before moving on to the profound understanding of reality through the practice of Vipassana meditation. Today in many meditation centers for lay people—such as those founded by U Ba Khin and the many centers around the world founded by his student S.N. Goenka—one is taught (through three days of *ānāpāna*, meditation on the breath) to arrive at a minimum level of concentration sufficient to initiate the practice of Vipassana. There are many reasons that it is more practicable for people of this modern era to learn Vipassana without having to pass through a long period of learning the technique of concentration.

These issues were considered in great detail and with much vigor by one of the most important teachers of meditation in modern Myanmar, Sayagyi U Ba Khin. The unique characteristic of his teaching arises from the fact that he was a lay teacher of meditation in an orthodox Buddhist country. According to tradition it wasn't permissible for a layman to instruct monks, and all his own teachings were specifically adapted for lay people.

The Historical Antecedents of U Ba Khin's Method

The credit goes to the venerable Ledi Sayadaw for his contribution in opening knowledge of the direct method of Vipassana meditation to lay people. (*Sayadaw* is a Burmese title meaning "respected teacher monk.") Ledi Sayadaw was a renowned scholar as well as a master of meditation. He wrote hundreds of *dīpanīs*, or manuals, explaining different aspects of the Buddha's teaching, several of which have been translated into English. In one of these works, *The Requisites of Enlightenment* (*Bodhipakkhiya Dīpanī*), he wrote:

> The seeds of *sīla* and *samādhi* can be obtained at will at any time. But the seeds of *paññā* (wisdom) ... can be obtained only when one encounters a Buddha *Sāsana* (era when Buddha's teachings are available). Outside of a Buddha *Sāsana*, one does not get the opportunity of even hearing the mere mention of words associated with *paññā*, though an infinite

number of *"suñña"* ("empty"—i.e., empty of a Buddha's teaching) world-cycles may elapse. Hence, those persons of the present day who are fortunate enough to be born into this world while a Buddha *Sāsana* flourishes, if they intend to accumulate the seeds of *magga-ñāṇa* (knowledge of the path) and *phala-ñāṇa* (knowledge of the fruits of the path) for the purpose of securing release from worldly ills in a future existence within a future Buddha *Sāsana*, should pay special attention to the knowledge of the *paramattha* (ultimate realities), which is extremely difficult for one to come across....

The "ultimate realities" mentioned are consciousness, the mental factors, the material qualities, and *nibbāna*. That is to say, one should develop a deep understanding of the impermanent nature of the mind-body phenomenon (which is the essence of Vipassana meditation) and the experience of *nibbāna*. Ledi Sayadaw goes on to say that if it is not possible to know this fruit of the Path, meditators should at least attain the first level of knowledge—deep insight into the insubstantiality and the impersonality of one's own body, composed of the elements of earth, air, fire and water. In fact, this will be enough to obtain a good harvest of the seeds of wisdom. Morality will help one to be born when Matteyya Buddha appears. (Matteyya is the name ascribed by tradition to the next Buddha.) But in order to attain maximum benefit these seeds of wisdom, developed through Vipassana meditation, must be present. Those who have not developed these seeds will not be able to achieve enlightenment, even if they hear the discourses of the future Buddha in person.

This sense of urgency motivated many monks, including Ledi Sayadaw, to spread the teaching of Vipassana in its simplest and most direct form, making it possible to practice with a minimum degree of concentration and in a way which could benefit even lay people. Ledi Sayadaw was actually one of the first to spread the essence of Vipassana meditation to lay people. As long as there was time and opportunity, he wanted people to begin working for their own ultimate salvation, and he recommended to everyone without exception at least to begin meditating at whatever level they could at that moment. Besides encouraging lay people to meditate himself, he began appointing his own lay students, such as Saya Thetgyi, the teacher of Sayagyi U Ba Khin, to begin teaching also.

Ledi Sayadaw, who was a famous scholar as well as meditation teacher, reemphasized that this direct method of Vipassana had its own base in the most important discourse of the Buddha, the *Mahāsatipaṭṭhāna Sutta*. His studies were helpful in clarifying many controversial points in the practice, contributing in this way to the development of Vipassana meditation not only in Buddhist countries but in the rest of the world as well. Without entirely eliminating the practice of mental concentration, the direct method of Vipassana—which is mere observation of the phenomena of one's own body and mind at the level of physical sensations—represented a new force, contributing to a resurgence of meditation practice which enabled lay people to be involved. Indeed, the only preparation one needs in order to practice this technique is to have the ability and the willingness. Furthermore, this method of Vipassana meditation can easily be included in the activities of daily life and is thus ideal for lay people, as well as for monks, who are looking for a simple, direct method which brings results here and now.

After the Second World War, interest in meditation for lay people spread rapidly, especially in Myanmar, resulting in the founding of hundreds of centers, many managed by monks, others by lay people. The spread of these centers accommodated the desire of many to meditate more intensively and for longer periods, in addition to making it easier to learn the technique without the need for a long and difficult preparation.

A Brief Biography of
U Ba Khin's Immediate Predecessors

Ledi Sayadaw (1846–1923)

The venerable Ledi Sayadaw was born in 1846 in Saing-pyin village, Dipeyin township in the Shwebo district (currently Monywa district) of northern Myanmar. In his village he attended the traditional monastery school where the *bhikkhus* (monks) taught the children to read and write in Burmese as well as how to recite many *Pāli* texts. At the age of eight he began to study with his first teacher U Nanda-dhaja Sayadaw, and he ordained as a *sāmaṇera* (novice) under the same Sayadaw at the age of fifteen. He took the name Ñāṇa-dhaja (the banner of knowledge). His monastic education included *Pāli* grammar and various texts from the *Pāli* canon.

Later on, under the care of Gandhama Sayadaw, the brilliant Sāmaṇera Ñāṇa-dhaja mastered the *Vedas* in eight months and continued his study of the *Tipiṭaka*. At the age of twenty, on 20 April 1866, he took the higher ordination to become a *bhikkhu* under his old teacher U Nanda-dhaja Sayadaw, who became his preceptor.

In 1867, just prior to the monsoon retreat, Bhikkhu Ñāṇa-dhaja left his preceptor and the Monywa district where he had grown up, in order to continue his studies in Mandalay.

Mandalay was the royal capital of Myanmar at that time, during the rule of King Min Don Min (who ruled from 1853-1878), and was the most important center of learning in the country. He studied there under several of the leading Sayadaws and learned lay scholars as well. He resided primarily in the Mahā-Jotikārāma monastery and studied with Ven. San-Kyaung Sayadaw, a teacher who is famous in Myanmar for translating the *Visuddhimagga* (Path of Purification) into Burmese.

During this time, Ven. San-Kyaung Sayadaw gave an examination of twenty questions for two thousand students. Bhikkhu Ñāṇa-dhaja was the only one who was able to answer all the questions satisfactorily. These answers were later published in 1880, under the title *Pāramī-Dīpanī* (Manual of Perfections). This was the first of many books to be published in Pāli and Burmese by Ven. Ledi Sayadaw.

During the time of his studies in Mandalay, King Min Don Min sponsored the Fifth Council, calling *bhikkhus* from far and wide to recite and verify the *Tipiṭaka*. The Council was held in Mandalay in

Venerable Ledi Sayadaw, 1846-1923

1871, and the authenticated texts were carved into 729 marble slabs that stand today (each slab housed under a small pagoda) surrounding the golden Kuthodaw Pagoda at the foot of Mandalay Hill. At this Council, Bhikkhu Ñāṇa-dhaja helped in the editing and translating of the *Abhidhamma* texts.

After eight years as a *bhikkhu,* having passed all his examinations, Ven. Ñāṇa-dhaja was qualified as a beginning Pāli teacher at the San-Kyaung monastery (also known as the Mahā-Jotikārāma monastery) where he had been studying.

For eight more years he remained there, teaching and continuing his own scholastic endeavours, until 1882 when he moved to Monywa. He was now thirty-six years old. At that time Monywa was a small district center on the east bank of the Chindwin River, which was renowned as a place where the teaching method included the entire *Tipiṭaka,* rather than just selected portions.

While he was teaching Pāli to the *bhikkhus* and *sāmaṇeras* at Monywa, his habit was to come to town during the day for his teaching duties. In the evening he would cross to the west bank of the Chindwin river and spend the nights in meditation in a small *vihāra* (monastery) on the side of Lak-pan-taung mountain. Although we do not have any definitive information, it seems likely that this was the period when he began practicing Vipassana in the traditional Burmese fashion: with *ānāpāna* (respiration) and *vedanā* (sensation).

The British conquered upper Myanmar in 1885 and sent the last king, Thibaw (who ruled from 1878-1885), into exile. The next year, 1886, Ven. Ñāṇa-dhaja went into retreat in Ledi forest, just to the north of Monywa. After a while many *bhikkhus* started coming to him there, requesting that he teach them. A monastery to house them was built and named Ledi-tawya monastery. From this monastery he took the name by which he is best known: Ledi Sayadaw. It is said that one of the main reasons that Monywa grew to be a larger town, as it is today, was because so many people were attracted to Ledi Sayadaw's monastery there. While he taught many aspiring students at Ledi-tawya, he retained his practice of retiring to his small cottage *vihāra* across the river for his own meditation.

When he had been in the Ledi forest monastery for over ten years, his main scholastic works began to be published. The first was *Paramattha-Dīpanī* (Manual of Ultimate Truth), published in

1897. His second book of this period was *Nirutta Dīpanī*, a book on Pāli grammar. Because of these books he gained the reputation as one of the most learned *bhikkhus* in Myanmar.

Though Ledi Sayadaw was based at the Ledi-tawya monastery, he travelled throughout Myanmar at times, teaching both medita-

tion and scriptural courses. It was during these trips up and down Myanmar that many of his published works were written. For example, he wrote the *Paṭicca-samuppāda Dīpanī* in two days while travelling by boat from Mandalay to Prome. He had with him no reference books but, because he had a thorough knowledge of the *Tipiṭaka,* he needed none. In the *Manuals of Buddhism* there are seventy-six manuals *(dīpanīs),* commentaries, essays, and so on, listed under his authorship, but this is not a complete list of his works.

Ledi Sayadaw is indeed a rare example of a *bhikkhu* who was able to excel in both *pariyatti* (the theory of Dhamma) as well as *paṭipatti* (the practice of Dhamma). Later he also wrote many books on Dhamma in Burmese. He said he wanted to write in such a way that even a simple farmer could understand. Before his time it was not usual to write on Dhamma subjects so that lay people could have access to them. Even while teaching orally, the *bhikkhus* would commonly recite long passages in Pāli and then translate the passage literally, which was very hard for the ordinary person to understand. It must have been that the strength of Ledi Sayadaw's practical understanding and the resultant *mettā* (loving-kindness) overflowed in his desire to spread Dhamma to all levels of society.

His reputation both as a scholar and a master meditation teacher grew to such an extent that the British government of India, which also ruled Myanmar (as Burma), conferred on him the title of *Aggamahāpaṇḍhita* (foremost great scholar). He was also awarded a Doctorate of Literature from the University of Yangon, and translations of several of his discussions on points of *Abhidhamma* were published in the "Journal of the Pali Text Society" in London.

In the last years of his life Venerable Ledi Sayadaw's eyesight failed him, perhaps because of the years he had spent reading, studying and writing, often with poor illumination. At the age of seventy-three he went blind and devoted the remaining years of his life exclusively to meditation and teaching meditation. He died in 1923 at the age of seventy-seven.

The Venerable Ledi Sayadaw was perhaps the outstanding Buddhist figure of his age. All who have come into contact with the path of Dhamma in recent years owe a great debt of gratitude to this scholarly, saintly monk who was instrumental in re-enlivening the traditional practice of Vipassana, making it more available for renunciates and lay people alike. In addition to this most important aspect of his teaching, his concise, clear and extensive scholarly work served to clarify the experiential aspect of Dhamma.

————————◇————————

Birds are first delivered from their mothers' wombs in the form of eggs. By breaking through the shells, they are delivered for a second time. Finally when they become full fledglings, endowed with feathers and wings, they are delivered from their nests and can fly wherever they please.

Similar is the case of meditators. They are first delivered from the distractions of the mind which have accompanied them throughout the beginningless *saṃsāra* (cycle of rebirth), through successfully setting up mindful body contemplation (mindfulness of the body—*kāyānupassanā*), or by accomplishing the work of tranquillity meditation.

Secondly, when they attain insight (*vipassanā*) into body, mind, aggregates (*rūpa, nāma, khandhā*) and so on, they are free from coarse forms of ignorance.

Finally, when the seven factors of enlightenment (*bojjhaṅga*) develop and mature, they become fully fledged by attaining the knowledge of the supramundane path (*lokuttara-magga-ñāṇa*) called *sambodhi*. Thus are they delivered from the state of worldlings (*puthujjana*), attaining the state of Noble Ones (*ariya*)—the supramundane: *nibbāna*.

> —*from "The Requisites of Enlightenment"*
> (Bodhipakkhiya Dīpanī)
> *by Venerable Ledi Sayadaw*
> (*translated from the original Burmese*)

Saya Thetgyi (1873–1945)

Saya Thetgyi (pronounced *Sa yá taji* in Burmese) was born on June 27, 1873, in the farming village of Pyawbwegyi, eight miles south of Yangon, and was given the name Maung Po Thet. He had two brothers and a sister. When Maung Po Thet was about ten years old, his father died, leaving their mother to care for the four children. His mother supported the family by making and selling vegetable fritters, and the shy little boy was made to go around the village selling the leftovers.

Because he was needed to help support the family, Maung Po's formal education was minimal—only about six years. His parents did not own any land or paddy (rice) fields, and used to collect for food the stalks of the paddy which were left over after harvesting.

When he was fourteen years old, Maung Po Thet started working as a bullock driver of a cart carrying paddy. He gave his daily wages to his mother. He was so small at the time that he had to take along a special box to stand on in order to get in and out of the cart.

As was customary, when he was about sixteen years old, Maung Po Thet married Ma Hmyin. His wife was the youngest of three daughters of a well-to-do landowner and paddy merchant. The couple had two children, a daughter and a son. Following custom, they lived in a joint family with Ma Hmyin's parents and sisters. The younger sister, Ma Yin, remained single and managed a successful small business. She was later instrumental in supporting U Thet in his practice and teaching of meditation. At around twenty-three years of age, U Thet began to practice meditation with a lay teacher, Saya Nyunt. From him he learned *ānāpāna* which he practiced for seven years.

U Thet and his wife had many friends and relatives living close by in the village. With many uncles, nephews, nieces, cousins and in-laws, they led an idyllic life of contentment in the warmth and harmony of family and friends. This rustic peace and happiness was shattered when a cholera epidemic struck the village in 1903. Many villagers died, some within a few days. They included U Thet's son, his teenage daughter, and other relatives. This calamity affected U Thet deeply. He could not find refuge anywhere, and he desperately wanted to find a way out of his misery. He asked permission from his wife and sister-in-law Ma Yin, as well as other relatives, to leave the village. Leaving them to manage the rice fields, he set out on a spiritual search, accompanied by a companion and follower, U Nyo.

U Thet wandered all over Myanmar in his fervent search, visiting mountain retreats and forest monasteries, studying with different teachers, both monks and laymen. Finally he followed the suggestion of his first teacher, Saya Nyunt, to go north to Monywa to practice with the venerable Ledi Sayadaw.

U Thet stayed with Ledi Sayadaw for seven years in all, during which time his wife and sister-in-law supported him by sending money each year from the harvest of the family farmland.

After seven years, accompanied by U Nyo, he returned to his village, but he did not return to his former householder's life. Ledi Sayadaw had advised him at the time of his departure to work diligently to develop his *samādhi* (concentration) and *paññā* (purifying wisdom) so that eventually he could begin to teach.

Accordingly, when U Thet and U Nyo reached Pyawbwegyi, they went straight to the *sālā* (rest-house) at the edge of the family farm, which they used as a Dhamma hall. Here they began to meditate continuously. They arranged for a woman who lived near the Dhamma hall to cook two meals a day while they continued their retreat.

U Thet continued in this way for one year. He made rapid progress in his meditation, and at the end of the period he felt the need for advice from his teacher. He could not speak to Ledi Sayadaw himself, but he knew that his teacher's books were in a cupboard at his home. So he went there to consult the manuals.

His wife and her sister had become quite angry with him for not returning to the house after such a long absence. His wife had even decided to divorce him. When the sisters saw U Thet approaching the house, they agreed neither to greet nor welcome him. But, as soon as he came in the door, they could not resist and found themselves welcoming him profusely. They talked for awhile, and U Thet asked for their forgiveness, which they freely granted.

They invited him for tea and a meal. He procured the books and explained to his wife that he was now living on eight precepts and would not be returning to the usual householder's life. From now on they would be as brother and sister.

His wife and sister-in-law invited him to come to the house each day for his morning meal and happily agreed to continue supporting him. He was extremely grateful for their generosity and told them that the only way he could repay them was to give them the Dhamma.

At first the people in the village were reluctant to come to him for instruction. They misinterpreted U Thet's zeal, thinking that perhaps after the grief of his losses and his absence from the village, he had lost his senses. But slowly they realized from his speech and actions that he was indeed a transformed person, one who was living in accordance with Dhamma.

U Thet started teaching *ānāpāna* to a group of about fifteen people in 1914, when he was forty-one years old. The students all stayed at the resthouse, some of them going home from time to time.

A year later U Thet took his wife, her sister and a few other family members to pay respects to his teacher. During this visit, Ledi Sayadaw gave his wooden staff to U Thet, saying: "Here, my great pupil, take my staff and go. Keep it well. I do not give this to you to make you live long, but as a reward, so that there will be no mishaps in your life. You have been successful. From today onwards, you must teach the Dhamma of *rūpa* and *nāma* (matter and mind) to six thousand people. The Dhamma known by you is inexhaustible, so propagate the *sāsana* (era of the Buddha's teaching). Pay homage to the *sāsana* in my stead."

Ledi Sayadaw summoned the monks of his monastery and told them: "This layperson is my great pupil U Po Thet... He is capable of teaching meditation like me... Learn the technique from him, and practice." U Thet taught Vipassana to about twenty-five learned monks of the monastery, at which point he became known as Saya Thetgyi (*saya*, meaning teacher; and *gyi*, a suffix denoting respect).

On returning to their village, Saya Thetgyi talked with his family about how to carry out Ledi Sayadaw's tall order. At first Saya Thetgyi thought that he must travel around the country teaching, but his sister-in-law suggested that he stay and continue teaching in his Dhamma hall in the resthouse. As his sister-in-law predicted, many did start coming, and Saya Thetgyi's reputation as a meditation teacher spread. He taught simple farmers and laborers as well as those who were well-versed in the Pāli texts. The village was not far from Yangon, which was the capital of Myanmar under the British, so government employees and urbanites, like U Ba Khin, also came.

From the time he returned from Ledi Sayadaw's center, Saya Thetgyi lived by himself and ate only one meal a day, in solitude and silence.

For thirty years he taught meditation to all who came to him, guided by his own experience and using Ledi Sayadaw's manuals as a reference. By 1945, when he was seventy-two, he had fulfilled his mission of teaching thousands. His wife had died; his sister-in-law had become paralyzed; and his own health was failing. So he distributed all his property to his nieces and nephews, setting aside fifty acres of rice paddy for the maintenance of his Dhamma hall.

He had twenty water buffaloes that had tilled his fields for years. He distributed them to people who he knew would treat them kindly, and sent them off with the invocation, "You have been my benefactors. Thanks to you the rice has been grown. Now you are freed from your work. May you be released from this kind of life for a better existence."

Saya Thetgyi moved to Yangon both for medical treatment and to be near his students there. One of them had established a meditation center on the northern slope of Shwedagon Pagoda. Nearby was a bomb shelter that had been built during the Second World War. Saya Thetgyi used this as his meditation cave. His students from Yangon, including U Ba Khin, came to see him as much as time permitted. Every night he would sit in meditation with his students, numbering about fifty. During these group meditations Saya Thetgyi did not speak, only silently meditated. During one of these group meditations, Saya Thetgyi, who had been sick with cold and fever, lay on his back and, after about an hour of labored breathing, he passed away.

His body was cremated on the northern slope of Shwedagon Pagoda, and Sayagyi U Ba Khin and his disciples later built a small pagoda on the spot. But perhaps the most fitting and enduring memorial to this singular teacher is the fact that the task given him by Ledi Sayadaw of spreading the Dhamma in all strata of society is continuing.

Playing With Fire

Among those who came to learn meditation from Saya Thetgyi was a Buddhist scholar, a very learned man. Unfortunately he seemed to be more interested in the theory of Vipassana than in experiencing it himself. Still, he completed his ten-day course successfully, and left well-pleased with what he had accomplished.

A few months later this man returned to visit Saya Thetgyi, and respectfully placed before him one or two volumes. "Sir," he said, "I have written a book explaining how to meditate, and I have dedicated it to you as my teacher."

Saya Thetgyi asked, "Are only these copies that you brought here dedicated to me?"

"Oh no, sir! All contain the dedication."

"Well, if you wish to dedicate them all to me, bring all the copies of your book here." The scholar happily agreed to do so, thinking perhaps that Saya Thetgyi would perform a ceremony to bless his work. After a few days he returned with a cartload of books.

"Are these all the copies of your book?" asked Saya Thetgyi.

"Yes, sir," the man replied proudly.

"Very well," said Saya Thetgyi, "Put them in the fallow field over there." The scholar did as Saya Thet directed, arranging the books in a neat pile.

"Now," said the teacher, "Go the kitchen and get a bottle of kerosene and some matches."

"Kerosene, sir? Matches?" The man was bewildered. What use could Saya Thetgyi have for these in the ceremony?

"Yes, kerosene and matches." Once again the scholar did as he was told, though somewhat reluctantly. When he returned with the bottle and matches, Saya Thetgyi said, "Good! Now sprinkle the kerosene over the books and set them alight."

The scholar could restrain himself no longer. "What, sir! You must be joking! I have labored so many months to write this book."

Saya Thetgyi replied, "You would have better used your time to meditate. How can you explain meditation to others unless you have meditated deeply yourself? And even if you yourself had understood it properly, how could you expect others to learn meditation from a book? They would only burn themselves as surely as children playing with fire. Better to burn the books!"

Webu Sayadaw (1896–1977)

Venerable Webu Sayadaw was one of the most highly respected monks of this century in Myanmar. He was notable in giving all importance to diligent practice rather than to scholastic achievement.

Webu Sayadaw was born in the village of Ingyinpin in upper Myanmar on February 17, 1896. He underwent the usual monk's training in the Pāli scriptures from the age of nine, when he became a novice, until he was twenty-seven. In 1923 (seven years after his ordination), he left the monastery and spent four years in solitude.

He practiced (and later taught) the technique of *ānāpāna-sati* (awareness of the in-breath and out-breath). He said that by working with this practice to a very deep level of concentration, one is able to develop *vipassanā* (insight) into the essential characteristics of all experience: *anicca* (impermanence), *anattā* (egolessness) and *dukkha* (unsatisfactoriness).

Webu Sayadaw was famous for his unflagging diligence in meditation and for spending most of his time in solitude. He was reputed to be an *arahant* (fully enlightened one), and it is said that he never slept.

For the first fifty-seven years of his life, Webu Sayadaw stayed in upper Myanmar, dividing his time among three meditation centers in a small area. After his first trip to Yangon, at the invitation of Sayagyi U Ba Khin, in 1953, he included southern Myanmar in his travels, visiting there to teach and meditate from time to time. He also went on pilgrimage to India and Sri Lanka. Webu Sayadaw spent his final days at the meditation center in the village where he was born. He passed away on June 26, 1977, at the age of eighty-one.

His First Encounter with Sayagyi U Ba Khin

At the beginning of 1941, an event occurred that had great importance for the life of U Ba Khin. He was promoted to the post of Chief Accounts Officer of the Burma Railways Board. One of his

duties was to travel on the Rangoon-Mandalay line, auditing the accounts of local stations. He travelled in a special carriage for the Chief Accountant, with full facilities for office work and sleeping overnight. His carriage would be attached to the main train, then detached at various stations.

One day in July, by error, his carriage was detached at a station in the town of Kyaukse, forty miles south of Mandalay. Although he was not scheduled to audit the accounts here, as Accounts Officer he was authorized to check the accounts of any station, and he proceeded to do so. When his work was over, he decided to visit the nearby Shwetharlyaung Hill and set out with the local station master. Sayagyi had heard that a monk named Webu Sayadaw, who had reached a high stage of development, was residing in the area. From the top of the hill they could see a cluster of buildings in the distance. They recognized this as the monastery of Webu Sayadaw and decided to go there.

At about 3:00 p.m. they arrived at the compound. An old nun sat pounding chilies and beans, and they asked her if they could pay respects to the Sayadaw. "This is not the time to see the reverend Sayadaw," she said. "He is meditating and will not come out of his hut until about six o'clock. This monk does not entertain people. He only comes out of his hut for about half an hour in the evening. If there are people here at this time, he may give a discourse and then return to his hut. He will not meet people at times they may wish to meet him."

U Ba Khin explained that he was a visitor from Yangon and that he did not have much time. He would like very much to meet Webu Sayadaw. Would it not be possible to pay respects outside? The nun pointed out the hut, a small bamboo structure, and the visitors went there together. Sayagyi knelt on the ground and said, "Venerable Sir, I have come all the way from lower Myanmar, Yangon, and wish to pay respects to you."

To everyone's astonishment, the door to the hut opened and the Sayadaw emerged, preceded by a cloud of mosquitoes. Sayagyi paid respects, keeping his attention in the body with awareness of *anicca*.

"What is your aspiration, layman?" Webu Sayadaw asked Sayagyi.

"My aspiration is to attain *nibbāna*, sir," U Ba Khin replied.

"*Nibbāna*? How are you going to attain *nibbāna*?"

"Through meditation and by knowing *anicca*, sir," said Sayagyi.

"Where did you learn to be aware of this *anicca*?"

Sayagyi explained how he had studied Vipassana meditation under Saya Thetgyi.

"You have been practicing Vipassana?"

"Yes, sir, I am practicing Vipassana."

"What sort of Vipassana?" Webu Sayadaw questioned him closely and Sayagyi gave the details. The Sayadaw was very pleased. He said, "I have been meditating in this jungle alone for years in order to experience such stages of Vipassana as you describe." He seemed astonished to encounter a householder who had reached advanced proficiency in the practice without being a monk.

Webu Sayadaw meditated with Sayagyi, and after some time said, "You must start teaching now. You have acquired good *pāramī* (accumulated merit), and you must teach the Dhamma to others. Do not let people who meet you miss the benefits of receiving this teaching. You must not wait. You must teach—teach now!"

With a Dhamma exhortation of such strength from this saintly person, U Ba Khin felt he had no choice but to teach. Back at the railway station, the assistant station master became his first student. Sayagyi instructed him in *ānāpāna* meditation in his railway carriage, using the two tables of the dining compartment as their seats.

Although Sayagyi did not begin to teach in a formal way until about a decade later, this incident was a watershed. It marked the point at which Sayagyi began to share his knowledge of meditation with others.

Questions and Answers

Q: What was the historical role U Ba Khin played in the development and spreading of this method of Vipassana meditation?

S.N. Goenka: U Ba Khin found himself continuing the work of teaching Vipassana meditation almost 2500 years after the Buddha taught, in accord with certain predictions—that the Dhamma in the form of Vipassana would begin to spread at this time. It was exactly then that U Ba Khin arrived to teach. As was said previously, his many societal obligations didn't leave him much time to dedicate to the spread of Vipassana meditation, but he taught a number of people who had such remarkable qualities that they became vehicles for the spread of Dhamma in the form of Vipassana.

Q: What are the main characteristics of U Ba Khin's teachings?

SNG: Meditators must start with *sīla*: that is, they must begin in their lives to respect certain basic moral principles. Then they must begin to develop *samādhi* (mental concentration), cultivating the awareness of the natural breath, only pure breath without adding other objects of concentration. And then they must begin to develop *paññā* (wisdom) through the observation of sensations on the body. Observing sensations with equanimity, without reacting, and understanding their characteristic of *anicca* (impermanence), one learns to stop generating mental impurities, which then allows those accumulated impurities finally to come to the surface and be eradicated. This is what U Ba Khin taught; this is what the Buddha taught; this is what I, myself, am teaching.

Q: What is the unique characteristic of Vipassana meditation as taught by U Ba Khin?

SNG: All importance is given to *bhāvāna-maya-paññā*, which is the wisdom that one develops through direct personal experience. With *suta-maya-paññā* (wisdom acquired by simply listening to someone else) or *cintā-maya-paññā* (wisdom obtained through reasoning and intellectual analysis), a person can purify the mind, but only to a certain degree. It is only with *bhāvāna-maya-paññā* (wisdom acquired through direct personal experience) that one can purify the mind at the deepest levels. The Buddha called the deepest mental conditioning *sankhāra anusaya kilesa*, that is, the conditioning hidden in our unconscious mind. He taught that only when these become eradicated could a person become completely liberated. And this could only be done through *bhāvāna-maya-paññā*, that is, with the wisdom derived from direct experience. And that direct experience can be acquired only by observing equanimously the physical sensations on the body. This is the basic contribution of the Buddha to humanity and this is what U Ba Khin continued to teach.

Q: How was the relationship between U Ba Khin and the monastic community of Myanmar?

SNG: He had excellent relations with the community of monks in Myanmar and had great respect for the monastic teachers, who also had a very good rapport with him. They had much loving-kindness for him and were proud of his teaching. They considered it a correct way of teaching Vipassana meditation. They were very happy for him, and naturally some of them would have preferred that U Ba Khin become a monk so that a great number of monks could participate in his courses. But U Ba Khin wasn't ready for this, simply because he wanted to spread Dhamma as well to all those who didn't consider themselves Buddhists. Teaching them in the robes of a monk could be interpreted as an attempt to convert them to a sect or religion. U Ba Khin was aware of this obstacle. He wanted lay people, householders, to learn this universal technique of purifying the mind of negativities and conditioning, so that they could become better lay people, better householders. For this he remained a lay teacher, in order to be an example, to be an inspiration.

Q: What type of Vipassana did U Ba Khin first learn? And what changes (if any) did he introduce in his teaching?

SNG: No changes. The same thing he learned, he passed on to future generations. No changes in the technique were made by anyone in this tradition.

Q: Do you think that U Ba Khin taught exactly what the Buddha taught? Did he adapt the Buddha's teachings to modern times? And if so, how and what did he change from the original teachings?

SNG: There was no change in the teaching, but U Ba Khin certainly made the way of presenting the teachings of the Buddha more adapted to the people who came to him. To the non-Buddhist, English-speaking Western people, who were more scientific minded, he would present the teaching in a more scientific way. So the explanation was made more palatable to those who were coming to learn, but the actual practical teaching remained the same.

Q: Why is your teaching called "in the tradition of Sayagyi U Ba Khin"? Did he inaugurate a tradition of Buddhism?

SNG: He always referred to the tradition of the Buddha, the tradition that was transferred to Myanmar and was continued down through the three generations of teachers we spoke about: Ledi Sayadaw, his disciple Saya Thetgyi, and finally U Ba Khin. We use the term "in the tradition of U Ba Khin" because he was the last teacher and was very well-known in his country, but this does not mean that this is a technique invented by him. It's an old technique which he was teaching in a modern way.

Q: Do you follow in your teachings the same path as U Ba Khin or have you introduced some changes?

SNG: No changes. It is not possible to change anything in the Buddha's teachings. You can make some change only if you become a super-Buddha. All those who are below the status of Buddha, below attaining the state of Buddhahood, should not make any change. In order to render the teaching clearer you needn't correct the essence; but the manner of teaching naturally can change. That is how it is that U Ba Khin, who had to teach modern Western students, explained things in a more scientific way, in a way that they could understand—as have I, for instance, when I came to India, and had to deal with a great number of people who belonged to different religious sects. Being myself originally from India and knowing the history of the religiosity and spirituality of the Indian people, when I face a person with such a past, I must understand what is behind this person and explain things in a way that enables them to better understand the teaching of the Buddha. This doesn't mean the technique is changed. It is only a way to explain things to people so that they can understand without any doubt.

Chapter Four

Characteristics of U Ba Khin's Method

For progressing in Vipassana meditation, a student must keep knowing anicca *as continuously as possible. The Buddha's advice to monks is that they should try to maintain the awareness of* anicca, dukkha *or* anattā *in all postures... Continuous awareness of* anicca, *and so of* dukkha *and* anattā, *is the secret of success.*

The last words of the Buddha just before he breathed his last and passed away into Mahā Parinibbāna *were: "Decay (or* anicca) *is inherent in all component things. Work out your own salvation with diligence."*

This is in fact the essence of all his teachings during the forty-five years of his ministry. If you will keep up the awareness of the anicca *that is inherent in all component things, you are sure to reach the goal in the course of time.*

—Sayagyi U Ba Khin,

U Ba Khin developed a direct approach to Vipassana meditation, making it possible to grasp it in a brief period of intensive practice and from then on to continue it as part of lay life. His method has been of great importance for the transmission of Dhamma in the West, because during twenty years of teaching at his center, he taught thousands of foreigners who needed no previous knowledge of Buddhism in order to immediately grasp this profound practice. Since U Ba Khin's death in 1971 several of his most committed students have carried on his work, both in Myanmar and abroad.

What is the purpose of Vipassana, this meditation of profound insight? Is it different in some way for someone who has dedicated his whole life to the practice than it is for someone who has a job and a family to support? In the broadest sense, there is no difference. The goal is the ending of suffering. The aim of the practice is the experience of "the *nibbānic* peace within," as U Ba Khin has explained it. But the benefits the practice offers also have to do with daily life, with the suffering born of inner tension, and with the anxiety and fears arising from the stress of modern life. The capacity to live, here and now, in a harmonious manner, able to manifest love and kindness, the capacity to execute one's daily duties without anger, greed or anxiety is attainable not only for monks but also for lay people.

U Ba Khin realized that his own students, unlike the monks, had many practical limitations and little time to dedicate to the practice. Moreover, they had to live in, and interact with, the world at large, outside the refuge of a monastery with much less control of their environment. Such conditions are generally hostile to correct moral conduct and good concentration which are requisites for deep understanding. For all these reasons, he gave them a method that enabled them to resist these pressures. Within the short period of ten days many of his students were able to experience at least a glimmer of the reality within and could continue to expand this consciousness through two hours of daily meditation after they left the center.

Understanding that the practice of *sīla* (morality) was fundamental, he always stressed the importance of observance of the five moral precepts which the Buddha prescribed for laymen: to refrain from killing, from stealing, from sexual misconduct, from lying and from the use of all intoxicants.

With the practice of *sīla* as a foundation, this technique has three particular qualities: first of all, development of a certain level of concentration. On this point U Ba Khin has written:

> *Samādhi* (concentration) is a way of training the mind to become tranquil, pure and strong, and therefore forms the essence of religious life, whether one be a Buddhist, a Jew, a Christian, a Hindu, a Muslim, or a Sikh. It is, in fact, the greatest common denominator of all religions. Unless one can get the mind freed from the impurities (*nīvarana*) and develop it to a state of purity, he can hardly identify himself with the *Brahmā* or God. Although different methods are used by people of different religions, the goal for the development of mind is the same, i.e., a perfect state of physical and mental calm. The student at the [Vipassana] center is helped to develop the power of concentration to one-pointedness by being encouraged to focus his attention on a spot on the upper lip at the base of the nose, synchronizing the inward and outward motion of respiration with silent awareness of in-breath and out-breath…. In the *ānāpāna* meditation technique [i.e., that of respiration mindfulness]which is followed at the center, one great advantage is that the respiration is not only natural, but also available at all times for the purpose of anchoring one's attention to it to the exclusion of all other thoughts. With a determined effort to narrow down the range of thought waves firstly to the area around the nose with respiration mindfulness and gradually, with the wavelength of respiration becoming shorter and shorter, to a spot on the upper lip with just the warmth of the breath, there is no reason why a good student in meditation should not be able to secure the one-pointedness of mind in a few days of training.

It was necessary for students to develop good mental concentration in a brief period of time, in order to have a certain degree of penetrative power to fully experience, rather than merely intellectualize, the inner truth. This was different from the traditional monastic practice according to which one must develop subtle concentration to the highest levels. The lay practitoner would seldom have either the time or the complete isolation required for such levels of *samādhi*. But at the same time U Ba Khin wasn't satisfied with a minimal practice of concentration. What interested him was attaining a level of concentration sufficient to work in the field of deep wisdom.

The second characteristic of U Ba Khin's teaching is the emphasis on *anicca*—impermanence. The Buddha said that all experience, all mundane phenomena, have three characteristics: impermanence, dissatisfaction (or suffering) and the absence of a personal self. Practicing awareness and observing only what is manifesting naturally, attention is to be focused on these three characteristics of reality. This practice results in eliminating false beliefs and weakening attachment. U Ba Khin taught that the most direct way of understanding these essential attributes is through the awareness of *anicca* (impermanence). He asserted that *anicca* is the most apparent and understandable of the three characteristics, and that perceiving *anicca* will automatically lead to the understanding of the other two.

The real goal of his method of teaching the technique of Vipassana is continuous observation of the changing, transitory physical phenomena within the framework of the body—the systematic observation of physical sensations. As the Buddha emphasizes repeatedly in the *Mahāsatipaṭṭhāna Sutta*, the subtle reality of arising-and-passing-away *(samudayavaya)* is inherent in every aspect of the mind-body phenomenon. U Ba Khin knew that this process is strong and easily discernible in the physical sensations of the body. His students were encouraged to place their concentrated attention upon these sensations in order to become sensitive to the process of change, the process that they could observe in the tactile experience of heat, cold, pain, numbness, pressure, etc. He taught them to simply observe the mutable nature of phenomena within the framework of the body. He always maintained that the continuity of the practice would bring spiritual as well as practical results. He was certain that a lay person was capable of actually experiencing the fruits of *nibbāna* in this very lifetime. And he encouraged people not to be satisfied merely with ritual practices or with books concerning the teachings.

The practice, as expressed by his student S.N. Goenka, is also an "art of living." U Ba Khin was so convinced of the power the method had to clear the mind that he strongly urged all the employees of his office in the Department of the Accountant General to take a meditation course conducted by him. For this purpose he set aside one part of the office for the practice of meditation. Sometimes during particularly chaotic government meetings, often with people full of contentious opinions, in the middle of the most heated discussions U Ba Khin would get up and stand for a few minutes gazing out the window. Then he would return to the meeting table. His colleagues thought that he was viewing the outside world, but U Ba Khin explained to those close to him that he was actually pausing to look inside, to re-establish his awareness in order to be in a better position to face the problems at hand in the meeting.

The third characteristic of U Ba Khin's method is the intensity of practice during brief periods of ten days in order to provide total immersion for people who have little time and must return immediately to the multitude of activities and responsibilities of daily life. For this reason U Ba Khin always emphasized for his students the practical and concrete aspects of the meditative work, reducing to a minimum theoretical and doctrinal explanations. For him it was and is a question of living the Dhamma—the natural law that regulates the universe—through one's own experience of applying a direct and intensive method.

Briefly outlining the method, it consists of the practice of morality, then concentrating the mind, beginning with awareness of the breath, and then directing the concentrated attention to various parts of the body, moving systematically throughout the whole physical structure in order to develop an increasingly thorough and subtle awareness of all the sensations arising there. The goal is to perceive with increasing clarity all the sensations as they manifest themselves, no matter what they may be, and by means of this perception, to develop an increasingly complete and penetrating awareness of the continuous arising-and-passing-away of physical and mental phenomena, of which the sensations are the manifestation. This is the observation of the body and of sensations, actually the first two arenas where awareness must be established, as they are described in one of the Buddha's primary discourses, the *Mahāsatipaṭṭhāna Sutta.*

The other two arenas (observation of the mind and of mental phenomena) are practiced in this method only to the extent necessary to maintain a continuity of awareness: all the thoughts, emotions, etc., that arise during the main practice of observing physical sensations in the body, would be noticed when arising, but the attention always remains focused on the body sensations, because it is through the clear perception of these and of their impermanent nature that the purification of the mind takes place. As the Buddha said: "Within this very fathom-long body containing the mind with its perceptions, I make known the universe, its origin, its cessation, and the way leading to its cessation." *(Aṅguttara-nikāya, Catukkanipāta 5.5, Rohitassa Sutta)*

Little by little, as perception of the corporeal processes becomes more subtle and precise, awareness increases of their instability and transitory nature. This is, in effect, the experience of *anicca*, of the radical impermanence of all that exists. In the terminology of U Ba Khin, this experience is described as "the activation of *anicca*." This activation, this awareness of impermanence at the level of direct experience—that gradually grows and expands throughout the body, inside and outside—clears the mind of desires, attachments, aversions, anxieties, fears, and tensions, reorganizing the old habit patterns of the mind. The benefits extend also to the physical body, often alleviating disorders and psychosomatic diseases.

What really happens can only be approximately described. Little by little, as the meditator penetrates more and more into the true nature of phenomena through the clear awareness of *anicca*—that is, through a direct cognizance of impermanence—the time comes when a different mental attitude arises, an element of experiential equanimity that has the effect of eliminating greed, aversion, anxiety, fear. As a consequence, the characteristic attractions and avoidances that give rise to our suffering lose their influence over us, and the attachment to what we erroneously consider our permanent personality diminishes. In the words of U Ba Khin:

> In the same way as fuel is burnt away by ignition, the negative forces (impurities or poisons) within are eliminated by the *nibbāna dhātu*, which [one] generates with the true awareness of *anicca* in the course of meditation....
>
> The experience of *anicca*, when properly developed, strikes at the root of one's physical and mental ills and removes gradually whatever is bad in [oneself], i.e., the causes of such physical and mental ills. This experience is not reserved for men who have renounced the world for the homeless life. It is for the householder as well. In spite of drawbacks which make a householder restless in these days, a competent teacher or guide can help a student to get the experience of *anicca* activated in a comparatively short time. Once he has got it activated, all that is necessary for him is to try to preserve it....

In order to develop it further, it is essential, after having completed a course, to practice regularly on one's own. However, U Ba Khin, being a very pragmatic man, didn't expect the impossible from an ordinary, busy individual:

> There is no need...to be activating the experience of *anicca* all the time. It should suffice if this could be confined to a regular period, or periods, set apart in the day or night for the purpose. During this time, at least, an attempt must be made to keep the attention focused inside the body, with awareness devoted exclusively to *anicca*. That is to say...awareness of *anicca* should go on from moment to moment so continuously as not to allow for the interpolation of any discursive or distracting thoughts, which are definitely detrimental to progress.

And speaking with all the authority that he had derived through his experience, U Ba Khin has been often quoted:

> We have no doubt whatsoever that definite results would accrue to those who would with an open mind sincerely undergo a course of training under a competent teacher—I mean results which will be accepted as good, concrete, vivid, personal, here-and-now—results which will keep them in good stead and in a state of well-being and happiness for the rest of their lives.

A brief practical description of these ten-day courses "in the tradition of U Ba Khin" can be found in the last chapter of this book.

Questions and Answers

Q: Why did U Ba Khin place so much emphasis on the understanding of *anicca*?

S.N. Goenka: Because this is what the Buddha taught. The Buddha explained that the teaching is about developing one's own wisdom, one's own *bhāvanā-mayā-paññā*, through observing sensations with the understanding of *anicca*, of their impermanence. It is only this experience, this understanding of impermanence, that can lead a person to penetrate the real truth of suffering, and this in turn leads to understanding the non-existence of the ego, understanding that there is no "I," no self.

Q: Why did U Ba Khin stress so much the continuity of practice, structuring the ten-day courses with such an intensive program?

SNG: Because this is what the teachings of the Buddha require— that the awareness of sensations with the understanding of *anicca* be maintained constantly, continuously, day and night. The period of a course is only ten days, which is a very short time. Therefore, for their own benefit, U Ba Khin suggested to his students that they maintain continuous awareness for as long as possible.

Q: Why did U Ba Khin give most importance to the observation of bodily sensations? And why the predominance of observing material phenomena—and thus the body with the base of sensations—as more important than observing mental phenomena?

SNG: Because when one speaks of observing the mind, most people understand that not as objectively experiencing the mind but as contemplating the mind, which would mean continuing to roll in it, continuing to react, and this is not the teaching of the Buddha. On the contrary, when one is working with body sensations, there is actually a direct, tangible, concrete experience that doesn't at all involve the imagination and is thus without any illusions. When the Buddha requires working with bodily sensations, physical sensations, this doesn't mean completely neglecting the mind—because it isn't the body that perceives the sensations, it is the mind. The sensations are on the body but they are felt and perceived by the mind. Mind and matter are both involved when a person observes sensations.

In fact, whatever arises in the mind manifests itself as a sensation in the body. One cannot emphasize this teaching enough. To observe only mental states will improve your faculty of observation, but this is not the whole truth. You are only observing your thoughts. But what is happening in the body at that moment? Both mind and body must be observed. When a thought arises, simultaneously there is a sensation in the body. And the sensation is actually the root of the problem. We do not react to the thoughts. It could seem that when we have a pleasant thought in the mind, craving begins, and when we have an unpleasant thought, aversion begins. But in fact, in keeping with the law of nature, that which we call a pleasant thought is nothing other than a pleasant sensation in the body. If you overlook the observation of physical sensations, you are working only at a superficial level. You can still derive some benefit from this, but it will not enable you to eradicate your impurities. The roots remain.

Q: Can you explain the Buddha's concept that the entire universe is contained within this very body?

SNG: Indeed, within this body turns the wheel of becoming. Within this body is the cause that puts into motion the wheel of becoming. And so within this body is also found the way to attain liberty from the wheel of suffering. For this reason investigation of the body is of utmost importance for a meditator whose goal is liberation from all conditioning. Unless one attains correct understanding of the direct physical reality within, of the reality which is the base of one's existence, the wheel of becoming within oneself continues to turn. Gradually, as correct understanding is developed, little by little the turning of the wheel slows down, until the point at which we end up liberated from the slavery of becoming.

Q: Can you explain in detail how our senses work within the body?

SNG: The five physical senses and the mind are all based upon the body. Through these six doors all of our contact with the external world occurs. For us the universe exists only when it comes into contact with one of these sense doors. A shape, for example, exists for us only when it comes into contact with the eye; otherwise for us, in fact, it has no existence. In the same way, a sound must come in contact with hearing and with the ear in order to really exist for us; a smell with the nose; a tactile object with the touch; a thought or a fantasy with the mind—otherwise they do not have for us any real existence. The entire universe manifests itself through these six doors which are found within the physical structure. For this reason it has been rightly said that the entire universe exists within this body. To investigate the reality within oneself in a scientific manner a meditator must set aside all beliefs, philosophies, imaginations and dogmas. To be able to arrive at knowing the ultimate reality within oneself, it is necessary to work only with the truth, and to accept as true only what one experiences directly. If one explores the truth in this way, all the mysteries of nature will be revealed.

Q: In what way must meditators approach the observation of their own bodies?

SNG: In the beginning the meditator finds gross, solid, apparent truth, that is, gross physical sensations, and from that point begins to penetrate these physical sensations, moving toward increasingly subtle truths, down to the most subtle, which was described by U Ba Khin as *kalāpa* (the smallest unit of matter, subatomic particles). Through direct experience the meditator realizes that contact of the eyes with a visible form gives rise to eye-consciousness—that is, to mental cognition of the fact that contact has occurred. Furthermore, the meditator realizes that the contact produces a vibration, a sensation that spreads throughout the body, as when you strike a bronze container at one point and the contact makes the entire vessel vibrate. When the contact has been acknowledged, the process of perception manifests: the visible form becomes recognized—for example, as a man or a woman, white or black, ugly or beautiful. Not only is the contact identified but it is also evaluated, as good or bad, positive or negative, pleasant or unpleasant. Finally if the sensation, due to the contact, is experienced as pleasant, the mind reacts with craving; if unpleasant, the mind reacts with aversion.

Then the meditator begins to understand clearly how these four parts of the mind—cognition, perception, sensation and reaction—actually work. Craving intensifies pleasant sensations, and pleasant sensations intensify craving. Aversion increases unpleasant sensations, and unpleasant sensations increase aversion. Whoever meditates properly will understand how, based on bodily sensations, the vicious circle begins and continues to manifest moment after moment. This is the wheel of becoming, of suffering.

The same process arises following contact of the ear with sound, the nose with smell, the tongue with taste, the body with a tangible object, the mind with a thought. In this way the wheel of becoming continues to turn, pushed by craving and aversion. In order to attain liberation from the wheel of becoming and gain real happiness, it is necessary to objectively observe this process that arises from bodily sensations.

Q: Now let's analyze the details of the technique. For concentrating the mind, why did U Ba Khin choose such a restricted area below the nostrils? And why did he insist on narrowing the area to the smallest point possible? Why did he suggest perceiving a sensation along with the awareness of respiration? Isn't *ānāpāna* only concentrating on respiration?

SNG: For the practice of Vipassana, and to carry the Buddha's teachings into the practice, awareness of body sensations is essential. For that reason, along with the work of observing the respiration as it comes in and as it goes out, it is necessary to begin perceiving sensations, feeling sensation in this small part of the body. The smaller the area, the more the mind grows sharp, penetrating and concentrated. Therefore, the more concentrated the mind is, the more sensitive it becomes and able to perceive sensation. If the mind is kept very distracted working on a larger area, it is more difficult to arrive at perceiving sensations, especially subtle sensations. For that reason it is only after two or three days of *ānāpāna*, in which concentration on respiration is practiced, that students are taught the observation of sensations.

Q: Why did U Ba Khin use the term "free flow," meaning to examine the whole body at once, to observe the entire body in one glance, from the top of the head to the tip of the toes, and in so doing observe all the physical sensations present in the body? This technique of observing sensations through the body is also called "sweeping." Is this a new technique different from the teaching of the Buddha?

SNG: It is only a different way to explain the same concept. When the entire solidity of the body and of the mind is dissolved, then it is possible to move one's attention from the head to the feet without any obstacle. In Pāli this stage is called *bhaṅga*, meaning dissolution, because there is no obstacle in any part. This situation can be called "free flow"—"free" because there is really no obstacle and we can pass our attention from head to feet and from feet to head, as a flow. Describing the work of the meditator at this stage, the Buddha used these words: "*sabba kāya paṭisamvedi assasissāmī,*" ti sikkhati; "*sabba kaya paṭisamvedi passasissāmī*", ti sikkhati ("Feeling the whole body I shall breathe in," thus he trains himself; "feeling the whole body I shall breathe out," thus he trains himself)—*(Dīgha-nikāya II.9, Mahāsatipaṭṭhāna Sutta)*

When one attains this state of *bhaṅga* (dissolution), then with every breath, inhalation or exhalation, it is possible to perceive the entire body. We can use different words to express this concept. If the people listening are able to understand in a certain way, then one can use different words, but this doesn't mean that something new has been invented with regard to the technique. Call it by whatever name, but the fact remains that such an experience is an important stage on the journey toward full liberation.

This term "free flow" can be explained by understanding that, at a certain stage, the entire solidity of the body dissolves. The apparent truth of the material body is solidity. We experience the body as solid. But as we keep observing it objectively, this solidity begins to dissolve, and we start experiencing the entire material structure as nothing but a mass of subatomic particles arising and passing away, arising and passing away, continuously. The entire body is just a mass of vibrations. At first, however, when we are still working with the solidity, we can't have this free flow of vibrations throughout the body, because there are blockages, such as intense pain, pressure, heaviness. Then we must continue to work observing the body part by part—"thus he trains himself"—and little by little all this solidity dissolves and we reach the state of total dissolution, where we perceive nothing but vibrations. Then our attention can move easily from head to feet and from feet to head without any obstruction.

Q: So the free flow occurs when there are no blockages anywhere and the whole body is without obstructions?

SNG: Exactly—only when there is no blockage of any type, not even mental. In fact, if there are strong emotions one can't have this free flow, because strong emotions always correspond to sensations of solidity and heaviness in the body. Only when emotions are dissolved at the mental level, and the solidity of the body is dissolved at the material level, then nothing remains but a mass of vibrations, a mass of energy moving in the body.

Q: There has been misunderstanding at times about these terms. How did such confusion ever arise regarding these expressions?

SNG: Perhaps the misunderstanding happened when U Ba Khin, in one of his discourses, expressed himself in the following way: "I have developed a technique that is very adapted to non-Buddhist people of the English tongue. Everybody can work with this method and obtain results. Come, try it for yourself and have the same results." This was his statement. Before U Ba Khin the teachers were instructing Burmese Buddhists who had their own way of understanding the teachings. But U Ba Khin had to deal with non-Buddhists and foreigners from the West, and for this reason he had to develop a way of explaining the technique that they would be able to understand. His own manner of presenting it was certainly unique, but the technique remained that taught by the Buddha.

Q: Why is so much emphasis placed on following a specific order of observing sensations in different parts of the body instead of leaving the mind to observe whatever is happening?

SNG: Because so much is required in such a short time. In our experience we have verified that those who work following a precise order have the possibility of experiencing their bodies open up most rapidly. Those who observe only sensations as they arise from time to time in different parts of the body generally observe only gross sensations, because these are predominant. The tendency of the mind is to observe only that which accompanies gross sensations, and in this way it takes a long time, sometimes years, before one can attain the stage of *bhaṅga,* or dissolution of the entire solidity of the body.

Q: How is this practice different from other forms of Vipassana?

SNG: I don't want to give opinions about other practices. But as I understand the teachings of the Buddha in the *Satipaṭṭhāna Sutta* and elsewhere, while the starting point can be different for different people, at a certain stage everyone must follow the same path towards *nibbāna.*

At the start of practice, Buddha gave different objects of meditation to different people, according to their mental conditioning, temperament, understanding, and capability. For example, for those who have great attachment to the body and to the passions of the body, the Buddha would have them contemplate a corpse, so they could come to understand that their body is also like that—made up of flesh and bones and blood and pus and mucus and so forth. Someone who is strongly attached to the body doesn't want to accept that the body is full of such unpleasantness, after all. What, then, would there be to develop an attachment toward?

One can start this way, but eventually one must reach the stage where one experiences *anicca* (impermanence), how things arise and pass away. This arising-and-passing-away should not be accepted at the intellectual or devotional level only; Buddha wanted us to experience it for ourselves. And it can be experienced only through sensation in the body. At the level of sensation, one finds, "Look, it has arisen, and look, it has passed away." Sensation arises, passes away; arises, passes away. When it is solidified, intensified, it arises and seems to stay for a while, but sooner or later it passes away.

When all solidity dissolves, it turns into subtle vibration, and every vibration becomes a wavelet that arises-and-passes away. So one experiences both solid sensations and subtle sensations arising and passing, arising and passing. Unless one experiences this directly, one hasn't understood the Buddha properly. Even before the Buddha, there were those who taught that the whole universe is impermanent, arising and passing. But Buddha discovered a technique by which one can experience it. And when we experience this impermanence directly, attachment, craving, and aversion go away, and the mind becomes purified. At a later stage, arising-and-passing occur so rapidly that one can't separate the one from the other. Then, after further purification of the mind, one reaches the stage of *nibbāna*. Whether one starts with contemplating a corpse, the material parts of the body, respiration, or some other object, the rest of the path must be the same.

PART TWO

The Writings of Sayagyi U Ba Khin

Chapter Five

The Essentials of Buddha-Dhamma in Meditative Practice

—Sayagyi U Ba Khin

U Ba Khin composed the following discourse in English particularly for his Western students. He read it to students on a number of occasions. After his death, the discourse was transcribed from an audio recording, and published under the above title.

Anicca, dukkha and *anattā*—impermanence, suffering and egolessness—are the three essential characteristics of things in the teaching of the Buddha. If you know *anicca* correctly, you know *dukkha* as its corollary and *anattā* as ultimate truth. It takes time to understand the three together.

Impermanence (*anicca*) is, of course, the essential fact which must be first experienced and understood by practice. Mere bookknowledge of the Buddha-Dhamma will not be enough for the correct understanding of *anicca* because the experiential aspect will be missing. It is only through experiential understanding of the nature of *anicca* as an ever-changing process within yourself that you can understand *anicca* in the way the Buddha would like you to understand it. As in the days of the Buddha, so too now, this understanding of *anicca* can be developed by persons who have no book-knowledge whatsoever of Buddhism.

To understand impermanence (*anicca*), one must follow strictly and diligently the Noble Eightfold Path, which is divided into the three groups of *sīla*, *samādhi* and *paññā*—morality, concentration and wisdom. *Sīla* or virtuous living is the basis for *samādhi* (control of the mind, mental concentration). It is only when *samādhi* is good that one can develop *paññā*. Therefore, *sīla* and *samādhi* are the prerequisites for *paññā*. By *paññā* is meant the understanding of *anicca*, *dukkha* and *anattā* through the practice of Vipassana, i.e., insight meditation.

Whether a Buddha has arisen or not, the practice of *sīla* and *samādhi* may be present in the human world. They are, in fact, the common denominators of all religious faiths. They are not, however, sufficient means for the goal of Buddhism—the complete end of suffering. In his search for the end of suffering, Prince Siddhārtha, the future Buddha, found this out and worked his way through to find the path which would lead to the end of suffering. After solid work for six years, he found the way out, became completely enlightened, and then taught men and gods to follow the path which would lead them to the end of suffering.

In this connection, we should understand that each action—whether by deed, word or thought—leaves behind an active force called *saṅkhāra* (or *kamma* in popular terminology), which goes to the credit or debit account of the individual, according to whether the action is good or bad. There is, therefore, an accumulation of *saṅkhāras* (or *kamma*) with everyone, which functions as the supply-source of energy to sustain life, which is inevitably followed by suffering and death. It is by the development of the power inherent in the understanding of *anicca*, *dukkha* and *anattā* that one is able to rid oneself of the *saṅkhāras* accumulated in one's own personal account.

This process begins with the correct understanding of *anicca* while further accumulations of fresh actions and the reduction of the supply of energy to sustain life are taking place simultaneously, from moment to moment and from day to day. It is, therefore, a matter of a whole lifetime or more to get rid of all one's *saṅkhāras*. He who has rid himself of all *saṅkhāras* comes to the end of suffering, for then no *saṅkhāra* remains to give the necessary energy to sustain him in any form of life. On the termination of their lives the perfected saints—i.e. the Buddhas and the *arahants*—pass into *parinibbāna*, reaching the end of suffering. For us today who take to Vipassana meditation it would suffice if we can understand *anicca* well enough to reach the first stage of an *ariya* (a noble person)— that is, a *sotāpanna* or stream-enterer—who will not take more than seven lives to come to the end of suffering.

The fact of *anicca*, which opens the door to the understanding of *dukkha* and *anattā* and eventually to the end of suffering, can be encountered in its full significance only through the teaching of a Buddha for as long as that teaching relating to the Noble Eightfold Path and the thirty-seven factors of enlightenment (*bodhipakkhiya dhammā*) remains intact and available to the aspirant.

For progress in Vipassana meditation, a student must keep knowing *anicca* as continuously as possible. The Buddha's advice to monks is that they should try to maintain the awareness of *anicca*, *dukkha* or *anattā* in all postures, whether sitting, standing, walking or lying down. Continuous awareness of *anicca*, and so of *dukkha* and *anattā*, is the secret of success. The last words of the Buddha just before he breathed his last and passed away into *mahāparinibbāna* were: "Decay (or *anicca*) is inherent in all component things. Work out your own salvation with diligence." This is in fact the essence of all his teachings during the forty-five years of his ministry. If you will keep up the awareness of the *anicca* that is inherent in all component things, you are sure to reach the goal in the course of time.

As you develop in the understanding of *anicca*, your insight into "what is true of nature" will become greater and greater, so that eventually you will have no doubt whatsoever of the three characteristics of *anicca*, *dukkha* and *anattā*. It is then only that you will be in a position to go ahead for the goal in view. Now that you know *anicca* as the first essential factor, you should try to understand what *anicca* is with real clarity, as extensively as possible, so as not to get confused in the course of practice or discussion.

The Knowledge of *Kalāpas*

The real meaning of *anicca* is that impermanence or decay is the inherent nature of everything that exists in the universe—whether animate or inanimate. The Buddha taught his disciples that everything that exists at the material level is composed of *kalāpas*. *Kalāpas* are material units very much smaller than atoms, which die out almost immediately after they come into being. Each *kalāpa* is a mass formed of the eight basic constituents of matter: the solid, liquid, calorific and oscillatory, together with color, smell, taste, and nutriment. The first four are called primary qualities, and are predominant in a *kalāpa*. The other four are subsidiaries dependent upon and springing from the former.

A *kalāpa* is the minutest particle in the physical plane—still beyond the range of science today.[†] It is only when the eight basic material constituents unite together that the *kalāpa* is formed. In other words, the momentary collocation of these eight basic elements of behavior, which makes a mass just for that moment, is known in Buddhism as a *kalāpa*. The life-span of a *kalāpa* is termed a "moment," and a trillion such moments are said to elapse during the wink of a man's eye. These *kalāpas* are all in a state of perpetual change or flux. To a developed student in Vipassana meditation they can be felt as a stream of energy.

The human body is not, as it may appear, a solid stable entity, but a continuum of matter (*rūpa*) coexisting with mentality (*nāma*). To know that our body is tiny *kalāpas* all in a state of change is to know the true nature of change or decay. This change or decay (*anicca*) occasioned by the continual breakdown and replacement of *kalāpas*, all in a state of combustion, must necessarily be identified as *dukkha*, the truth of suffering. It is only when you experience impermanence (*anicca*) as suffering (*dukkha*) that you come to the realization of the truth of suffering, the first of the Four Noble Truths basic to the doctrine of the Buddha.

[†] At the time U Ba Khin composed this essay the popular undersanding of subatomic particles and particle physics was still slight. Today we identify *kalāpas* as subatomic particles, in a constant state of oscillation between matter and energy.

Why? Because when you realize the subtle nature of *dukkha* from which you cannot escape for a moment, you become truly afraid of, disgusted with, and disinclined towards your very existence as mentality-materiality (*nāma-rūpa*), and look for a way of escape to a state beyond *dukkha*, and so to *nibbāna*, the end of suffering. What that end of suffering is like, you will be able to taste, even as a human being, when you reach the level of a *sotāpanna*—a stream-enterer—and develop well enough by practice to attain the unconditioned state of *nibbāna*, the peace within. But even in terms of everyday, ordinary life, no sooner than you are able to keep up the awareness of *anicca* in practice will you know for yourself that a change is taking place in you for the better, both physically and mentally.

Before entering upon the practice of Vipassana meditation (that is, after *samādhi* has been developed to a proper level), a student should acquaint himself with the theoretical knowledge of material and mental properties (i.e., of *rūpa* and *nāma*). For in Vipassana meditation one contemplates not only the changing nature of matter, but also the changing nature of mentality, of the thought-elements of attention directed towards the process of change going on within matter. At times the attention will be focused on the impermanence of the material side of existence (i.e., upon *anicca* in regard to *rūpa*); and at other times on the impermanence of the thought-elements or mental side (i.e., upon *anicca* in regard to *nāma*). When one is contemplating the impermanence of matter, one realizes also that the thought-elements simultaneous with that awareness are also in a state of transition or change. In this case one will be knowing *anicca* in regard to both *rūpa* and *nāma* together.

All I have said so far relates to the understanding of *anicca* through bodily feeling of the process of change of *rūpa* (or matter) and also of thought-elements depending upon such changing processes. You should know that *anicca* can also be understood through other types of feeling as well. *Anicca* can be contemplated through feeling:

1. by contact of visible form with the sense organ of the eye;

2. by contact of sound with the sense organ of the ear;

3. by contact of smell with the sense organ of the nose;

4. by contact of taste with the sense organ of the tongue;

5. by contact of touch with the sense organ of the body;

6. and by contact of mental objects with the sense organ of the mind.

One can thus develop the understanding of *anicca* through any of the six sense organs. In practice, however, we have found that of all types of feeling, the feeling by contact of touch with the component parts of the body in a process of change, covers the widest area for introspective meditation. Not only that, the feeling by contact of touch (by way of friction, radiation and vibration of the *kalāpas* within) with the component parts of the body is more evident than other types of feeling. Therefore a beginner in Vipassana meditation can come to the understanding of *anicca* more easily through bodily feeling of the change of *rūpa*, or matter. This is the main reason why we have chosen bodily feeling as a medium for quick understanding of *anicca*. It is open to anyone to try other means, but my suggestion is that one should be well-established in the understanding of *anicca* through bodily feeling before any attempt is made through other types of feeling.

The Levels of Knowledge

There are ten levels of knowledge in Vipassana, namely:

1. *sammasana*: theoretical appreciation of *anicca*, *dukkha* and *anattā* by close observation and analysis;

2. *udayabbaya*: knowledge of the arising and dissolution of *rūpa* and *nāma* by direct observation;

3. *bhaṅga*: knowledge of the rapidly changing nature of *rūpa* and *nāma* as a swift current or stream of energy; in particular, clear awareness of the phase of dissolution;

4. *bhaya*: knowledge that this very existence is dreadful;

5. *ādīnava*: knowledge that this very existence is full of evils;

6. *nibbidā*: knowledge that this very existence is disgusting;

7. *muñcitakamyatā*: knowledge of the urgent need and wish to escape from this very existence;

8. *patisaṅkhā*: knowledge that the time has come to work for full realization of deliverance with *anicca* as the base;

9. *saṅkhārupekkhā*: knowledge that the stage is now set to get detached from all conditioned phenomena (*saṅkhāra*) and to break away from egocentricity;

10. *anuloma*: knowledge that would accelerate the attempt to reach the goal.

These are the levels of attainment which one goes through during the course of Vipassana meditation. In the case of those who reach the goal in a short time, they can be known only in retrospect. Along with one's progress in understanding *anicca*, one may reach these levels of attainment—subject, however, to adjustments or help at certain levels by a competent teacher. One should avoid looking forward to such attainments in anticipation, as this will distract from the continuity of awareness of *anicca* which alone can and will give the desired reward.

The Experience of *Anicca* in Daily Life

Let me now deal with Vipassana meditation from the point of view of a householder in everyday life and explain the benefit one can derive from it—here and now—in this very lifetime.

The initial object of Vipassana meditation is to activate the experience of *anicca* in oneself and eventually to reach a state of inner and outer calmness and balance. This is achieved when one becomes engrossed in the feeling of *anicca* within. The world is now facing serious problems which threaten all mankind. It is just the right time for everyone to take to Vipassana meditation and learn how to find a deep pool of quiet in the midst of all that is happening today. *Anicca* is inside of everybody. It is within reach of everybody. Just a look into oneself and there it is—*anicca* to be experienced. When one can feel *anicca*, when one can experience *anicca*, and when one can become engrossed in *anicca*, one can and will cut oneself off from the world of ideation outside. *Anicca* is, for the householder, the gem of life which he will treasure to create a reservoir of calm and balanced energy for his own well-being and for the welfare of the society.

The experience of *anicca*, when properly developed, strikes at the root of one's physical and mental ills and removes gradually whatever is bad in him, i.e., the causes of such physical and mental ills. This experience is not reserved for men who have renounced the world for the homeless life. It is for the householder as well. In spite of drawbacks which make a householder restless in these days, a competent teacher or guide can help a student to get the experience of *anicca* activated in a comparatively short time. Once he has got it activated, all that is necessary is for him to try to preserve it; but he must make it a point, as soon as time or opportunity presents itself for further progress, to work for the stage of *bhaṅgañāṇa* (knowledge of *bhaṅga*).

However, there is likely to be some difficulty for one who has not reached the stage of *bhaṅga*. It will be just like a tug-of-war for him between *anicca* within, and physical and mental activities outside. So it would be wise for him to follow the motto of "Work while you work, play while you play." There is no need for him to be activating the experience of *anicca* all the time. It should suffice if this could be confined to a regular period, or periods, set apart in the day or night for the purpose. During this time, at least, an attempt must be made to keep the attention focused inside the body, with awareness devoted exclusively to *anicca*. That is to say, his awareness of *anicca* should go on from moment to moment so continuously as not to allow for the interpolation of any discursive or distracting thoughts, which are definitely detrimental to progress. In case this is not possible, he will have to go back to respiration-mindfulness, because *samādhi* is the key to the contemplation of *anicca*. To get good *samādhi*, *sīla* (morality) has to be perfect, since *samādhi* is built upon *sīla*. For a good experience of *anicca*, *samādhi* must be good. If *samādhi* is excellent, awareness of *anicca* will also become excellent.

There is no special technique for activating the experience of *anicca* other than the use of the mind adjusted to a perfect state of balance and attention projected upon the object of meditation. In Vipassana the object of meditation is *anicca*, and therefore in the case of those used to focusing their attention on bodily feelings, they can feel *anicca* directly. In experiencing *anicca* in relation to the body, it should first be in the area where one can easily get his attention engrossed, changing the area of attention from place to place, from head to feet and from feet to head, at times probing into the interior. At this stage it must clearly be understood that no attention is to be paid to the anatomy of the body, but to the formations of matter—the *kalāpas*—and the nature of their constant change.

If these instructions are observed, there will surely be progress, but the progress depends also on *pāramī* (i.e., one's disposition for certain spiritual qualities) and devotion of the individual to the work of meditation. If he attains high levels of knowledge, his power to understand the three characteristics of *anicca*, *dukkha* and *anattā* will increase and he will accordingly come nearer and nearer to the goal of the *ariya* or noble saint—which every householder should keep in view.

This is the age of science. Man of today has no utopia. He will not accept anything unless the results are good, concrete, vivid, personal, and here-and-now.

When the Buddha was alive, he said to the people of Kālāma:

> Now look, you Kālāmas. Be not misled by report or tradition or hearsay. Be not misled by proficiency in the scriptural collections, or by reasoning or logic, or reflection on and approval of some theory, or because some view conforms

with one's inclinations, or out of respect for the prestige of a teacher. But when you know for yourselves: these things are unwholesome, these things are blameworthy, these things are censured by the wise; these things, when practiced and observed, conduce to loss and sorrow—then do ye reject them. But if at any time you know for yourselves: these things are wholesome, these things are blameless, these things are praised by the intelligent; these things, when practiced and observed, conduce to welfare and happiness—then, Kālāmas, do ye, having practiced them, abide.

The time clock of Vipassana has now struck—that is, for the revival of Buddha-Dhamma Vipassana in practice. We have no doubt whatsoever that definite results will accrue to those who would with an open mind sincerely undergo a course of training under a competent teacher—I mean results which will be accepted as good, concrete, vivid, personal, here-and-now—results which will keep them in good stead and in a state of well-being and happiness for the rest of their lives.

May all beings be happy and may peace prevail in the world.

The Importance of Understanding *Anicca*

—*Vipassana Research Institute*

The following article, from the Vipassana Research Institute (VRI), explains in greater detail the importance of the concept of anicca. *VRI was founded in 1985 with the aim of conducting research into the sources of the technique of Vipassana meditation using the words of the Buddha. The Buddha's words are preserved in the* Tipitaka, *the collected books of the Buddha's teachings as they were faithfully transmitted, first by oral tradition and later recorded in writing in three collections. VRI is adjacent to the Vipassana International Academy in Igatpuri, India. It is now one the biggest centers in the world for the practice of Vipassana.*

> *Sabbe saṅkhārā aniccā'ti;*
> *yadā paññāya passati,*
> *atha nibbindati dukkhe—*
> *esa maggo visuddhiyā.*

> "Impermanent are all compounded things."
> When one observes this with wisdom,
> then one becomes detached from suffering;
> this is the path of purification.

Dhammapada, 277

Anicca

Change is inherent in all phenomenal existence. There is nothing animate or inanimate, organic or inorganic that we can label as permanent, since even as we affix that label on something it is undergoing metamorphosis. Realizing this central fact of life by direct experience within himself, the Buddha declared: "Whether a fully Enlightened One has arisen in the world or not, it still remains a firm condition, an immutable fact and fixed law that all formations are impermanent, subject to suffering, and devoid of substance." *Anicca* (impermanence), *dukkha* (suffering), and *anattā* (insubstantiality) are the three characteristics common to all sentient existence.

Of these, the most important in the practice of Vipassana is *anicca*. As meditators, we come face to face with the impermanence of ourselves. This enables us to realize that we have no control over this phenomenon, and that any attempt to manipulate it creates suffering. We thus learn to develop detachment, an acceptance of *anicca*, an openness to change. This enables us to live happily amid all the vicissitudes of life. Hence the Buddha said:

> In one who perceives impermanence... the perception of insubstantiality is established. And in one who perceives insubstantiality, egotism is destroyed; (as a result) even in the present life one attains liberation.
>
> —*Khuddaka-nikāya, Udāna 4.1, Meghiya Sutta*

The direct perception of *anicca* leads automatically to a grasp of *anattā* and also of *dukkha*, and whosoever realizes these facts naturally turns to the path that leads out of suffering.

Given the crucial importance of *anicca*, it is not surprising that the Buddha repeatedly stressed its significance for the seekers of liberation. In the *Mahā-satipaṭṭāna Sutta* (the principal text in which he explained the technique of Vipassana) he described the stages in the practice, which must in every case lead to the following experience:

> [The meditator] dwells observing the phenomenon of arising...dwells observing the phenomenon of passing away...dwells observing the phenomenon of arising-and-passing away.
>
> —*Dīgha -nikāya, 2.9, Mahāsatipaṭṭhāna Sutta*

We must recognize the fact of impermanence not merely in its readily apparent aspect around and within us. Beyond that we must learn to see the subtle reality that every moment we ourselves are changing, that the "I" with which we are infatuated is a phenomenon in constant flux. Through this experience we can easily emerge from egotism and so from suffering.

Elsewhere the Buddha said:

> The eye, O meditators, is impermanent. What is impermanent is unsatisfactory. What is unsatisfactory is substanceless. What is substanceless is not mine, is not I, is not my self. This is how to regard eye with wisdom as it really is.

The same formula applies to the ear, nose, tongue, body and mind—to all the bases of sensory experience, every aspect of a human being. Then the Buddha continued:

> Seeing this, oh meditators, the well-instructed noble disciple becomes satiated with the eye, ear, nose, tongue, body and mind (i.e., with sensory existence altogether). Being satiated he does not have the passion for them. Being passionless he is set free. In this freedom arises the realization that he is freed.
>
> —*Saṃyutta-nikāya, 2.1, Ajjhattānicca Sutta*

In this passage the Buddha makes a sharp distinction between knowing by hearsay and knowing by personal insight. One may be a *sutavā*, that is, someone who has heard about the Dhamma and accepts it on faith or perhaps intellectually. This acceptance, however, is insufficient to liberate anyone from the cycle of suffering. To attain liberation one must see truth for oneself, must experience it directly within oneself. This is what Vipassana meditation enables us to do.

If we are to understand the unique contribution of the Buddha, we must keep this distinction firmly in mind. The truth of which he spoke was not unknown before his time; it was current in India in his time. He did not invent the concepts of impermanence, suffering and insubstantiality. His uniqueness lies in having found a way to advance from merely hearing truth to experiencing it.

One text that shows this special emphasis of the teaching of the Buddha is the *Bāhiya Sutta*, found in the *Saṃyutta Nikāya*. In it is recorded an encounter between the Buddha and Bāhiya, a wanderer in search of a spiritual path. Although not a disciple of the Buddha, Bāhiya asked him for guidance in his search. The Buddha responded by questioning him as follows:

> What do you think, Bāhiya: is the eye permanent or impermanent?
>
> —Impermanent, sir.
>
> That which is impermanent, is it a cause of suffering or happiness?
>
> —Of suffering, sir.
>
> Now, is it fitting to regard what is impermanent—a cause of suffering, and by nature changeable—as being "mine," being "I," being one's "self"?
>
> —Surely not, sir.
>
> —*Saṃyutta-nikāya 2.69, Bāhiya Sutta*

The Buddha further questioned Bāhiya about visual objects, eye consciousness and eye contact. In every case this man agreed that these were impermanent, unsatisfactory, not-self. He did not claim to be a follower of the teaching of the Buddha, and yet he accepted the facts of *anicca*, *dukkha* and *anattā*. The *sutta* thus documents that, among at least some of the contemporaries of the Buddha, ideas were accepted that we might now regard as having been unknown outside his teaching. The explanation, of course, is that for Bāhiya and others like him the concepts of impermanence, suffering and egolessness were simply opinions that they held—in Pāli, *maññā*. To such people the Buddha showed a way to go beyond beliefs or philosophies, and to experience directly their own nature as impermanent, suffering, insubstantial.

What, then, is the way he showed? In the *Brahmajāla Sutta* the Buddha provides an answer. There he lists all the beliefs, opinions and views of his time, and then states that he knows something far beyond all views:

> For having experienced as they really are the arising of sensations and their passing away, the relishing of them, the danger in them and the release from them, the Enlightened One, O meditators, has become liberated, being free from all attachment.

> —*Dīgha-nikāya, 1.1, Brahmajāla Sutta*

Here the Buddha states quite simply that he became enlightened by observing sensations as the manifestation of impermanence. It behooves anyone who aspires to follow the teachings of the Buddha to do likewise.

Impermanence is the central fact that we must realize in order to emerge from our suffering, and the most immediate way to experience impermanence is by observing our sensations. Again the Buddha said:

> There are three types of sensations, O meditators [all of which are] impermanent, compounded, arising owing to a cause, perishable, by nature passing away, fading and ceasing.

> —*Saṃyutta-nikāya, 2.211, Anicca Sutta*

The sensations within ourselves are the most palpable expressions of the characteristic of *anicca*. By observing them we become able to accept the reality, not merely out of faith or intellectual conviction, but out of our direct experience. In this way we advance from merely hearing about the truth to experiencing it within ourselves.

When we thus encounter truth face to face, it is bound to transform us radically. As the Buddha said:

> When a meditator thus dwells aware with proper understanding, diligent, ardent and self-controlled, then if pleasant bodily sensations in him arise, he understands, "This pleasant bodily sensation has arisen in me, but it is dependent, it is not independent. Dependent on what? On this body. But this body is impermanent, compounded, arising from conditions. Now how could pleasant bodily sensations be permanent that arise dependent on an impermanent, compounded body, itself arising owing to conditions?"

—*Saṃyutta-nikāya, 2.209, Paṭhamagelañña Sutta*

He dwells experiencing the impermanence of sensations in the body, their arising, falling and cessation, and the relinquishing of them. As he does so, his underlying conditioning of craving is abandoned. Similarly, when he experiences unpleasant sensations in the body, his underlying conditioning of aversion is abandoned; and when he experiences neutral sensations in the body, his underlying conditioning of ignorance is abandoned.

In this way, by observing the impermanence of bodily sensations, a meditator approaches ever closer to the goal of the unconditioned *(nibbāna)*.

Upon reaching this goal, Koṇḍañña, the first person to become liberated through the Buddha's teaching, declared: *Yaṃ kiñci samudayadhāmmaṃ sabbaṃ te nirodha-dhammaṃ*—"Everything that has the nature of arising also has the nature of ceasing." It is only by experiencing fully the reality of *anicca* that he was eventually able to experience a reality that does not arise or pass away. His declaration is a signpost to later travelers on the path, indicating the way they must follow to reach the goal themselves.

At the end of his life the Buddha declared: *Vaya-dhammā saṅkhārā*—"All created things are impermanent." With his last breaths he reiterated the great theme of which he had spoken so often during his years of teaching. He then added: *Appamādena sampādetha*—"Strive diligently." To what purpose, we must ask, are we to strive? Surely these words, the last spoken by the Buddha, can only refer to the preceding sentence. The priceless legacy of the Buddha to the world is the understanding of *anicca* as a means to liberation. We must strive to realize impermanence within ourselves, and by doing so we fulfill his last exhortation to us, we become the true heirs of the Buddha.

Chapter Six

What Buddhism Is

—*Sayagyi U Ba Khin*

In 1951, when Sayagyi was the Accountant General of Burma, he was requested by a religious study group to lecture on Buddhism. The study group was headed by the information officer and the economic and finance officer of the Special Technical and Economic Division of the U.S. government. Sayagyi presented a series of three lectures in Yangon (at the Methodist Church, Signal Pagoda Road) which were later published as a booklet entitled "What Buddhism Is." The following is abridged.

Lecture No. 1 (September 23, 1951)

I consider it a great privilege to be in your midst today and to have this opportunity of addressing you on the subject of "What Buddhism Is." At the outset, I must be very frank with you. I have not been to a university, and I have no knowledge of science except as a man on the street. Nor am I a scholar in the theory of Buddhism with any knowledge of the Pāli language in which the *Tipiṭaka* (known as, literally, the "Three Baskets" of Buddha Dhamma) are maintained. I must say, however, that I have read in Burmese to some extent the treatises of Buddhism by well-known and learned Buddhist monks. As my approach to Buddhism is more by practical than by theoretical means, I hope to be able to give you something of Buddhism which is not easily available elsewhere. I must admit, however, that for the time being I am just a student of practical Buddhism and also an experimentalist trying to learn through Buddhism the truth of the nature of forces. As this has to be done as a householder and within a limited time available amidst the multifarious duties of a responsible officer of government, the progress is rather slow, and I do not claim for a moment that what I am going to say is absolutely correct. I may be right or wrong. But when I say a thing, I assure you that it is with sincerity of purpose, with the best of intentions and with conviction.

Lord Buddha said in the *Kālāma Sutta:*

> Do not believe in what you have heard;
> do not believe in the traditions, because they have been
> handed down for generations;
> do not believe in anything because it is rumored and spo-
> ken by many;
> do not believe merely because a written statement of some
> old sage is produced;
> do not believe in conjectures;
> do not believe in that as truth to which you have become
> attached by habit;
> do not believe merely the authority of your teachers and
> elders.
> After observation and analysis, when it agrees with reason
> and is conducive to the good and gain of one and all, then
> accept it and live up to it.

Pray do not, therefore, believe me when I come to the philosophical issues until and unless you are convinced of what I say, either as a sequel to proper reasoning or by means of a practical approach.

> To abstain from evil;
> To do good;
> To purify the mind:
> These are the teachings of all the Buddhas.

This extract taken from the *Dhammapada* gives in brief the essence of Buddhism. It sounds simple but is so difficult to practice.

One cannot be a true Buddhist unless he puts the doctrine of Buddha into practice. Buddha said:

> Ye, to whom the truths I have perceived have been made known by me, make them surely your own; practice them, meditate upon them, spread them abroad; in order that the pure religion may last long and be perpetuated for the good and the gain and the weal of gods and men.

Before I take up the teachings of Buddha, which form the basic foundation of Buddhism, I propose to acquaint you, first of all, with the life story of Gotama Buddha. For this purpose, I feel it my duty to give you a background of certain Buddhist concepts which may be foreign to most of you. I propose, therefore, to give you a short and descriptive explanation of such concepts in Buddhism, as to the universe, the world system, the planes of existence, etc. These will, no doubt, give you some food for thought. I would however, appeal to you to give a patient hearing and to pass over these matters for the time being, i.e., until we come to the question time for discussion.

Universe

The Buddhist concept of the universe may be summed up as follows:

There is the *Okāsa Loka* (the universe of space) which accommodates *nāma* and *rūpa* (mind and matter). In this mundane world it is *nāma* and *rūpa* which predominate under the influence of the law of cause and effect. The next is the *Saṅkhāra Loka* (the universe of mental forces), creative or created. This is a mental plane arising out of the creative energies of mind through the medium of bodily actions, words and thoughts. The third and the last is the *Satta Loka* (the universe of sentient beings). These beings are the products of mental forces. We may rather call these three as a "three-in-one" universe, because one is inseparable from another. They are, so to say, interwoven and interpenetrating.

What will interest you most are the *cakkavālas* or world systems, each with its thirty-one planes of existence. Each world system corresponds to the human world with its solar system and other planes of existence. There are millions and millions of such world systems, simply innumerable. Ten thousand such world systems closest to us are within the *Jāti-Khetta* (or the field of origin) of a Buddha. In fact when the renowned *sutta* (or sermon) *Mahā Samaya* (meaning the "Great Occasion") was preached by Buddha in the *Mahāvana* (forest) near the town of Kapilavatthu, not only the *brahmās* and *devas* of our world system, but those of all of the ten thousand world systems were present to listen to the teachings of Buddha. Lord Buddha can also send his thought-waves charged with boundless love and compassion to the sentient beings of a hundred crores (thousand million) of such world systems within the *Anākhetta* (or the field of influence). The remainder of the world systems are in the *Visaya Khetta* (or infinite space) beyond the reach of Buddha's effective thought waves. You can very well imagine from these concepts of Buddhism the size of the universe as a whole. The material insignificance of our world in the *Okāsa loka* (universe of space) is simply terrifying. The human world, as a whole, must be just a speck in space.

Now I will give you an idea of the thirty-one planes of existence in our world system which, of course, is the same as in any of the other world systems. Broadly they are:

(i) *Arūpa Loka*—immaterial world of brahmās;

(ii) *Rūpa Loka*—fine material world of brahmās;

(iii) *Kāma Loka*—sensuous world of devas, mankind and lower beings.

The *Arūpa Loka* is comprised of four *brahmā* worlds of immaterial state, i.e., without *rūpa* or matter. The *Rūpa Loka* is comprised of sixteen *brahmā* worlds of fine material state. The *Kāma Loka* is comprised of:

(a) Six *deva lokas* (or celestial worlds), viz.:

(i) *Catumahārājika*

(ii) *Tāvatiṃsa*

(iii) *Yāmā*

(iv) *Tusita*

(v) *Nimmānarati*

(vi) *Paranimmita-vasavatti*

(b) The human world

(c) The four lower worlds, viz:

(i) *Niraya*   (hell)

(ii) *Tiricchāna*   (animal world)

(iii) *Peta*   (ghost world)

(iv) *Asura*   (demon world)

These planes of existence are pure or impure, cool or hot, luminous or dark, light or heavy, pleasant or wretched—according to the character of the mental forces generated by the mind or the volition (*cetanā*) of a series of actions, words and thoughts. For example, take the case of a religious man who suffuses the whole universe of beings with boundless love and compassion. He must be generating such mental forces as are pure, cooling, luminous, light and pleasant—forces which normally settle down in the *brahmā* worlds. Let us now take the reverse case of a man who is dissatisfied or angry. As the saying goes, "Face is the indication of mind": the impurity, heat, darkness, heaviness and wretchedness of his mind are immediately reflected in the person, visible even to the naked eye. This is due, I may say, to the generation of the evil mental forces of *dosa* (anger) which go down to the lower world of existence. The same is the case with the mental forces arising out of *lobha* (greed) or *moha* (delusion). In the case of meritorious deeds such as devotion, morality and charity which have, at their base, attachment to future well-being, the mental forces generated are those that will normally be located in the sensuous planes of devas and of mankind. These, ladies and gentlemen, are some of the concepts in Buddhism relevant to the life story of Gotama Buddha which I will presently begin.

Preparation

Gotama Buddha is the fourth of the five Buddhas to arise in the world cycle which is known as *bhadda-kappa*. His predecessors were Buddhas Kakusandha, Konāgamana and Kassapa. There were also innumerable Buddhas who had arisen in earlier *kappas* (ages) and who had preached the self-same Dhamma which gives deliverance from suffering and death to all matured beings. Buddhas are all compassionate, glorious and enlightened.

A hermit by the name of Sumedha was inspired by Buddha Dīpaṅkara; so much so that he took the vow to make all the necessary preparations to become a Buddha in the course of time. Buddha Dīpaṅkara gave him his blessings and prophesied that he would become a Buddha by the name of Gotama. From then onwards, existence after existence, the *Bodhisatta* (i.e., would-be Buddha) conserved mental energies of the highest order through the practice of ten *pāramīs*, or virtues towards perfection, viz.:

1. *dāna*   (virtue in alms-giving)

2. *sīla*   (morality)

3. *nekkhamma*   (renunciation)

4. *paññā*   (wisdom)

5. *viriya*   (perseverance)

6. *khanti*   (forbearance)

7. *sacca*   (truthfulness)

8. *adhiṭṭhāna*   (determination)

9. *mettā*   (all-embracing love)

10. *upekkhā*   (equanimity)

It is, therefore, a most enduring task to become a Buddha. Utmost strength of willpower is necessary to even think of it. The *Bodhisatta's* preparatory period came to an end with the life of King Vessantara who excelled any living being in alms-giving. He gave away his kingdom, his wife and his children and all his worldly possessions, for the consummation of his solemn vow taken before the *Dīpaṅkara* Buddha. The next existence was in *Tusita* (one of the celestial planes) as glorious Setaketu Deva, until he got his release from that plane and took conception in the womb of Māyā Devi, the Queen of King Suddhodana of Kapilavatthu, a place near modern Nepal.

When the time was drawing nigh for her confinement, the Queen expressed her desire to go to the place of her own parents for the event. King Suddhodana accordingly sent her there with befitting retinues and guards. On the way, a halt was made at the Lumbinī *sāla* forest. She got down from the palanquin and enjoyed the cool breeze and fragrance of the *sāla* flowers. While holding out her right hand to a branch of the nearby *sāla* tree for a flower, all of a sudden and unexpectedly, she gave birth to a son who was to become the all-enlightened Buddha. Simultaneously, the natural order of things in the cosmos was revolutionized in many respects and thirty-two wonderful phenomena were vivified. All material worlds were shaken from the foundation. There were unusual illuminations in the solar system. All the beings of material planes could see each other. The deaf and dumb were cured. Celestial music was heard everywhere, and so on.

At that moment, Kāḷa Devala, the hermit teacher of King Suddhodana, was having a discourse with celestial beings of *Tāvatiṃsa*. He was a hermit of fame who had mastery of the eight *samāpattis* (attainments) which gave him supernormal powers. Knowing of the birth of a son to the King due to the rejoicing in all the *rūpa* and *kāma* worlds, he hurried back to the palace and desired the baby to be brought before him for blessings. When the King placed the baby before his teacher for the occasion, Devala at once understood that the baby was no other than the embryonic Buddha. He smiled at this knowledge but cried almost immediately thereafter, because he foresaw that he would not live to hear his teachings, and that even after his death he would be in the *arūpa brahmā loka* (immaterial plane of *brahmās*) whence he would have no relationship with any of the material planes. He missed the Buddha and his teachings miserably.

On the fifth day, the child was named Siddhattha in the presence of renowned astrologer-palmists who agreed that the child had all the characteristics of a Buddha to come. The mother Queen, however, died a week after confinement and the child was taken care of by his maternal aunt, Pajāpatī Gotamī.

Siddhattha spent his early years of life in ease, luxury and culture. He was acclaimed to be a prodigy both in intellect and strength. The King spared no pains to make the course of his life smooth. Three separate palaces were built to suit three seasons with all the necessities that would make the Prince sink in sensuality. That was because the King, out of paternal affection, desired his son to remain in worldly life as a king rather than as an enlightened Buddha. The King Suddhodana was overly watchful that his son be in such environments as would give him no chance of higher philosophical ideas. In order to make sure that the thought of the Prince never turned in this direction, he ordered that nobody serving him or in his association was ever to speak a single word about such things as old age, sickness or death. They were to act as if there were no unpleasant things in this world. Servants and attendants who showed the least sign of becoming old, weak or sickly were replaced. On the other hand, dancing, music and enjoyable parties were held right through, to keep him under a complete shade of sensuality.

The Great Renunciation

As days, months and years passed, however, the monotony of the sensual surroundings gradually lost hold of the mind of Prince Siddhattha. The mental energies of virtue conserved in all his innumerable earlier lives for the great goal of Buddhahood were automatically aroused. At times, when the world of sensuality lost control over his mind, his inner self worked its way up and raised his mind to a state of purity and tranquillity with the strength of *samādhi*. The war of nerves began.

An escape from sensuality and passion was his first consideration. He wanted to know what existed outside the walls of the palace beyond which he had not even once visited. He wished to see nature as it is, and not as man has made it. Accordingly he decided to see the royal park, outside the palace walls. On the way to the park, in spite of precautions taken by the King to clear the roads of unpleasant sights, he saw in the very first visit an old man bent with age. Next he saw a sick person in the agony of a fatal malady. Thereafter he encountered a human corpse. On the last trip he came across a monk.

All these set his mind to serious thinking. His mental attitude was changed. His mind became clear of impurities and tuned up with the forces of his own virtues conserved in the *saṅkhāra loka* (plane of mental forces). By then his mind had become freed from hindrances, and was tranquil, pure and strong. It all happened on the night when a son had been born to his queen, a new fetter to bind him down. He was, however, immune from anything which would tend to upset the equilibrium of his mind. The virtues of determination worked their way towards a strong resolve, and he made up his mind to seek the way of escape from birth, old age, suffering and death. It was midnight when the solemn determination was made. He asked his attendant Channa to keep his stallion Kanthaka ready. After a parting look at his wife and the newly-born babe, Prince Siddhattha broke away from all the ties of family and of the world and made the Great Renunciation. He rode across the town to the river Anomā which he crossed, never to return until his mission had been achieved.

The Search for Truth

After this Great Renunciation, Prince Siddhattha went around in the garb of a wandering ascetic with a begging bowl in his hands in search of possible teachers. He placed himself under the spiritual guidance of two renowned brahmin teachers, Āḷāra and Uddaka. Āḷāra laid stress on the belief in *ātman* (soul) and taught that the soul attained perfect release when freed from material limitations.

This did not satisfy the Prince. He next went to Uddaka who placed too much emphasis on the effect of *kamma* and the transmigration of soul. Both could not get out of the conception of "soul," and the Prince ascetic felt that there was something else to learn. He therefore left both of them to work out the way to emancipation on his own. By that time, of course, he had learned the eight *samāpattis* and had become an adept in the exercise of all supernormal powers, including the ability to read events of many *kappas* to come, as well as a similar period from the past. These were all in the mundane field and they did not much concern the Prince ascetic, whose ambition was an escape from this mundane field of birth, suffering and death.

He was later joined by five ascetics, one of whom (Koṇḍañña by name) was the astrologer-palmist who had foretold on the fifth day of his birth that Siddhattha would surely become a Buddha. These ascetics served him well throughout the six years, during which he was engaged in fasting and meditation, subjecting himself to various forms of rigorous austerities and discipline until he was reduced to almost a skeleton. One day, in fact, he fell down in a swoon through exhaustion. When he survived this condition, he changed his method, followed a middle course and found that the way for his enlightenment was clearer.

Attainment of Buddhahood

It was on the eve of the full moon of *Vesākha* [equivalent to the month of May] just 2,562 years ago, that Prince Siddhattha, wandering ascetic, sat cross-legged beneath a *bodhi* tree on the bank of the river Nerañjarā in the forest of Uruvelā (near present-day Bodh Gayā), with the strongest of determinations not to rise from that posture on any account until he gained the truth and enlightenment, the Buddhahood, even if the attempt might mean the loss of his very life.

The great event was approaching. The Prince ascetic mustered up all his strength of mind to secure that one-pointedness of mind which is so essential for the discovery of truth. The balancing of the mind, the Prince found on this occasion, was not so easy as hitherto. There was not only the combination of the mental forces of the lower planes with those of the higher planes all around him, but also interferences strong enough to upset, off and on, the equilibrium of his mind. The resistance of the impenetrable masses of forces against the radiation of the light normally secured by him was unusual (perhaps because it was a final bid for Buddhahood and Māra, the supreme controller of evil forces, was behind the scene). The Prince, however, worked his way through slowly but surely, backed up by the mental forces of virtues which must inevitably have come back to him at the right moment.

He made a vow and called upon all the *brahmās* and *devas* who had witnessed the fulfillment of his ten great perfections to join hands with him in the struggle for supremacy. This done, the association with the transcendingly pure mental forces of the *brahmās* and *devas* had a salutary effect. The thick masses of forces, which seemed impenetrable, broke away; and with a steady improvement in the control over the mind, they were wiped out once and for all. All the hindrances having been overcome, the Prince was able to raise his power of concentration and put the mind into a state of complete purity, tranquillity and equanimity. Gradually, the consciousness of true insight possessed him. The solution to the vital problems which confronted him made its appearance in his consciousness as an inspiration. By introspective meditation on the realities of nature in his own self, it came vividly to him that there is no substantiality, as there seems to be, in the human body, and that it is nothing but the sum total of innumerable millions of *kalāpas* (subatomic particles), each about 1/46,656th part of a particle of dust from the wheel of a chariot in summer. On further investigation, he realized that this *kalāpa* also is matter in constant change or flux; and, similarly, that the mind is a representation of the mental forces (creative) going out and the mental forces (created) coming into the system of an individual continually and throughout eternity.

Buddha then proclaimed that his eye of wisdom had arisen when he got over the substantiality of his "own self." He saw by means of the lens of *samādhi* the *kalāpas* on which he next applied the law of *anicca* (impermanence), and reduced them to non-entity or habitual behavior patterns—doing away with what we in Buddhism call *paññatti* (apparent truth); and coming to a state of *paramattha* (nature of forces) or, in other words, "ultimate reality."

Accordingly, he came to a realization of the perpetual change of mind and matter in himself (*anicca*) and as a sequel thereto, the truth of suffering (*dukkha*). It was then that the egocentrism in him broke down into the void and he got over to a stage beyond "suffering"—i.e., *dukkha-nirodha* (the extinction of suffering) with no more traces of *attā* (attachment to self) left behind. "Mind and matter" were to him but empty phenomena which roll on forever, within the range of the law of cause and effect and the law of dependent origination. The truth was realized. The inherent qualities of the embryonic Buddha then developed, and complete enlightenment came to him by the dawn of the *Vesākha* day.

"Verily, Prince Siddhattha attained *sammā sambodhi* and became the Buddha, the Awakened One, the Enlightened One, the All-knowing One. He was awake in a way compared with which all others were asleep and dreaming. He was enlightened in a way compared with which all other men were stumbling and groping in the dark. His knowing was with the knowledge compared with which, what all other men know is but a kind of ignorance."

Ladies and gentlemen, I have taken so much of your time today. I thank you all for the patient listening. I must also thank the clergy of the church for their kind permission given to me for this address.

Lecture No. 2 (September 30, 1951)

Last Sunday, I gave you a brief outline—a very brief one, too—of the life of our Lord Buddha up to the moment of his attainment of Buddhahood. I am going to tell you today what his teachings are.

Buddhist teachings are preserved in what we call the *Tipiṭaka*, consisting of *Suttas* (discourses), *Vinaya* (laws of discipline for the Saṅgha (monks) and *Abhidhamma* (philosophical teachings). We have the *Tipiṭaka* in Pāli in several volumes which will require an intelligent Pāli scholar some months just to read through. I propose, therefore, to confine myself today only to essentials—i.e., the fundamental truths of Buddhism.

Before Lord Buddha took upon himself the task of spreading the Dhamma, he remained in silent meditation for a continuous period of forty-nine days—seven days under the *bodhi* tree, and seven days each in six other spots nearby, enjoying from time to time the peace of supreme *nibbāna* and at other times going deeper, in investigation, into the most delicate problems of *paramattha dhamma* (ultimate realities). Upon the complete mastery of the law of *paṭṭhāna* (the law of relations) in which infinite modes of relations between thought-moments are dealt with, there emerged from his body brilliant rays in six colors, which eventually settled down as a halo of six colored rays around his head. He passed these seven-times-seven days of meditation without food. It is beyond us all to be without food for forty-nine days. The fact remains that throughout the period he was on a mental plane, as distinct from the physical plane wherein mankind normally resides. It is not the material food that maintains the fine material and life continuum of beings in the fine material worlds of *brahmās*, but the *jhānic pīti* (rapture arising from deep meditation), which in itself is a nutriment. This was the case with the Buddha whose existence during this long period was on a mental rather than physical plane. Our experiments in this line of research have firmly convinced us that for a man of such high intellectual and mental development as the Buddha, this is a possibility.

It was at daybreak on the fiftieth day of his Buddhahood when he arose from this long spell of meditation. Not that he was tired or exhausted, but, as he was no longer in the mental plane, he felt a longing for food. At that time, two traders from a foreign land were travelling in several carts loaded with merchandise through the Uruvelā forest. A *deva* of the forest who was their relative in one of the previous existences advised them to take the opportunity of paying homage to the all-enlightened Buddha who had just arisen from his meditation. They accordingly went to the place where the Buddha was seated, illumined by the halo of six colored rays. They could not resist their feelings. They lay prostrate in worship and adoration before Buddha and later offered preserved rice cakes with honey for the first meal of the Buddha. They were accepted as his lay disciples. Upon requesting that they might be given some tokens for their worship, Buddha presented them with eight strands of hair from his head.

You will be surprised to know that these two traders were Tapussa and Bhallika of Okkalāpa, which today is known as Rangoon where you are at this moment. And the renowned Shwedagon, which you have all probably visited, is the pagoda in which was enshrined all the eight hair relics of Buddha under the personal direction of the then ruler of Okkalāpa, 2,540 years ago. It has been preserved and renovated until now by successive Buddhist kings and devotees. Unfortunately, however, these two traders of Okkalāpa, who had the privilege of becoming the first lay disciples of the Buddha, were disciples only by faith, without a taste of the Buddha Dhamma in actual practice which alone could give them deliverance from suffering and death. Faith is, no doubt, a preliminary requisite; but it is the practice of the teachings which really counts. The Buddha therefore said:

> The path must be trodden by each individual;
> Buddhas do but point the way.

Teachings of the Buddha

Buddhism is not a religion according to its dictionary meaning because it has no center in God, as is the case in all other religions. Strictly speaking, Buddhism is a system of philosophy coordinated with a code of morality, physical and mental. The goal in view is the extinction of suffering and death.

The Four Noble Truths taught by the Buddha in his first sermon known as *Dhamma-cakka-pavattana Sutta* (the discourse to set in motion the Wheel of Dhamma) form the basis on which is founded this system of philosophy. In fact, the first three of the Four Noble Truths expound the philosophy of Buddha while the fourth (the Noble Eightfold Path, which is a code of morality-cum-philosophy) serves as a means for the end. This first sermon was given to the five ascetics, led by Koṇḍañña, who were his early companions in search of truth. Koṇḍañña was the first disciple of the Buddha to practice to become an *arahant* (a holy one gone beyond the limitations of all fetters).

Now we come to the Four Noble Truths. They are as follows:

1. *dukkha-sacca*   (truth of suffering)
2. *samudaya-sacca*   (truth of the origin of suffering)
3. *nirodha-sacca*   (truth of the extinction of suffering)
4. *magga-sacca*   (truth of the path leading to the extinction of suffering)

To come to a complete understanding of the fundamental concepts in the philosophy of Buddha, emphasis is laid on the need for the realization of the truth of suffering. To bring home this point, Lord Buddha tackled the problem from two different angles.

First, by a process of reasoning, he made his disciples understand that life is a struggle. Life is suffering; birth is suffering; old age is suffering; illness is suffering; death is suffering. The influence of sensuality, however, is so strong in mankind that they are normally apt to forget themselves, to forget what they will have to pay thereby. Just think for a moment how life exists in the prenatal period; how from the moment of birth the child has to struggle for existence; what preparations he has to make to face life; what he has to struggle with as a man until he breathes his last.

You can very well imagine what life is. Life is indeed suffering.

The more one is attached to self, the greater is the suffering. In fact, what pains and sufferings a man has to undergo are suppressed in favor of momentary sensual pleasures, which are but occasional spotlights in darkness. But for the *moha* (delusion), which keeps him away from the truth, he surely would have worked out his way for emancipation from the rounds of life, suffering and death.

Secondly, the Buddha made it known to his disciples that the human body is composed of *kalāpas* (subatomic units), each dying out simultaneously as it arises. Each *kalāpa* is a mass formed of the following nature-elements:

1. *paṭhavī*   extension   (lit., earth)

2. *āpo*   cohesion   (lit., water)

3. *tejo*   radiation   (lit., heat and cold)

4. *vāyo*   motion   (lit., air)

5. *vaṇṇo*   color

6. *gandho*   smell

7. *raso*   taste

8. *ojā*   nutritive essence

The first four are called *mahā-bhūtas*—i.e., essential material qualities—which are predominant in a *kalāpa*. The other four are merely subsidiaries which are dependent upon and born out of the former. A *kalāpa* is the minutest particle noticeable in the physical plane. It is only when the eight nature-elements (which have merely a characteristic of behavior) are together that the entity of a *kalāpa* is formed. In other words, the coexistence of these eight nature-elements of behavior makes a mass, which in Buddhism is known as a *kalāpa*. These *kalāpas*, according to the Buddha, are in a state of perpetual change or flux. They are nothing but a stream of energies, just like the light of a candle or an electric bulb. The body (as we call it), is not an entity as it seems to be, but is a continuum of matter and life-force coexisting.

To a casual observer a piece of iron is motionless. The scientist knows that it is composed of electrons all in a state of perpetual change or flux. If this is so with a piece of iron, what will be the case with a living organism, say a human being? The changes taking place inside a human body must be more violent. Does man feel the rocking vibrations within himself? Does the scientist who knows that all the electrons are in a perpetual state of change or flux ever feel that his own body is but energy and vibration? What will be the repercussion on the mental attitude of the man who introspectively sees that his own body is mere energy and vibration?

To quench thirst one may easily just drink a glass of water from a village well. Supposing his eyes are as powerful as microscopes, he would surely hesitate to drink the very same water in which he must see the magnified microbes. Similarly, when one comes to the realization of perpetual change within himself (*anicca*—impermanence), he must come to the understanding, as a sequel thereto, of the truth of suffering as a consequence of the sharp sense of feeling the radiation, vibration and friction of the atomic units within. Indeed life is suffering, both within and without, to all appearances and in ultimate reality.

When I say "life is suffering," as the Buddha taught, please be so good as not to run away with the idea that, if it is so, life is miserable, life is not worth living and the Buddhist concept of suffering is a terrible concept which will give you no chance of a reasonably happy life. What is happiness? For all that science has achieved in the field of materialism, are the peoples of the world happy? They may find sensual pleasures off and on, but in their heart of hearts they are not happy when they realize what has happened, what is happening and what may happen next. Why? This is because, while man has mastery of matter, he is still lacking in mastery over his mind.

Pleasure born of sensuality is nothing compared with the *pīti* (rapture) born of the inner peace of mind which can be secured through a process of Buddhist meditation. Sense pleasures are preceded and followed by troubles and pains as in the case of a rustic who finds pleasure in cautiously scratching the itches over his body, whereas *pīti* is free from such troubles and pains either way. Looking from a sensual field, it will be difficult for you to appreciate what that *pīti* is like. But, I know, you can also enjoy and have a taste of it for comparative valuation. There is therefore nothing to suppose that Buddhism teaches something which will make you feel miserable with the nightmare of suffering. But please take it from me that it will give you an escape from the normal conditions of life, a lotus as it were, in a pond of crystal water, immune from its fiery surroundings. It will give you that "peace within" which will satisfy you that you are getting beyond not only the day-to-day troubles of life, but slowly and surely beyond the limitation of life, suffering and death.

What, then, is the origin of suffering? The origin of it, the Buddha said, is *taṇhā* (craving). Once the seed of desire is sown, it grows into greed and multiplies into craving or lust, either for power or material gains. The man in whom this seed is sown becomes a slave to these cravings; and he is automatically driven to strenuous labors of mind and body to keep pace with them until the end comes. The final result must surely be the accumulation of the evil mental force generated by his own actions, words and thoughts which are motivated by the *lobha* (desire) and *dosa* (aversion) inherent in him.

Philosophically speaking again, it is the mental forces of actions (*saṅkhārā*) which react in the course of time on the person originating them, which are responsible for the stream of mind and matter, the origin of suffering within.

Path Leading to the Extinction of Suffering

What, then, is the path leading to the extinction of suffering? The path is none other than the Noble Eightfold Path taught by the Buddha in his first sermon. This Eightfold Path is divided into three main stages, namely: *sīla*, *samādhi* and *paññā*.

Sīla (precept)

    1. right speech

    2. right action

    3. right livelihood

Samādhi (concentration of mind)

    4. right exertion

    5. right attentiveness

    6. right concentration

Paññā (wisdom-insight)

    7. right aspiration

    8. right understanding

Sīla

The three characteristic aspects of *sīla* are as follows:

    1. *sammā-vācā*   (right speech)

    2. *sammā-kammanta*   (right action)

    3. *sammā-ājīva*   (right livelihood)

By right speech is meant: speech which must be true, beneficial and neither foul nor malicious.

By right action is meant: fundamentals of morality which are opposed to killing, stealing, sexual misconduct and drunkenness.

By right livelihood is meant: ways of living by trades other than those which increase the suffering of all beings (such as slave trading, the manufacturing of weapons, and traffic in intoxicating drugs).

These represent generally the code of morality as initially pronounced by the Buddha in his very first sermon. Later, however, he amplified it and introduced separate codes for monks and lay disciples.

I need not worry you with what has been prescribed for monks. I will just let you know what the code of morality (the precepts for a Buddhist lay disciple) is. This is called the *Pañca Sīla* (Five Precepts). They are:

1. *pāṇātipātā*—abstention from killing any sentient beings. (Life is the most precious for all beings; and in prescribing this, Buddha's compassion extends to all beings.)

2. *adinnādānā*—abstention from taking what is not given. (This serves as a check against improper desire for possessions.)

3. *kāmesu-micchācārā*—abstention from sexual misconduct. (Sexual desire is dormant in man. It is irresistible to almost all. Unlawful sexual indulgence is therefore one which the Buddha prohibited.)

4. *musāvādā*—abstention from telling lies. (This precept is included to fulfill, by the way of speech, the essence of truth.)

5. *surāmeraya*—abstention from intoxication. (Intoxication causes a man to lose his steadfastness of mind and reasoning power so essential for the realization of truth.)

The *Pañca Sīla* are therefore intended to control actions and words and to serve as a foundation for *samādhi* (concentration of mind).

Samādhi

Ladies and gentlemen, we now come to the mental aspect of Buddhism which I'm sure will greatly interest you. In the second stage of the Noble Eightfold Path (that is, *samādhi*) are included:

1. *sammā-vāyāma*   (right exertion)
2. *sammā-sati*   (right attentiveness)
3. *sammā-samādhi* (right concentration)

Right exertion is of course the prerequisite for right attentiveness. Unless one makes a concerted effort to narrow down the range of thoughts of his wavering and unsteady mind, he cannot expect to secure that attentiveness of mind which in turn helps him bring the mind by right concentration to a state of one-pointedness and equanimity. It is here that the mind becomes freed from hindrances, pure and tranquil; illumined within and without. The mind in such a state becomes powerful and bright. Outside, it is represented by light which is just a mental reflex, with the light varying in degrees from that of a star to that of the sun. To be plain, this light which is reflected before the mind's eye in complete darkness is a manifestation of the purity, tranquillity and serenity of mind.

The Hindus work for it. To go from light into the void and come back to it, is truly *Brāhmanic*. The New Testament, in Matthew, speaks of "body full of light." We also hear of Roman Catholic priests meditating regularly for this very miraculous light. The holy Qur'an, too, gives prominence to the "manifestation of divine light."

This mental reflex of light denotes the purity of mind within, and the purity of mind forms the essence of a religious life whether one be a Buddhist, Hindu, Christian or Muslim. Indeed the purity of mind is the greatest common denominator of all religions. Love, which alone is the means for the unity of mankind, must be supreme, and it cannot be so unless the mind is transcendently pure. A balanced mind is necessary to balance the unbalanced minds of others: "As a fletcher makes straight his arrow, a wise man makes straight his trembling and unsteady thought, which is difficult to guard, difficult to hold back." So said the Buddha. Exercise of mind is as necessary as exercise of the physical body. Why not, then, give exercise to mind and make it strong and pure so that you may enjoy the *jhānic* peace within? When inner peace begins to permeate the mind, you will surely progress in the knowledge of truth.

Believe it or not, it is our experience that under a proper guide, this inner peace and purity of mind can be secured by one and all, irrespective of their religion or creed, providing they have sincerity of purpose and are prepared to submit to the guide for the period of trial.

When by continued practice, one has complete mastery over his mind, he can enter into *jhānic* states (meditative states of deep absorption) and gradually develop himself to acquire *samāpattis* (attainments) which will give him supernormal powers the same as those exercised by Kāḷa-Devala, the hermit teacher of King Suddhodana. This, of course, must be tried in penance and away from human habitations, but is rather dangerous for those who still have traces of passion in them. Anyway, such a practice, which gives supernormal powers in this mundane field, was not encouraged by Buddha, whose sole object of developing *samādhi* was to have the purity and strength of mind essential for the realization of truth. We have in Buddhism forty different methods of concentration of which the most outstanding is *ānāpāna*, i.e., concentration on the incoming and outgoing breath, the method followed by all Buddhas.

Paññā

Ladies and gentlemen, I will now take up the philosophical aspect of Buddhism in the third stage of the Noble Eightfold Path: *paññā* (insight).

The two characteristic aspects of *paññā* are:

1. *sammā-saṅkappa* (right aspiration)

2. *sammā-diṭṭhi*   (right understanding)

Right understanding of the truth is the aim and object of Buddhism. Right aspiration is the analytical study of mind and matter, both within and without, in order to come to the realization of truth.

You have heard of *nāma* and *rūpa* (mind and matter) so many times, I owe you a further explanation.

Nāma is so called because of its tendency to incline towards an object of the senses. *Rūpa* is so called because of its impermanence due to perpetual change. The nearest terms in English to *nāma* and *rūpa* therefore are mind and matter. I say "nearest" because the meaning is not exact.

Nāma, strictly speaking, is the term applied to the following:

1. consciousness   (*viññāṇa*)
2. feeling   (*vedanā*)
3. perception   (*saññā*)
4. volitional energies   (*saṅkhāra*)

These together with *rūpa* in the material state make what we call the *pañca-khandhas* (five aggregates). It is with the five aggregates that the Buddha summed up all the mental and physical phenomena of existence (which in reality is a continuum of mind and matter coexisting, but which to a layman is his personality or ego).

In *sammā-saṅkappa* (right aspiration), the disciple who, by then, has developed the powerful lens of *samādhi*, focuses his attention into his own self and by introspective meditation makes an analytical study of the nature: first, of *rūpa* (matter) and then of *nāma* (mind and mental properties). He feels (and at times he also sees) the *kalāpas* in their true state. He begins to realize that both *rūpa* and *nāma* are in a constant state of change—impermanent and fleeting. As his power of concentration increases, the nature of forces in him becomes more and more vivified. He can no longer get out of the impression that the *pañca khandhas* (five aggregates) are suffering within the law of cause and effect. He is now convinced that, in reality, all is suffering within and without, and that there is nothing such as ego. He longs for a state beyond suffering. So eventually getting out of the bonds of suffering, he moves from the mundane to the supramundane state and enters the stream of *sotāpanna*, the first of the four stages of *ariyas* (noble ones). Then he becomes free from: (1) ego; (2) doubts; (3) attachment to rules and rituals.

The second stage is *sakadāgāmi*, on coming to which, sensuous craving and ill will become attenuated. He ceases to have any passion or anger when he reaches the third stage of *anāgāmi*. The stage of *arahat* is the final goal.

Each of the *ariyas* can feel what *nibbāna* is like, even as a human being, for any number of times as he may choose, by going into the fruition stage of *sotāpanna*, etc., which gives him the *nibbānic* peace within.

This peace within which is identified with *nibbāna* has no parallel because it is supramundane. Compared to this, the *jhānic* peace within (which I mentioned earlier in dealing with *samādhi*) is negligible because, while the *nibbānic* peace within takes one beyond the thirty-one planes of existence, the *jhānic* peace within will still keep him within these planes—for example, in the fine material world of the *brahmās*.

Ladies and gentlemen, just a word more. What I have said here are just some of the fundamental aspects of Buddhism. With the time at my disposal, I hope I have given you my best.

To come to a state of purity of mind with a light before you; to go to the *jhānic* state at will; to experience, for yourselves, *nibbānic* peace within: these are all within your reach.

Why not, then, try for the first two at least which are within the confines of your own religion? I am prepared to give any help that you may require.

May I again express my gratitude to you all for the patient listening.

Lecture No. 3 (October 14, 1951)

My talk on "What Buddhism Is" will not be complete without a reference, though in brief, to the law of *paṭicca samuppāda* (the Law of Dependent Origination) and the law of *paṭṭhāna* (the law of relations, or cause and effect).

It will be recalled that in summing up my first lecture, I mentioned how Prince Siddhattha, the wandering ascetic, realized the truth and became Buddha. Lest you forget, I will repeat that portion again.

"Verily, Prince Siddhatta attained *sammā sambodhi* and became Buddha, the Awakened One, the Enlightened One, the All-knowing One. He was awake in a way compared with which all others were asleep and dreaming. He was enlightened in a way compared with which all other men were stumbling and groping in the dark. His knowing was with the knowledge compared with which, what all other men know is but a kind of ignorance."

All religions, no doubt, claim to show the way to truth. In Buddhism, as long as one has not realized the truth, i.e., the Four Noble Truths, he is in ignorance. It is this ignorance (*avijjā*) that is responsible for the generation of mental forces (*saṅkhārā*) which regulate the life continuum (*viññāṇa*) in all sentient beings. Just as the life continuum is established in a new existence, mind and matter (*nāma* and *rūpa*) appear automatically and correlatively. These, in turn, are developed into a vehicle or body with sense centers (*saḷāyatanā*).

These sense centers give rise to contact (*phassa*); and the contact of these sense centers with sense objects gives rise to sense impressions [sensations] (*vedanā*) which have the effect of arousing desire (*taṇhā*) followed closely by attachment or clinging to desire (*upādāna*). It is this attachment or clinging to desire which is the cause of becoming (*bhava*) or existence, with the attendant birth, old age, illness, death, anxiety, agony, pains, etc., all of which denote "suffering." In this way Buddha traced the origin of suffering to ignorance.

The Buddha said:

> Ignorance is the origin of mental forces;
> mental forces, the origin of the life continuum;
> life continuum, the origin of mind and matter;
> mind and matter, the origin of sense centers;
> sense centers, the origin of contact;
> contact, the origin of impression [sensation]
> impression [sensation], the origin of desire;
> desire, the origin of attachment;
> attachment, the origin of becoming (existence);
> becoming (existence), the origin of birth;
> birth, the origin of old age, illness, death, anxiety,
> agony, pains, etc. (which are all suffering).

This chain of origination is called the Law of Dependent Origination. The root cause for all these is therefore *avijjā* or ignorance (i.e., ignorance of the truth). It is true superficially that desire is the origin of suffering. This is so simple. When you want a thing, desire is aroused. You have to work for it or you suffer for it. But this is not enough. The Buddha said, "The five aggregates which are nothing but mind and matter also are suffering." The truth of suffering in Buddhism is complete only when one realizes the truth by seeing mind and matter as they really are (both within and without) and not as they seem to be.

The truth of suffering is therefore something which must be experienced before it can be understood. For example, we all know from science that everything that exists is nothing but vibration caused by the whirling movement of an infinite number of electrons. But how many of us can persuade ourselves to believe that our own bodies are subject to the same law? Why not then try to feel them as they really are, in so far as it relates to yourself? One must be above the mere physical condition for this purpose. He must develop mental energy powerful enough to see things in their true state. With developed mental power, one can see through-and-through, more than what one can see with the help of the latest scientific instruments. If that be so, why should one not see what is happening precisely in his own self—the atoms, the electrons and whatnot—all changing fast and yet never ending. It is, of course, by no means easy.

In reality our "suffering within" is a sequel to the keen sense of feeling the vibration, radiation and friction of the atomic units experienced through the process of introspective meditation called Vipassana, with the aid of the powerful lens of *samādhi*. Not knowing this truth is indeed ignorance. Knowing this truth in its ultimate reality means destruction of the root cause of suffering: that is, ignorance, with all the links in the chain of causation ending with what we call "life," with its characteristics of old age, illness, anxiety, agony, pains, and so on.

So much for the Law of Dependent Origination and the root cause of suffering.

Let us now turn our attention to the causal law of relations as expounded by the Buddha in the law of *Paṭṭhāna* of the *Abhidhamma Piṭaka*. This is the law, in the course of the analytical study of which, six colored rays emerged from the person of Buddha during his uninterrupted meditation for forty-nine days (soon after the attainment of Buddhahood). We have five volumes of about five hundred pages of Pāli text on this very delicate subject. I will give here only just an idea of the law.

There are twenty-four types of relations on which the fundamental principles of cause and effect in Buddhism are based. These are as follows:

1. condition   (*hetu*)
2. object   (*ārammaṇa*)
3. dominance   (*adhipati*)
4. contiguity   (*anantara*)
5. immediate contiguity (*samanantara*)
6. coexistence   (*sahajāta*)

7. reciprocity   (*aññamañña*)
8. dependence   (*nissaya*)
9. sufficing condition   (*upanissaya*)
10. antecedence   (*purejāta*)
11. consequence   (*pacchājāta*)
12. succession   (*āsevana*)
13. action   (*kamma*)
14. effect   (*vipāka*)
15. support   (*āhāra*)
16. control   (*indriya*)
17. ecstasy   (*jhāna*)
18. means   (*magga*)
19. association   (*sampayutta*)
20. dissociation   (*vippayutta*)
21. presence   (*atthi*)
22. absence   (*natthi*)
23. abeyance   (*vigata*)
24. continuance   (*avigata*)

I will explain to you now about the correlation of *hetu* (condition) and *kamma* (action) and the effect produced by their causes as I understand them.

Hetu is the condition of the mind at one conscious moment of each *kamma* action, whether physical, vocal or mental. Each *kamma* therefore produces a condition of mind which is either moral, immoral or neutral. This is what in Buddhism we call *kusala dhamma*, *akusala dhamma* and *abyākata dhamma*. These *dhammas* are mere forces (i.e., mental forces), which collectively create the universe of mental forces.

Moral (*kusala*) forces are positive forces generated from *kammas* (actions, words and thoughts) motivated by such good deeds as alms-giving, welfare work, devotion, purification of mind, and so on.

Immoral (*akusala*) forces are negative forces generated from *kammas* (actions, words and thoughts) motivated by desire, greed, lust, anger, hatred, dissatisfaction, delusion, and so on.

Neutral (*abyākata*) forces are neither moral nor immoral, as in the case of an *arahat* who has got rid of all traces of ignorance (*avijjā*). In the case of an *arahat*, contact (*phassa*) of sense objects with sense centers produces no sense impressions (*vedanā*) whatsoever, just as no impression is possible on flowing water which is ever-changing. To him, the whole framework of the body is but an ever-changing mass and any impression thereon automatically breaks away with the mass.

Let us now address the moral and immoral forces generated by conditioned actions with the planes of existence. For this purpose, I will classify the planes of existence roughly as follows:

Arūpa and *Rūpa Brahmā* Planes

These are beyond the range of sensuality. Supreme love, supreme compassion, supreme joy at the success and greatness of others, and supreme equanimity of mind are the four qualities of mind which generate transcendently pure, brilliant and extremely pleasing, cool and light mental forces which find their location in the highest of the planes of existence. This is the reason why in these planes matter is superfine and there is nothing but radiance. The vehicles or bodies of the *brahmās* cannot be identified with matter, but with radiation or light.

Sensuous Planes

These consist of:

1. planes of celestial beings

2. human world

3. planes of lower forms of existence

Planes of Celestial Beings

All good or meritorious deeds, words or thoughts which have a taint of desire for future well-being create moral mental forces which are considerably pure, luminous, pleasant and light. These find their location in the higher planes of celestial beings where matter is fine, luminous, pleasant and light. These celestial beings therefore have astral bodies varying in fineness, luminosity and color according to the planes to which they belong. Ordinarily they live in heavenly bliss until their own moral mental forces are consumed; then they revert to the lower planes of existence.

Planes of the Lower Forms of Existence

(I will come to the human world last.)

All malicious, evil, demeritorious actions, words and thoughts create mental forces which are by nature impure, dark, fiery, heavy and hard. The most impure, dark, fiery, heavy and hard mental forces should therefore find their place in hell, the lowest of the four planes of existence.

The matter in these planes must therefore be hard, crude, unpleasant and hot. The human world is just above the concentration of these forces, which are meant for consumption (to be experienced) by those beings destined for the lower forms of existence. These beings, with the exception of those in the animal world, are invisible to the ordinary human eye but visible to those who have developed the higher powers of *samādhi* and secured the divine eye. Here suffering—both physical and mental—predominates. This is just the reverse of what happens in the planes of celestial beings.

Human World

Now I come to the human world, this half-way house between heaven and hell. We experience pleasure and pain mixed together in degrees, as determined by our own past *kamma*. From here, we can, by developing our mental attitude, draw in our own mental forces from the higher planes. It is also from here that we can go down to the depths of depravity and tune up with the forces of the lower order.

There is no such constancy as in the other planes of existence. One may be a saint today, but he can be a rogue thereafter. He may be rich today, but he may soon become poor. The vicissitudes of life here are very conspicuous. There is no man who is stable, no family which is stable, no community which is stable, no nation which is stable.

All are subject to the law of *kamma*. As this *kamma* comes out of "mind" which is ever-changing, the effects of *kamma* must necessarily also be changing.

As long as man has inherent impurities in him and dies with the mental attitude tuned up with the mental forces of a plane of lower existence; then, at the last moment of his death, the next existence is automatically in that lower plane (to clear, one might say, his debit account of mental forces there).

On the other hand if, at the moment of death, his mental attitude is associated with the forces in the human world, the next existence can be in the human world again. If, however, his mental attitude at the last moment of death is associated with the reminiscence of his good deeds, the next existence will normally be in the celestial world (where one enjoys the credit balance of his own mental forces in that plane). One goes to the *brahmā* world, if at the moment of death his mind is not sensual, but is pure and tranquil.

This is how *kamma* plays its role in Buddhism with mathematical precision.

These, ladies and gentlemen, are the essential teachings of Buddha. How these teachings affect the individual depends on how one takes them.

The same applies to the family, the community or the people in general. We have Buddhists in faith and Buddhists in practice. Yet there is another class of Buddhists who are simply labelled "Buddhists" at birth. Only Buddhists in actual practice can secure the change in mental attitude and outlook. Let them only observe the Five Precepts; they are the followers of the teachings of Buddha. If this were followed by all the Buddhists in Burma, there would be no internecine strife such as we are having here in Burma. But there is another disturbing factor: that is, the bodily requirements. One must have the bare necessities of life. Life is more precious to him than anything else. The tendency therefore is to break the laws of discipline, whether religious or governmental, for one's self-preservation and for the preservation of others depending on him.

What is most essential is the generation of pure and good mental forces to combat the evil mental forces which dominate mankind. This is by no means easy. One cannot rise to the level of pure mental attitude without the help of a teacher. If we want effective power to combat these forces, we must work for it according to Dhamma. Modern science has given us, for what it is worth, the atomic bomb, the most wonderful and yet at the same time the most dreadful product of man's intelligence. Is man using his intelligence in the right direction? Is he creating good or bad mental forces, according to the spirit of Buddhism? It is our will that decides how and upon what subject we shall use intelligence. Instead of using intelligence only for the conquest of atomic energy in matter without, why not use it also for the conquest of atomic energy within?

This will give us the "peace within" and enable us to share it with all others. We will then radiate such powerful and purified mental forces as will successfully counteract the evil forces which are all around us. Just as the light of a single candle has the power to dispel darkness in a room, so also the light developed in one man can help dispel the darkness in several others.

To imagine that good can be done by the means of evil is an illusion, a nightmare. The case in point is that of Korea. For all the loss of lives on both sides, now over one million, are we nearer to, or further away, from peace? These are the lessons which we have learned. Change of mankind's mental attitude through religion alone is the solution. What is necessary at the moment is mastery over the mind and not only mastery over matter.

In Buddhism we differentiate between *loka dhātu* and *dhamma dhātu*. By *dhātu* is meant the nature-elements or forces. *Loka dhātu* is therefore matter (with its nature-elements) within the range of the physical plane. *Dhamma dhātu*, however, comprises mind, mental properties and some aspects of nature-elements which are not in the physical but in the mental plane. Modern science deals with what we call *loka dhātu*. It is just a base for *dhamma dhātu* in the mental plane. A step further and we come to the mental plane; not with the knowledge of modern science, but with the knowledge of Buddha-Dhamma in practice.

At least Mr. H. Overstreet, author of *The Mature Mind* (W. W. Norton & Co., Inc., New York) is optimistic about what is in store for mature minds. He writes:

> The characteristic knowledge of our century is psychological. Even the most dramatic advances in physics and chemistry are chiefly applications of known methods of research. But the attitude toward human nature and human experience that has come in our time is new.
>
> This attitude could not have come earlier. Before it came, there had to be long preparation. Physiology had to be a developed science; for the psychological person is also physiological. His makeup, among other things, is a matter of brain tissue, of nerves, of glands, of organs of touch, smell and sight. It was not until about seventy years ago that physiology was sufficiently developed to make psycho-physical research possible, as in the laboratories of the distinguished German psychologist, William Wundt. But before physiology there had to be a developed science of biology. Since brain, nerves, glands and the rest depend upon all processes, the science of the living cell had to have its maturing before a competent physiology could emerge.
>
> But before biology, there had to be chemistry; and before chemistry, physics; and before physics, mathematics. So the long preparation goes back into the centuries.
>
> There is, in short, a time clock of science. Each science has to wait until its hour strikes. Today, at least, the time clock of science strikes the hours of psychology, and a new enlightenment begins.

To be sure, the interests explored by this latest of the sciences are themselves old; but the accuracy of research is new. There is, in brief, a kind of iron logic that is in control. Each science has to wait for its peculiar accuracy until its predecessor has supplied the data and tools out of which its accuracy can be made.

The time clock of science has struck a new hour: a new insight begins to be at our service.

May I say that it is the Buddha Dhamma which should be studied by one and all for a new insight into the realities of human nature. In Buddhism we have the cure for all the mental ills that affect mankind. It is the evil forces of the mind, past and present, that are responsible for the present state of affairs all over the world.

Nowadays, there is dissatisfaction almost everywhere. Dissatisfaction creates ill feeling. Ill feeling creates hatred. Hatred creates enmity. Enmity creates war. War creates enemies. Enemies create war. War creates enemies, and so on. It is now getting into a vicious cycle. Why? Certainly because there is lack of proper control over the mind.

What is man? Man is, after all, mental forces personified. What is matter? Matter is nothing but mental forces materialized, a result of the reaction of the moral (positive) and immoral (negative) forces.

Buddha said: *Cittena niyate loko* (the world is mind-made). Mind therefore predominates everything. Let us then study the mind and its peculiar characteristics and solve the problem that is now facing the world.

There is a great field for practical research in Buddhism. Buddhists in Burma will always welcome whoever is anxious to have the benefit of their experience.

Ladies and gentlemen, I have made an attempt to give you the best of what I know about Buddhism. I shall be glad to give any interested person further explanation on any point that he may wish to discuss. I am grateful to you for the kind attendance and the interest taken in my lectures. May I again thank the clergy of the church for the permission so kindly given for this series of lectures.

Peace to all beings.

Questions and Answers

Q: More than all the Buddhist interpretations of the universe, it seems that the most important understanding for the practice is the realization of the Four Noble Truths.

S.N. Goenka: Yes, because these Four Noble Truths are universal truths. Nobody can deny the First Noble Truth, the reality of suffering. Association with undesirables [undesirable objects, people, situations] and disassociation from the desirable brings suffering. So the First Noble Truth, the truth of suffering, of misery, is universal. The Second Noble Truth, the cause of misery, looks different from the inside and from the outside. It seems that I am miserable because something happened outside that I didn't want to happen, or something didn't happen according to my wishes. But deep inside, everyone can realize: "The misery I am suffering is caused by my reaction of craving or aversion. I like something, and I generate craving. I dislike something, and I generate aversion." This Second Noble Truth is common to all.

So, too, the way to come out of misery is common to all, because you have to eradicate the root of your misery, where craving and aversion start. At a gross level, a good way to do that is to practice *sīla*—that is, don't perform any action, physical or verbal, that will disturb or harm other beings, because simultaneously it will harm you. Then work with *samādhi;* control your mind. But mere control is not sufficient; you must go deep and purify your mind. Once it is purifed, craving and aversion are gone, and you have reached the stage where there is no misery at all. It's all so scientific; people accept it so easily. Of course, if we keep fighting over dogma, difficulties arise. But I say, just practice and see: Are you suffering or not? Isn't this the cause of the suffering? And isn't it eradicated by practicing in this way?

Q: Perhaps at the intellectual level one can come to understand this reasoning about the Four Noble Truths, but how is it possible to explain, in a way that is understandable for the common person, that life is suffering and that the practical realization of this Noble Truth can lead to freedom from suffering?

SNG: This is *dukkha*—this is a universally bitter truth which cannot be eliminated by ignoring it or by turning away from it. We cannot close our eyes to it and wish it away. We cannot make it go by any speculation or argument. To accept the reality of *dukkha* is to accept the truth. When we accept the truth of *dukkha*, only then can we seek a way to come out of it.

Can there be any impediment to accepting the truth of *dukkha*? How evident is this truth, how clear is this fact? How the lives of all living beings are infused with *dukkha*! We cannot even imagine how great is the suffering of all sentient beings. In this tiny span of time while I am engaged in speaking these sentences, on this earth countless smaller beings are being devoured and crushed in bloody jaws; they are being ruthlessly swallowed without any pity. Can we ever measure their agony, their pain, their *dukkha*?

Even if we leave aside the suffering of the sentient beings of the animal kingdom, how immeasurable and limitless is the *dukkha* of man alone? In this one moment of existence, how many sick people in the hospitals of the world are groaning in agony? How many, having sensed impending death, are crying in vain, in fear and anguish? How many, at the loss of their wealth, prestige, their position, their power, are beset at this moment with pain? Who can have any reason for not accepting the truth of suffering while living in this universe where there is suffering everywhere?

We certainly do not wish to say that in life there is only *dukkha* and not a vestige of any pleasure. But are the pleasures of the senses really something that can be called happiness? Does not that glitter of happiness contain within it the shadow of pain? There is no sensual pleasure which is permanent, unchanging, everlasting. There is not a single pleasure in the sensual sphere which one can enjoy with satisfaction forever. All pleasures are impermanent, are changing, must come to an end. Whatever is impermanent is unsatisfactory, after all. When we get attached to something because it seems pleasurable to us, how great is the sorrow when that pleasure is no more; the pain becomes intense.

In the eyes of the world, a person may be considered very happy or even consider himself very happy. How long do people enjoy such pleasures? How quickly does the momentary brightness turn to darkness! As much as a person gets involved in and attached to these pleasures, to the same degree he involves himself in inevitable suffering. But one who enjoys pleasantness with detachment—clearly understanding its impermanent nature—is always safe from the suffering when pleasure ends. Therefore while enjoying these pleasures, if we are aware of their changing, impermanent nature, if we are aware of the inherent *dukkha* in them, then we remain free of the pain that comes along when these pleasures end. To see *dukkha* in our pleasures is to see the truth which destroys *dukkha;* this is a righteous way of life which ensures our well-being.

The purpose of seeing the truth of *dukkha* is that as soon as the *dukkha* raises its head, we see it, we apprehend it, and at once extinguish the fire of this *dukkha* so it cannot spread. If we are aware of the *dukkha* involved in attachment to pleasure, then we will not allow the fire to spread. While enjoying the pleasure we will tend not get tense or excited, and when the pleasure ends, even then we won't become miserable, because all along we have understood the ephemeral nature of pleasure. So, the ceasing of the pleasure does not necessarily become a cause for suffering.

Everyone, without any exception, experiences some of the truth of suffering, but it is only when the suffering is experienced and observed objectively, rather than indulged in, that the truth of it becomes beneficial. Then it becomes a Noble Truth. To cry, to whimper, to writhe in pain because of some physical suffering is, no doubt, seeing the truth of suffering, but to observe and understand the suffering underlying the apparent enjoyment of boisterous laughter, wine and song is to really see the Noble Truth of suffering.

As long as we are unable to observe the real nature of sense pleasures, we shall continue to cling to them, we shall continue to yearn for them—and this is, after all, the main cause of all our suffering.

So, if we are to fully understand, fully comprehend *dukkha*, then we have to understand and consider the subtle reality. At the level of experience, within the framework of one's own body, one observes the transitory, impermanent nature of reality and thus realizes the nature of the entire mind-matter universe. The world of the senses is impermanent, and whatever is impermanent is suffering.

To understand and to observe this reality is to comprehend, to appreciate the First Noble Truth; and it is this understanding of the Noble Truth of suffering which can take us toward freedom from all suffering.

Q: Often we are able to understand and accept at the intellectual level what has been said but still miss what the deepest cause of our suffering is.

SNG: At the root of all our suffering there is always some attachment, there is always some craving. Let us try to understand desire more thoroughly, more completely and in greater depth.

We are constantly experiencing an infinity of cravings. We see a form with our eyes which seems beautiful, and our desire is stimulated. We hear something, we smell something, taste something, touch something tangible which is pleasant, and at once desire it. Our attachment raises its head. Similarly, when we recall some sense pleasure which gave us intense pleasure—we at once become desirous of experiencing it again. Or if we imagine some sense pleasure which we have not so far experienced, then the craving to experience it manifests itself.

The desire for the objects of these six senses arises because the objects of the senses make us restless. For what we do not possess there arises a strong craving. We get only dissatisfaction from what we have. Where there is clinging there is dissatisfaction, and where there is dissatisfaction there has to be clinging. Dissatisfaction with what is and craving for what is not, both these keep us miserable.

Even if we were to realize the suffering of greed and clinging at an intellectual level, still we could not come out of this misery by means of such intellectual knowledge. Throughout life we have been involved in a spirit of greedy competition. Right from childhood—since youth, when we stepped into life—the constant desire has been to get ahead of others. In the mad spirit of competition life has become a free-for-all—the law of the jungle, survival of the fittest prevails. Life has become tense and full of restlessness and striving.

But where do we find happiness and well-being in this rat-race when before we achieve the object of our desire we are disturbed with discontentment. In our efforts to achieve, we lose the equilibrium of our minds. And having succeeded in our achievement, instead of enjoying the satisfaction of possession, we become still more agitated to acquire more, to hoard more.

All such activity—which in its beginning begets anxiety, restlessness, tensions, suffering; which brings more of these undesirable states of mind as it expands; and which ends in more suffering—how could this seeming progress at the material level usher in an era of peace and prosperity?

This does not mean that householders should shun all material activity and spend their lives in poverty. People must work to eliminate their own poverty as well as that of others too. They should really work hard, but also maintain a balanced mind while they are engaged in work. If, under the influence of attachment and craving, they were to lose their human dignity, peace and equilibrium, despite having amassed material wealth they certainly would not have achieved any real happiness. To achieve real happiness one must maintain equilibrium of the mind, reasonableness of the mind.

The disease of clinging and competition spreads like an infectious illness and constantly keeps on spreading throughout humanity. Mankind thus loses peace and tranquillity. This inordinate competition and desire thus becomes the breeding ground for our misery, not our happiness. Peace lies in keeping it at bay. Peace lies in keeping it at arm's length, peace lies in keeping ourselves beyond the reach of the tentacles of inordinate craving and useless competition, and in keeping our mind always balanced and equanimous.

Q: In face of these situations which we encounter daily, what is the way to end the suffering and agitation that is in us?

SNG: If a thing arises due to a certain cause, it can certainly be eradicated by eradicating the cause. Suffering, we have seen, arises because of craving and aversion. If these are completely eliminated, then as a matter of course, suffering will also be eliminated.

It is easy to accept this truth at the theoretical level but so difficult to realize it at the experiential level. And unless one experiences in practice the eradication of the causes, the resultant end of suffering can never be attained. A truly liberated person does not merely expound the theory of the eradication of suffering; he shows the way to achieve this end. Thus, the way to come out of misery is essentially practical, not merely theoretical.

To eradicate the sources of suffering—craving and aversion—one must know how and where they arise. Through personal experience, a liberated person discovers and then teaches that they always arise whenever there is a sensation. And a sensation arises whenever there is contact of a sense-object with a sense-door—of material vision with the eyes; of sound with the ears; of odor with the nose; of taste with the tongue; of touch with the body; of thought with the mind.

We must eradicate craving and aversion at their source—that is, where the sensation arises. To do so, we must develop the ability to be aware of all the sensations within the body. For this purpose we should train our minds to become sharp and sensitive enough to feel the sensations at all levels. Along with this distinct awareness, we must also develop the faculty of maintaining equanimity towards all the sensations—pleasant, unpleasant, and neutral. If we maintain this awareness and equanimity, we will certainly not react; when sensation arises, one will not again generate craving or aversion.

Q: So the way to liberate the mind is essentially practical; but how does one develop these mental qualities of awareness and equanimity you have just pointed out?

SNG: A way was found which could be understood and practiced. It is the Fourth Noble Truth, i.e., the Noble Eightfold Path.

To start with, one should at least abstain from vocal and physical actions which contribute to one's mental agitation. One should refrain from speaking lies, harsh words, or slanderous talk, or idle gossip. One should refrain from killing, stealing, sexual misconduct, and intoxicants. One should avoid a means of livelihood which causes harm to others. With the base of this morality (*sīla*), one makes proper efforts and begins to develop awareness of sensations, at least in one small area of the body. To do so, one sits quietly with closed eyes, observing the flow of inbreath and outbreath at the entrance to the nostrils. Working for some time with this awareness of respiration, one develops the ability to keep the mind fixed on a single object of attention: the area below the nostrils, above the upper lip. With this heightened concentration (*samādhi*), one becomes capable of experiencing the natural, normal, physical sensations in this area.

The mind is now sharp enough to begin experiencing sensations throughout the physical structure.

Systematically, diligently, and repeatedly, one moves the attention through the body, gradually strengthening awareness of sensations, increasing one's ability not to react to them. With this training—the awareness of the reality, in the present moment, and equanimity—the pattern of thought begins to change, from thoughts of craving, aversion, ignorance to thoughts of Dhamma, or the way out of suffering.

But thinking, even of Dhamma, will not lead to liberation from suffering. For that, one must continue developing awareness and equanimity. Without elation about pleasant sensations or depression in the face of unpleasant ones, one understands not merely intellectually but experientially that these sensations are nothing but manifestations of the contact of mind and matter—phenomena which are as impermanent and ephemeral as the sensations themselves. Something so ephemeral as these sensations cannot be a basis for real happiness; rather, they will be a source of misery. One also starts realizing at the experiential level that the entire mental phenomenon, the physical phenomenon, and the combination of these two is certainly not "I," not "mine," not "my soul." In this way, by experiencing reality as it is, in its nature, with its true characteristics, the meditator develops real wisdom (*paññā*), and emerges from illusions and delusions.

Thus, by maintaining awareness and equanimity, one gradually weakens the old habits of craving and aversion. Even when reaction does occur, it is less intense and passes more quickly. It no longer has such a powerful impact on the mind.

The more one remains fully aware and equanimous, not allowing new reactions of craving and aversion to occur, the more one gives an opportunity to one's stock of old reactions, of suppressed mental defilements, to rise to the conscious level of the mind, one by one, to be eradicated. Layer after layer, these past conditionings come to the surface. By maintaining equanimity, one eradicates them and thus finds relief from misery.

Whatever amount of defilements are eradicated, to that degree he is free of suffering. Step by step, remaining aware and not reacting, one advances on the path, until sooner or later one reaches the stage when the entire accumulation of past reactions has been eradicated, and the habit of reaction itself has disappeared. Freed from all craving, aversion, ignorance—past, present and future—one experiences total freedom from suffering.

To reach this stage, one has to work and work strenuously. Simply reading articles, or engaging in discussions or debates, will not suffice. The only way to achieve liberation is by one's own efforts—the effort to observe the reality of oneself, within the framework of one's body, without reacting to it.

This is the way to achieve the end of suffering.

Q: We have examined the theoretical and practical importance of awakening in us the awareness of *anicca*—that is, the direct experience of the impermanent nature of every mental and physical phenomenon. U Ba Khin also emphasized this practical aspect in our daily lives. Can you describe in practical terms what is happening in the body and in the mind, how this law of cause and effect works, and how this change can help us?

SNG: The Buddha said that understanding the Dhamma is nothing other than understanding the law of cause and effect. You have to realize this truth within yourself. In a ten-day course you have the opportunity to learn how to do this. This investigation of truth pertaining to matter, pertaining to mind and pertaining to the mental concomitants, the mental contents, is not merely for the sake of curiosity, but to change your mental habit pattern at the deepest level of the mind. As you keep proceeding you will realize how the mind influences matter, and how matter influences the mind.

Every moment, within the framework of the body, masses of subatomic particles—*kalāpas*—arise and pass away, arise and pass away. How do they arise? The cause becomes clear as you investigate the reality as it is, without influence from any past conditioning or philosophical beliefs. The material input, the food that you have taken, becomes a cause for these *kalāpas* to arise. You will also find that *kalāpas* arise and pass away due to the climatic atmosphere around you. You also begin to understand the formation of the mind-matter structure: how matter helps matter to arise and dissolve, arise and dissolve. Similarly, you understand how mind helps matter to arise and dissolve. You will also notice that at times matter arises from the mental conditioning of the past—that is, the accumulated *sankhāras* (conditioning) of the past. By the practice of Vipassana all of this starts to become clear. In ten days you do not become perfect in this understanding but a beginning is made. You learn to observe: At this moment, what type of mind has arisen and what is the content of this mind? The quality of the mind is according to the content of the mind. For example, when a mind full of passion (or a mind full of anger, or a mind full of fear) has arisen, you will notice that as it arises it helps to generate these subatomic particles.

When the mind is full of passion, within this material structure, subatomic particles of a particular type arise, and there is a bio-chemical secretion that starts flowing throughout the body with the stream of the blood or otherwise. This type of biochemical flow, which starts because a mind full of passion has arisen, is called *kāmāsava* (lit.: sensual flow).

Now, as a very objective scientist, you proceed further, simply observing the truth as it is, observing how the law of nature works. When this secretion of *kāmāsava* starts, since it is the biochemical produced by passion, it influences the next moment of the mind with more passion. Thus this *kāmāsava* turns into a craving of passion at the mental level, which again stimulates *kāmāsava*, a flow of passion at the physical level. One starts influencing the other, starts stimulating the other, and the passion keeps on multiplying for minutes together, at times for hours together. The behavior pattern of the mind of generating passion is strengthened because of the repeated generation of passion.

And not only passion but also fear, anger, hatred, and craving—every type of impurity that comes in the mind simultaneously generates an *āsava* (flow). And this *āsava* keeps stimulating that particular negativity, that particular impurity, resulting in a vicious cycle of suffering. You may call yourself a Hindu, or a Muslim, or a Jain, or a Christian—it makes no difference—the process is such, the law is such, that it is applicable to one and all. There is no discrimination.

Mere understanding at the intellectual level will not help to break this cycle, and may even create difficulties. Your beliefs from a particular tradition may look quite logical, yet these beliefs will create obstacles for you. The intellect has its own limitation. You cannot realize the ultimate truth merely at the intellectual level. The ultimate truth is limitless, infinite, while the intellect is finite. It is only through experience that we are able to realize that which is limitless, infinite. Even those who have accepted this law of nature intellectually are not able to change the behavior pattern of their minds, and as a result they are far away from the realization of the ultimate truth.

This behavior pattern is at the depth of the mind. What is called the "unconscious mind" is actually not unconscious; at all times it remains in contact with this body. And along with this contact of the body a sensation keeps arising, because every chemical that flows in your body generates a particular type of sensation. You feel a sensation—pleasant, unpleasant or neutral, whatever it is—and with the feeling of this sensation, you keep reacting. At the depth of your mind you keep reacting with craving, with aversion, with craving, with aversion. You keep generating different types of *sankhāras*, different types of negativities, different types of impurities, and the process of multiplication continues. You can't stop it because there is such a big barrier between the conscious and the unconscious mind. When you practice Vipassana you break this barrier. Without Vipassana the barrier remains.

At the conscious level of the mind, at the intellectual level of the mind, one may accept the entire theory of Dhamma, of truth, of law, of nature. But still one keeps rolling in misery because one does not realize what is happening at the depth of the mind. Sensations are there in your body every moment. Every contact results in a sensation. This isn't a philosophy, it is the actual truth which can be verified by one and all.

On the surface the mind keeps itself busy with outside objects, or it remains involved with games of intellectualization, imagination, or emotion. That is the job of your "tiny mind" (*paritta citta*), the surface level of the mind. Therefore you do not feel what is happening deep inside, and you do not feel how you are reacting to what is happening at the deeper level of the mind.

By Vipassana, when that barrier is broken, one starts feeling sensations throughout the body, not merely at the surface but also deep inside because throughout the entire physical structure, wherever there is life, there is sensation. And by observing these sensations you start realizing the characteristic of arising and passing, arising and passing. By this understanding you start to change the habit pattern of the mind.

Say, for example, you are feeling a particular sensation which may be due to the food you have eaten, which may be due to the atmosphere around you, which may be due to your present mental actions, or which may be due to your old mental reactions that are giving their fruit. Whatever it may be, a sensation is there, and you are trained to observe it with equanimity and not to react to it; but you keep on reacting because of the old habit pattern. You sit for one hour, and initially you may get only a few moments when you do not react, but those few moments are wonderful moments. You have started changing the habit pattern of your mind by observing sensation and understanding its nature of impermanence. This stops the blind habit pattern of reacting to the sensation and multiplying the vicious cycle of misery. Initially in an hour you get a few seconds, or a few minutes of not reacting. But eventually, by practice, you reach a stage where throughout the hour you do not react at all. At the deepest level you do not react at all. A deep change is coming in the old habit pattern. The vicious cycle is broken: your mind was reacting to the chemical process which was manifesting itself as a sensation, and as a result, for hours together, your mind was flooded with a particular impurity, a particular defilement. Now it gets a break for a few moments, a few seconds, a few minutes. As the old habit of blind reaction becomes weaker, your behavior pattern is changing. You are coming out of your misery.

Again, this is not to be believed because the Buddha said so. It is not to be believed because I say so. It is not be believed because your intellect says so. You have to experience it yourself. People coming to these courses have found by their experience that there is a change for the better in their behavior.

Q: The method you have just described is very practical, but can everybody benefit from it—even those who suffer from severe addictions, such as to drugs or alcohol?

SNG: When we talk of addiction, it is not merely to alcohol or to drugs, but also to passion, to anger, to fear, to egotism: all of these are addictions. All these are addictions to your impurities. At the intellectual level you understand very well: "Anger is not good for me. It is dangerous. It is so harmful." Yet you are addicted to anger, you keep generating anger. And when the anger has passed, you keep repenting: "Oh! I should not have done that. I should not have gotten angry." Meaningless! The next time some stimulation comes you become angry again. You are not coming out of it, because you have not been working at the depth of the behavior pattern of your mind. The anger starts because of a particular chemical that has started flowing in your body, and with the interaction of mind and matter—one influencing the other—the anger continues to multiply.

By practicing this technique, you start observing the sensation which has arisen because of the flow of a particular chemical. You do not react to it. That means you do not generate anger at that particular moment. This one moment turns into a few moments, which turn into a few seconds, which turn into a few minutes, and you find that you are not as easily influenced by this flow as you were in the past. You have slowly started coming out of your anger.

People who have come to these courses go back home and apply this technique in their daily lives by their morning and evening meditation and by continuing to observe themselves throughout the day—how they react or how they maintain equanimity in different situations. The first thing they will try to do is to observe the sensations. Because of the particular situation, maybe a part of the mind has started reacting, but by observing the sensations their minds become equanimous. Then whatever action they take is an action; it is not a reaction. Action is always positive. It is only when we react that we generate negativity and become miserable. A few moments observing the sensation makes the mind equanimous, and then it can act. Life then is full of action instead of reaction.

This practice morning and evening, and making use of this technique in daily life—both of these start to change the behavior pattern. Those who used to roll in anger for a long time find their anger decreases. When anger does come, it cannot last for a long period because it is not so intense. Similarly, those who are addicted to passion find that this passion becomes weaker and weaker. Those who are addicted to fear find the fear becoming weaker and weaker. Different kinds of impurities take different amounts of time to come out of. Whether it takes a long time to come out of them, or a short time, the technique will work, provided it is practiced properly.

Whether you are addicted to craving—or aversion, or hatred, or passion, or fear—the addiction is to a particular sensation that has arisen because of the biochemical flow (*āsava*). This type of matter results in reaction at the mental level, and the reaction at the mental level again turns into this biochemical reaction. When you say that you are addicted, you are actually addicted to the sensation. You are addicted to this flow, this biochemical flow.

The *āsava* of ignorance is the strongest *āsava*. Of course there is ignorance even when you are reacting with anger or passion or fear; but when you get intoxicated with alcohol or drugs, this intoxication multiplies your ignorance. Therefore it takes time to feel sensations, to go to the root of the problem. When you get addicted to liquor, or addicted to drugs, you cannot know the reality of what is happening within the framework of the body. There is darkness in your mind. You cannot understand what is happening inside, what keeps on multiplying inside. We have found that in cases of alcohol addiction, people generally start benefiting more quickly than people who are addicted to drugs. But the way is there for everyone to come out of misery, however addicted they may be, however ignorant they may be. If you keep working patiently and persistently, sooner or later you are bound to reach the stage where you start feeling sensations throughout the body and can observe them objectively. It may take time. In ten days you may only make a slight change in the habit pattern of your mind. It doesn't matter; a beginning is made and if you keep practicing morning and evening, and take a few more courses, the habit pattern will change at the deepest level of the mind and you will come out of your ignorance, out of your reaction.

We keep advising people who are addicted to smoking—even ordinary tobacco smoking—that if an urge arises in the mind, not to take the cigarette and start smoking. We advise them: "Wait a little." Just accept the fact that an urge to smoke has arisen in the mind. When this urge arises, along with it there is a sensation in the body. Start observing this sensation, whatever the sensation may be. Do not look for a particular sensation. Any sensation at that time in the body is related to the urge to smoke. And by observing the sensation as impermanent, *anicca*, it arises, it passes; it arises, it passes; and in ten minutes, fifteen minutes, this urge will pass away. This is not a philosophy but the experiential truth.

Similarly, for those who are addicted to alcohol or addicted to drugs, when an urge arises, we advise them not to succumb immediately, but to wait ten or fifteeen minutes, and accept the fact that an urge has arisen, and observe whatever sensation is present at that time. By applying these instructions, they have found that they are coming out of their addictions. They may not be successful every time, but if they are successful even one time out of ten, a very good beginning has been made because the root has started changing. The habit pattern lies at the root of the mind, and the root of the mind is strongly related to the sensations on the body: mind and matter are so interrelated, they keep on influencing each other.

If this law, this law of nature, is merely accepted intellectually, or devotionally, the benefit will be minimal—it may inspire you to practice. But the real benefit accrues through the actual practice. It is a long path, a lifetime job. Even a journey of ten thousand miles must start with the first step. For one who has taken the first step it is possible that one will take the second step, the third step, and like this, step by step, one will reach the final goal of full liberation.

Chapter Seven

The Real Values of True Buddhist Meditation

—Sayagyi U Ba Khin

In December 1961, the Prime Minister of the State of Israel, David Ben Gurion, visited Myanmar. A delegation of Israeli press representatives also came to report on this event. Sayagyi was asked to address a gathering of these journalists, who were invited to tea at the International Meditation Center. Those who attended the talk were already acquainted with the booklet "What Buddhism Is."

From discussions with one of the journalists prior to the talk, Sayagyi concluded that the Israelis were more interested in the present values of Buddhist meditation than in what would be gained in an afterlife. Accordingly, he named his paper "The Real Values of True Buddhist Meditation" and drew from the wealth of his own personal experiences, and those of his students, to illustrate this point. Included was an extensive set of charts, graphs and examples drawn from Sayagyi's active career in government service, demonstrating the productive potential of a calm and balanced mind. Presented here is an abridged introductory portion of the paper, which was published by the Buddha Sāsana Council Press, Rangoon, in 1962.

The Foundation of a Buddhist

A Buddhist is a person who takes refuge in the Buddha, the Dhamma and the Saṅgha.

We have four categories of Buddhists, namely:

1. *bhaya* (a Buddhist because of danger);

2. *lābha* (a Buddhist because of need for gratification);

3. *kula* (a Buddhist because of birth);

4. *saddhā* (a Buddhist because of faith).

Buddhists may be further divided into two classes, namely:

1. those who intend to make a bid for release in this very life;

2. those who are just accumulating the virtues *(pāramī)* with a view to becoming:

   a) a Buddha (enlightened person; one who has discovered the way to liberation, has practised it, and has reached the goal by his own efforts);

   b) a *Pacceka* Buddha ("lone" or "silent" Buddha, who is unable to teach the way he has found to others);

   c) *agga sāvaka* (chief disciple);

   d) *mahā sāvaka* (leading disciple);

   e) *arahat* (liberated being; one who has destroyed all his mental impurities)

Amongst those who intend to make a bid for release in the same lifetime, there are four types of individuals, namely:

1. *ugghātitaññu:* An individual who encounters a Buddha in person and who is capable of attaining the holy path and holy truth through the mere hearing of a short discourse.

2. *vipañcitaññu:* An individual who can attain the Path and the Fruits only when a discourse is expounded to him at some considerable length.

3. *neyya:* An individual who has not the capability of attaining the Path and the Fruits through the hearing of either a short or long discourse, but who must make a study of the teachings

and practice the provisions contained therein for days, months and years in order that he may attain the Path and the Fruits.

In this connection, to a question raised by Bodhi Rājakumāra, Buddha said:

> I cannot say what exactly should be the time for the complete realization of the truth. Even assuming that you renounce the world and join the order of my Saṅgha, it might take you seven years or six years or five years or four years or three years or two years or one year, as the case may be. Nay, it can be six months or three months or two months or one month. On the other hand, I do not also discount the possibility of attainment of *arahat*-ship in a fortnight or seven days or in one day or even in a fraction of a day. It depends upon so many factors.

4. *padaparama:* An individual who, though he encounters a Buddha *sāsana* (era when Buddha's teachings are available), and puts forth the utmost possible effort in both the study and practice of the Dhamma, cannot attain the Paths and the Fruits within this lifetime. All that he can do is to accumulate habits and potentials. Such a person cannot obtain release from *saṃsāra* (the cycle of rebirth) within his lifetime. If he dies while practicing *samatha* for *samādhi* (calm), or Vipassana for *paññā* (insight), and secures rebirth either as a human being or a *deva* in his next existence, he can attain the Path and the Fruits in that existence within the present Buddha *sāsana*.

It is therefore to be assumed that only those quite matured in the accumulation of virtues (*pāramī*), such as those of the four types of individuals referred to above, will be *inclined* to make that bid for release and take seriously to courses of Buddhist meditation. As a corollary, we have no doubt that whoever is determined to follow strictly and diligently the Noble Eightfold Path through a course of Buddhist meditation under the guidance of a *qualified* teacher, is an individual of either [the third or fourth] type.

The Essence of Buddha-Dhamma

The Buddha-Dhamma is subtle, deep, and difficult to understand. It is by strictly and diligently following the Noble Eightfold Path that one can:

1. come to the realization of the truth of suffering or ill,

2. annihilate the cause of suffering and then

3. come to the end of it.

Only the accomplished saint, only the *arahat*, can fully understand the truth of suffering or ill. As the truth of suffering is realized, the causes of suffering become automatically destroyed, and so, one eventually comes to the end of suffering or ill. What is most important in the understanding of the Buddha-Dhamma is the realization of the truth of suffering or ill through a process of meditation in accordance with the three steps of *sīla*, *samādhi* and *paññā* of the Noble Eightfold Path. As the Buddha put it:

> It is difficult to shoot from a distance, arrow after arrow, through a narrow keyhole and miss not once. It is more difficult to shoot and penetrate with the tip of a hair, split a hundred times, a piece of hair similarly split. It is still more difficult to penetrate to the fact that 'all this is suffering or ill.'

He, who has by the practice of Buddha-Dhamma passed into the four streams of sanctity and enjoyed the four fruitions, can appreciate the six attributes of the Dhamma, namely:

1. The Dhamma is not the result of conjecture or speculation, but the result of personal attainments, and it is precise in every respect.

2. The Dhamma produces beneficial results here and now for those who practice it in accordance with the techniques evolved by the Buddha.

3. The effect of Dhamma on the person practicing it is immediate in that it has the quality of simultaneously removing the causes of suffering with the understanding of the truth of suffering.

4. The Dhamma can stand the test of those who are anxious to do so. They can know for themselves what the benefits are.

5. The Dhamma is part of one's own self, and is therefore susceptible of ready investigation.

6. The fruits of Dhamma can be fully experienced by the [noble disciples who have reached the stages of a liberation].

The Fruits of the Path of Meditation

Whoever is desirous of undergoing a course of training in Buddhist meditation must go along the Noble Eightfold Path. This Noble Eightfold Path was laid down by the Buddha in his first sermon to the five ascetics (*pañca vaggiyā*) as a means to the end, and all that is necessary for the student is to follow strictly and diligently the three steps of *sīla*, *samādhi*, and *paññā*, which form the essence of the said Noble Eightfold Path.

Sīla (precepts, moral conduct)

1. right speech

2. right action

3. right livelihood

Samādhi

4. right exertion

5. right attentiveness

6. right concentration

Paññā (wisdom-insight)

7. right contemplation

8. right understanding

The fruits of meditation are innumerable. They are embodied in the discourse on the advantages of a *samaṇa's* life (*Sāmaññaphala Sutta*). The very object of becoming a *samaṇa* or monk is to follow strictly and diligently the Noble Eightfold Path and enjoy not only the fruits (*phala*) of *sotāpatti, sagadāgāmi, anāgāmi* and *arahata†*, but also to develop many kinds of faculties. A layman who takes to meditation to gain insight into the ultimate truth, also has to work in the same way; and if his potentials are good, he may also enjoy a share of those fruits and faculties.

Only those who take to meditation with good intentions can be assured of success. With the development of the purity and the power of the mind backed by the insight into the ultimate truth of nature, one might be able to do a lot of things in the right direction for the benefit of mankind.

The Buddha said:

> O monks, develop the power of concentration. He who is developed in the power of concentration sees things in their true perspective.

This is true of a person who is developed in *samādhi*. It must be all the more so in the case of a person who is developed not only in *samādhi* but also in *paññā* (insight).

It is a common belief that a man, whose power of concentration is good and can secure a perfect balance of mind at will, can achieve better results than a person who is not so developed. There are, therefore, definitely many advantages that accrue to a person who undergoes a successful course of training in meditation, whether he be a religious man, an administrator, a politician, a businessman or a student.

My own case may be cited as an example. If I have to say something here about myself it is with a sincere desire, and with no other motive whatsoever, to illustrate just what practical benefits

---

†The four stages of liberation: the stream-enterer, once-returner, non-returner and the fully liberated one.

can accrue to a person practicing Buddhist meditation. The events are factual and, of course, one cannot deny the facts.

These are as follows:

I took up Buddhist meditation seriously from January 1937. My life sketch in "Who is Who" of the *Guardian* Magazine, December 1961 gives an account of the duties and responsibilities of government, which I have been discharging from time to time. I retired from the service of government from 26 March, 1953, on attaining the age of fifty-five years but was re-employed as from that date until now in various capacities, most of the time holding two or more separate posts equivalent to those of heads of departments. At a time I was holding three separate sanctioned appointments of the status of head of a department for nearly three years, and on another occasion four such sanctioned posts simultaneously for about a year.

In addition, there were also a good number of special assignments either as member of standing committees in the departments of Prime Minister and National Planning or as chairman or member of ad hoc committees.

Dr. Elizabeth K. Nottingham in her paper entitled "Buddhist Meditation in Burma" asked: "May it (meditation) not possibly help to create a reservoir of calm and balanced energy to be used for the building of a 'welfare state' and as a bulwark against corruption in public life?"

To this question, my answer would definitely be "Yes." I can say this with conviction, because the achievements in all spheres of work happened to be most outstanding in spite of the fact that each of the posts (viz., Director of Commercial Audit, Chairman of the State Agricultural Marketing Board, and Principal, Government Institute for Accounts and Audit) is a challenge to any senior officer of government.

I was appointed Director of Commercial Audit (i.e., as head of the Directorate of Commercial Audit with effect from 11 June,

1956 to reorganize the Directorate which was formed on 4 October, 1955) with a staff of just fifty men including only three qualified accountants. The problem was to reorganize the Directorate and raise the standard of its efficiency to cope with the work of audit of transactions of the developing Boards and Corporations of Burma.

Next, I was appointed Chairman of the State Agricultural Marketing Board on 21 June, 1956, (just ten days after appointment as Director of Commercial Audit) to take charge of the affairs of the Board, which were found to be deteriorating, with the accounts in arrears for five years, the surplus stock at the end of the preceding year at 1.7 million tons and the market price of rice fallen from 60 pounds [sterling] per ton in 1953 to 34 pounds per ton in 1956. There was also the problem of disunity between the officers and members of the subordinate ranks.

In 1958, acting upon the recommendation of the Boards Enquiry Commission (headed by the Prime Minister) of which I was a member, the establishment of a Government Institute for Accounts and Audit was mooted. Burma was extremely short of accountants and account clerks. The result was that with the exception of two organizations of pre-war origin, the accounts of boards and corporations were badly in arrears (i.e., for two to four years), apart from a large number of irregularities which came to notice. I was accordingly charged, in addition to my own existing duties, with the responsibility of establishing a State Institute of Government Accounts and Audit for the purpose of giving training to the officers and staff of all the boards and corporations in Burma. I assumed charge of the post of Principal of this institute with effect from1 April, 1958 for spade work, and the Institute was formally opened by the Prime Minister on 11 July, 1958.

The results of these undertakings will surely illustrate what "a reservoir of calm and energy" one can create with Buddhist meditation to be used for the building of a "welfare state."

Human Relations

As to how loving-kindness reinforced with the power of truth could do something tangible in the matter of human relations, let me cite a few of my own experiences.

I was required by the Prime Minister to investigate into the many irregularities suspected in the State Agricultural Marketing Board (S.A.M.B.), and was accordingly appointed on 15 August, 1955, as chairman of the S.A.M.B. Special Enquiry Committee. The reports made by me led to further enquiries by the Bureau of Special Investigations, and their enquiries led to the arrest of four officers of the Board (including the General Manager) during the time of the annual conference of the Board's officers.

This was so much resented by the officers in conference that they submitted resignations en masse from their appointments under the Board. This action by the officers created an impasse, and the situation became aggravated when the Union of Employees of the Board gave support to their cause through the medium of their all-Burma annual conference being held at Pegu. The government decided to accept their resignations, and this decision upset most of the officers, who half-heartedly had taken that course of action. Eventually, after some negotiations by third parties, they withdrew their resignations and surrendered themselves to the government for a token penalty.

It was in this atmosphere that I had to join the State Agricultural Marketing Board as its chairman, before I could forget their slogans denouncing the Special Enquiry Committee and the Bureau of Special Investigations. However, I had no grudge against anybody, because I had worked for the best interests of the country and was sure that I could prevail upon them my point of view that my acceptance of the offer of the post of Chairman of the Board was to save the situation of the Board and the country at that critical juncture, and to work for the efficiency and welfare of the employees, as well as other people connected with the business of the Board.

In point of fact, after a few meetings with the representatives of these bodies, I should say I had really turned the tide. There was a reunion between the officers and the staff, and coordination between the Board and the millers and other traders. New plans were drawn up and improved techniques introduced. The results happened to be what nobody would have dared even to think of. I recommended very strongly two officers of the Board for their wholehearted cooperation and unrelenting efforts which made for the success of the undertaking. The government was very kind to grant the title of *Wunna Kyawhtin* (a title given to acknowledge meritorious government service) to them, one of whom was the Deputy General Manager (administration) and the other, President of the State Agricultural Marketing Board Employees' Union. Employees' unions normally run counter to government, and I presume such a case in which the president of an employees' union was awarded a title, must be rare.

For the Directorate of Commercial Audit, the case is not at all difficult. There is a Buddhist society, many of the members of which are my disciples in meditation, and there is also a social club, where there is brotherly feeling among all the officers and staff of the Directorate. Religious functions are held annually where one and all join hands for the common objective, and twice a year they pay homage to the Directorate, both as teacher and as the head of the organization. The social club arranges annual trips in a chartered launch or other means to out-stations for relaxation where members of the employees' families also join, and a pleasant atmosphere is created for all. All these help to promote understanding with each other and pave the way for efficiency in the Directorate.

For the Institute of Accounts and Audit where teachers with extraordinary patience and goodwill are required, apart from their qualifications and teaching experience, the vice-principal and the lecturers are mostly those who have taken courses of meditation at the center. To whatever types the students may belong, the good intentions of the teachers prevail upon them and the response of the students in all the classes has been consistently excellent. From the date of the inception of the Institute, there was not a single complaint from the students. On the other hand, at the close of each course of study there are parties held by the students in honor of the principal and the teachers, where they invariably express their gratitude for the kindness shown to them and the pains taken to help them understand their lessons thoroughly.

I have no doubt, therefore, that meditation plays a very important role in the development of the mind to enable one to have the best in human relations.

Byproducts

What I am going to state here is about the very minor by-products of meditation relating to physical and mental ills. This is not the age for showing miracles, such as rising into the air, or walking on the surface of water, which would be of no direct benefit to the people in general. But if the physical and mental ills of men could be removed through meditation, it should be something for one to ponder.

According to the Buddhist way of thinking, each action, whether by deed, word or thought, produces and leaves behind a force of action (*saṅkhāra*) which goes to the credit or debit account of the individual according to its good or bad objective. This invisible something which we call *saṅkhāra* is the product of the mind with which each action is related. It has no element of extension. The whole universe is permeated with the forces of action of all living beings. The inductive theory of life has the origin, we believe, in these forces, each individual absorbing continually the forces of his own actions, at the same time releasing new forces of actions by deeds, words and thoughts; creating, so to say, an unending cycle of life with pulsation, rhythm and vibration as its symbol.

Let us take the forces of good actions as positive and the forces of bad actions as negative. Then we get what we may call the positive and negative reaction, which is ever taking place everywhere in the universe. It is taking place in all animate and inanimate objects, in my body, in your body and in the bodies of all living beings.

When one can understand these concepts through a proper course of meditation, he knows nature as it truly is. With the awareness of the truth of *anicca* and/or *dukkha* and/or *anattā*, he develops in him what we may call the sparkling illumination of *nibbāna dhātu*, a power that dispels all impurities or poisons—the products of bad actions, which are the sources of his physical and mental ills. In the same way as fuel is burned away by ignition, the negative forces (impurities or poisons) within are eliminated by the *nibbāna dhātu*, which he generates with the true awareness of *anicca* in the course of meditation. This process of elimination should go on until such time as both the mind and body are completely cleansed of such impurities or poisons.

Among those who have taken courses of meditation at the center are some who were suffering from complaints such as hypertension, tuberculosis, migraine, thrombosis, etc. They became relieved of these even in the course of ten days. If they maintain the awareness of *anicca* and take longer courses at the center, there is every likelihood of the diseases being rooted out in course of time. Since anything which is the root cause of one's own physical and mental ills is *samudaya* (an arisen phenomenon), and this *samudaya* can be removed by the *nibbāna dhātu* which one generates in true Buddhist meditation, we make no distinction between this or that disease. One aspect of meditation is *samudaya pahātabba*, which literally means "for the removal of the causes of suffering."

A note of caution is necessary here. When one develops *nibbāna dhātu*, the impact of this *nibbāna dhātu* upon the impurities and poisons within his own system will create a sort of upheaval, which must be endured. This upheaval tends to increase the sensitivity of the radiation, friction, and vibration of the atomic units within. This will grow in intensity, so much so that one might feel as though his body were just electricity and a mass of suffering. In the case of those who have diseases such as those mentioned above, the impact will be all the stronger and, at times, almost explosive. Nevertheless, enduring it, he becomes alive to the fact that a change is taking place within himself for the better, and that the impurities are gradually diminishing, and that he is slowly but surely getting rid of the disease.

Mankind, today, is facing the danger of radioactive poisons. If such poisons absorbed by a man exceeds the maximum permissible concentration (m.p.c.), he enters the danger zone. I have a firm belief that the *nibbāna dhātu* which a person develops in true Buddhist meditation, is power, which will be strong enough to eradicate the radioactive poisons, if any, in him.

Revolution with a View to *Nibbāna*

—Sayagyi U Ba Khin

The following has been reproduced and abridged from the Myanmar magazine The "Light of the Dhamma." This discourse was given by Sayagyi in 1950 on the full moon day of July, the day known as Dhammacakka *day. This day is celebrated because it was during this time of year that the Buddha gave his first discourse to his five companions: the* Dhammacakka-pavattana Sutta *(lit., revolving the wheel of Dhamma). In this discourse the Buddha outlines the Four Noble Truths explaining in detail the Noble Eightfold Path; in other words, the very core of his teaching.*

The Discourse on the Revolution

The discourse I am going to deliver tonight is a discourse on revolution that is apt and proper for the occasion of *Dhammacakka* day. Some may think that it is a discourse that supports the revolution of a group of persons to free themselves from being suppressed by another group of persons. It is not so. The discourse on revolution that I am going to deliver is a supramundane revolution against one's own polluted mind for the attainment of freedom from the rounds of birth and death, which leads to the realization of *nibbāna* (the ultimate reality).

It will not be taken wrongly if it is said that the *Dhammacakka* discourse was delivered by the Buddha who personally revolted against the bondage of the mundane world to gain enlightenment and reach the full extinction of defilements (*sa-upādisesa nibbāna*) so that all the beings—human, *deva* and *brahmā*—might be able to revolt against the bondage of their mundane worlds and reach *nibbāna*.

To Gain Freedom from the Three Types of Mundane Worlds

The Buddha revolted against the three types of mundane worlds and gained enlightenment in the early hours of Vesākha day (the full moon of May). He was not satisfied with this achievement only, for because of the perfections (*pāramīs*) that he had fulfilled for the benefit of all beings, he also had to impart the method of revolt for all beings to fight for the attainment of their freedom from the three worlds.

Nibbāna—Freedom in Reality

In this revolution with the view to *nibbāna*, there are so many obstructions which are on the side of ignorance (*avijjā*) that there seems to no way of escape for us. With the perfections accumulated the Buddha had to defend and fight against the five divisions of Māra's army, viz., the evil (*devaputta māra*), the defilements (*kilesa māra*), the aggregates (*khandha māra*), the death (*maccu māra*), and the kamma formations (*abhisaṅkhāra māra*). They suppress and imprison us, so that there is no outlet of escape for us.

Before the Buddha delivered the first sermon, during the seven weeks after the enlightenment, he took no nourishment. He was in deep contemplation on the profound details of the Dhamma. It is not an easy matter to save beings from the world entwined in ignorance (*avijjā*). When all the beings were viewed with the Buddha's eye, after the seventh week, he deliberated whether to deliver the profound Dhamma to beings enmeshed in the defilements. That is why the great *brahmā* Sahampati, accompanied by *devas* and *brahmās*, offered the jewelled garland and entreated the Buddha to deliver the Dhamma, beginning with the Pāli words: *Desetu Bhagavā dhammaṃ, desetu sugato* (May the blessed one teach the Dhamma; may the supremely good one teach the Dhamma).

After promising the great *brahmā* Sahampati that he would teach the Dhamma, he looked to see who among the living human beings had the ability to understand and benefit by the Dhamma. He saw the five ascetics who served him while he practiced *Dukkharacariya* (the rigorous ascetic practices). So the Buddha went to the deer park near Vārānasi where the five ascetics were, and during the first watch of the night delivered the *Dhammacakka* discourse beginning with *Dveme bhikkhave antā pabbajitena nasevitabbā* (These two extremes, bhikkhus, should not be followed by one who has given up the world). This discourse is the way to the transformation of a new personality. In other words, the Noble Path revolts against the mundane path and leads to *nibbāna*. At the end of the discourse the leader of the five ascetics, Koṇḍañña, became a *sotāpanna* (stream-enterer), i.e., transformed into a new being as a noble person.

At that time the *devas* and *brahmās* who came from the ten thousand universes also became established in their lives as noble beings (*ariyas*). To become an *ariya* means to grasp the true essence of the elements of *nibbāna* and to be free from mental defilements. The realization of *nibbāna* is becoming a new being, changing from an ordinary worldling to a noble being. It is not possible to transform a person to such a new life by ordinary means of preparation. The Buddha achieved this by the fulfillment of the perfections (*pāramīs*) developed through countless aeons. This culminated in the wisdom of omniscience and other wisdoms, and the turning of the wheel of Dhamma.

Why is it called *Dhammacakka*?

The reason why this very first discourse is called the *Dhammacakka* discourse is this, as mentioned in the *Dhammacakka Kathā* of *Paṭisambhidā-magga*:

> *Dhammapavatanti kenatthena dhammacakkaṃ, dhammañca pavatteti cakkañcati.*

In what sense is the setting going of Dhamma called *dhammacakka*? It is the setting going of truth (*dhamma*) and the wheel (*cakka*) of the teaching.[†]

It is the origin of the Four Noble Truths and it also causes the continuous rotation of the noble Dhamma of the Four Noble Truths. The rotation of the wheel of Dhamma is called the *Dhammacakka*.

The essence of the *Dhammacakka* is the Four Noble Truths, which are: *dukkha sacca* (the truth of suffering); *samudaya sacca* (the truth of the origin of suffering); *nirodha sacca* (the truth of the cessation of suffering); *magga sacca* (the truth of the noble path that leads to the cessation of suffering).

Of these Four Noble Truths, the noble path (*magga sacca*) which constitutes the Noble Eightfold Path is of the utmost importance. Although the Buddha delivered eighty-two thousand discourses, as occasions arose during the forty-five years of his ministry, the basic practical aspect of his teaching is the Noble Eightfold Path.

The Path of Revolution

The Noble Eightfold Path is composed of three aspects of practical work: morality, concentration and wisdom (*sīla*, *samādhi*, and *paññā*).

The path of morality (*sīla*) consists of three subdivisions: right speech (*sammā vācā*), right action (*sammā kammanta*) and right livelihood (*sammā ājīva*).

The path of concentration (*samādhi*) consists of three subdivisions: right effort (*sammā vāyāma*), right mindfulness (*sammā sati*), right concentration (*sammā samādhi*).

[†] Here, according to the commentaries, the word *cakka* (literally, "wheel") has the additional meaning of "the dispensation of Buddha." Therefore, this line from *Paṭisambhidā-magga* is indicating that the first discourse of Buddha, in which the basic outline of the entire teaching is laid out, is called *Dhammacakka-pavattana* because two things are set forth or set going: *dhammañca pavatteti* (the truth is set forth) and *cakkañca pavatteti* (the dispensation is set going). The usual translation, "the rotation of the wheel of Dhamma," implies these two meanings metaphorically.

The path of wisdom (*paññā*) consists of two subdivisions: right thought (*sammā saṅkappa*) and right view (*sammā diṭṭhi*).

As soon as *sīla*, *samādhi* and *paññā*—with *paññā* as the leading factor—are properly combined in practice, one is sure to reach the noble path. If one has not reached the path, it is because *sīla*, *samādhi* and *paññā* are not yet properly balanced. The path prepared with these three aspects of practice, is the revolutionary path of the Buddha.

Mind is Supreme

In the path of morality, consisting of right speech, right action and right livelihood, the bodily actions and speech should be bound and restrained. Bodily actions and speech are usually controlled by greed, hatred and delusion (*lobha*, *dosa* and *moha*) which are in turn the servants of craving, conceit and wrong view (*taṇhā*, *māna* and *micchā-diṭṭhi*). These unwholesome qualities have accompanied us as our habitual inclinations through the cycle of births (*saṃsāra*). The bodily action (*kāya kamma*) and verbal action (*vaci kamma*) are the paths of the revolution that should really and truly be revolted against.

Here, as the saying goes, *Mano pubbaṅgamā dhammā* (mind is the master of the bodily actions and verbal actions). Again, as it is said: *Papasmiṃ ramati mano* (the mind delights in dwelling in evil). It cannot be revolted against by ordinary means but only with great zeal.

May all beings be able to muster immense zeal!

Discipline the Mind

In the Noble Path of right effort, right mindfulness and right concentration, the mind that gives rise to unwholesome bodily actions and verbal actions, should be securely restrained. Then it cannot run amok but will stay calm and collected.

Right concentration cannot be achieved unless there is right effort and right mindfulness, to keep the mind calm and still. To achieve right concentration, mindfulness should be developed with right effort. I want you to believe that with the help and guidance of a person who is competent to help, *samādhi* (concentration) can be rapidly established. The Buddha had to resist and fight against the evil (*devaputta māra*) while he was establishing the first stage of *samādhi* under the bodhi tree. After conquering the evil with the *samādhi* thus established, he subjugated the defilements (*kilesa māra*) and the death (*maccu māra*) with ease. Similarly, nowadays under the guidance and guardianship of a person who is highly developed in the perfections (*pāramīs*) and who can, to a certain degree, guard against the dangers of the evil (*devaputta māra*), *samādhi* can be established within a short period.

There are six types of character or nature (*carita*) affecting all human beings, but it is not possible to know which type a person belongs to, since we do not have the ability to do so. But it is a sure fact that no one is free from delusion (*mohacarita*), which is none other than ignorance itself. That is why one cannot argue that it is an unnatural process to establish *samādhi* by practicing *ānāpāna sati* (awareness of the in- and out-breathing). This practice is suitable for persons with the nature and habitual inclination of delusion (*moha*). But people may not believe that it is relatively easy to establish *samādhi* by the practice of *ānāpāna*.

It is true that it will be difficult to subjugate the mind, to keep it refined and proper and to make it stay where one keeps it—the mind that throughout this cycle of rebirth (*saṃsāra*) has freely and wantonly wandered, the mind without a custodian, the incessantly restless, mercurial mind. But for those who do not look forward to worldly benefits, but want only the attainment of *nibbāna*, should they meet the right teacher, it becomes an easy matter.

There are many people who have experienced the clearly shining acquired image (*uggaha nimitta*) after the first attempt at meditation and the counter image (*paṭibhāga nimitta*) quite soon afterwards. That is why I would like to request those persons who are practicing Dhamma for the realization of *nibbāna*, not to overlook the *sīla-samādhi-paññā* triad.

The True Nature

Right thought (*sammā saṅkappa*) is the contemplation of the true nature of the aggregates, sense bases and elements. The knowledge of the true nature after such contemplation is to be called the path of right view (*sammā diṭṭhi*). Then the problem arises: what is meant by "true nature"?

The true nature is this: the mind and matter (*nāma* and *rūpa*) of the five aggregates are incessantly and infallibly breaking down and passing away. This is the true nature of impermanence (*anicca*). The mind and matter of the five aggregates does not possess even a particle of satisfactoriness and is totally unsatisfactory. This is the true nature of unsatisfactoriness (*dukkha*). The mind and matter of the five aggregates has nothing to indicate that there is any substantiality such as me, mine and self. This is the true nature of egolessness, impersonality (*anattā*).

These true natures are all within the body (which is but one fathom long) of the people who are now listening to this discourse. One must penetrate with one's basic concentration and insight wisdom into this body. One must look critically at the true nature of mind and matter, to remove the conceptual beliefs that are blocking the path. One must repeatedly study the true nature of impermanence, the true nature of suffering, the true nature of egolessness of the five aggregates. And one must develop the ten insight knowledges of Vipassana†. This process is called *vipassanā*.

These practices are said to be insight wisdom which removes conceptual truth to reach the ultimate truth (from *paññatti* to *paramattha*). Fundamentally, it is to be believed that if the triad of *sīla*, *samādhi* and *paññā* is diligently practiced, the Four Noble Truths will be comprehended and *nibbāna* will be realized. At the present time when Vipassana is more widely practiced, if there is a strong base of *samādhi*, it is certain that *nibbāna* is not far off.

---

† For an explanation of the ten insight knowledges, see "The Essentials of Buddha-Dhamma in Meditative Practice," pp. 116-117.

But those persons who are dazed by the evil (*devaputta māra*) will think that nothing can be done; they will give up and take the easy way out. When the Buddha saw and admonished the monk Kolita (who was later known as Mahā Moggallāna) for being drowsy during meditation, he said, "Kolita, for a person who is looking for the happiness of *nibbāna*, why do you want to associate with such undesirables as *thīna-middha* and *pamāda* (sloth, torpor and indolence)?"

So get rid of sloth, torpor and indolence with their repercussions and practice the Noble Eightfold Path, the Noble Path which is annunciated in the *Dhammacakka*.

Throughout *saṃsāra* (the cycle of rebirth), for the mind which believes that the compounded mind and body (*nāma-rūpa*) is:

nicca (permanent)—revolt against such a mind to open up the realization and knowledge of impermanence (*anicca vijjā ñāṇa*)

sukha (pleasurable)—revolt against such a mind to open up the realization and knowledge of suffering (*dukkha vijjā ñāṇa*)

attā (self)—revolt against such a mind to open up the realization and knowlege of non-self (*anattā vijjā ñāṇa*).

To Peace and Tranquillity

In brief, from today onwards, may you be able to practice with the utmost effort, to accomplish the supramundane wisdom (*lokuttara ñāṇa*), by revolting against the conceptualized mundane world (*loka*).

May those persons who make the effort and practice, receive and be engulfed by the *dhammadhātu*, *bodhidhātu*, and *nibbānadhātu* (the vibration of Dhamma, *bodhi*, or enlightenment, and *nibbāna*, respectively) of the Buddha.

May they, by their established *sīla*, *samādhi* and *paññā*, utterly destroy the evils that are the colonizers of *saṃsāra*, viz., craving, conceit, and wrong view (*taṇhā*, *māna* and *micchā-diṭṭhi*) and attain swiftly and directly the full extinction of defilements (*sa-upādisesa nibbāna*), which is beyond all the nature of compounded things (*saṅkhāra dhamma*).

May they, with the radiant rays of *nibbāna* that they have received, deliver peace and tranquillity throughout this universe.

Questions and Answers

Q: We've talked quite a bit about *anicca*, impermanence. What about the teaching of *anattā*, which is ordinarily understood as "no self" or "no abiding self"? Ordinarily we think that we need a self in order to function in the world. We have expressions like "self-esteem" and "self-confidence," and we believe that "ego strength" is a measure of a person's ability to cope with daily life. What does this "no self" teaching mean?

S.N. Goenka: For those who haven't experienced that stage of "no self," it's true that in the apparent world there must be an ego, and this ego must be stimulated. If I don't crave something, I won't get the stimulation I need to function. In my courses, whenever I say that craving and attachment are harmful, people say that if there were no attachment, no craving, what would be the fun of living? There would be no life. We'd all be like vegetables.

As a family man who has done business in the world, I can understand their concerns. But I also understand that when you work with this technique and reach the stage where the ego dissolves, the capacity to work increases many-fold. When you lead a very ego-centered life, your whole attitude is to do as much as possible for yourself. But this attitude makes you so tense that you feel miserable. When, as a result of doing Vipassana, the ego dissolves, then by nature the mind is full of love, compassion, and goodwill. You feel like working, not only for your own benefit, but for the benefit of all. When the narrow-minded ego stimulation goes away, you feel so much more relaxed, and so much more capable of working. This is my own experience, and the experience of so many who have walked on this path.

This technique does not make you inactive. A responsible person in society is full of action. What goes away is the habit of blind reaction. When you work with reaction, you generate misery. When you work without reaction, you generate positive feeling.

Q: U Ba Khin was a person with an important social role and was part of the government of his country. What was his opinion of subjects like war, famine, etc.?

SNG: In society there are many important issues; it isn't possible, in the name of Vipassana or any other kind of meditation, to close one's eyes and escape. It is necessary to make one's own contribution. The Buddha used to say: "If you are hungry you cannot practice Dhamma, you cannot practice meditation." This is a very important point.

All wars are harmful. But to have only the idealistic goal of keeping society away from such war doesn't help. Every individual must liberate himself from his own internal tensions. The tensions in society, in nations, between individuals—all exist because of impurities in the minds of individuals.

Man is a social being. It is neither possible nor profitable for him to live separated from society. Whatever contribution he makes to the society while being a member of it, in terms of making the social fabric more peaceful and harmonious, is the yardstick of his merit as a useful member of society. The basis of any healthy, harmonious society is always the healthy and harmonious individuals who populate it. Disharmonious people not only remain tense and unhappy themselves, but also make other people around them ill-at-ease because of their tensions and disharmony. Therefore, it is obvious that if we wish to produce a society which is happy, healthy and harmonious, we will also have to make each individual happy, healthy and harmonious. Only if each individual has a pure, peaceful mind can we expect peace in the society. Dhamma is a unique way for attaining peace for the individual, and hence is a way to attain peace and harmony for the society and the world.

Q: What role can the Vipassana meditator play in the area of social action—for example, helping others, the poor, the hungry, the neglected, the homeless, the sick, etc.?

SNG: To help others is absolutely essential for everyone who follows the path of Dhamma. For the meditator, naturally, the main goal is purification of the mind. But one indication that the mind is purifying is an increase in the volition to help others. A pure mind will always be filled with love and compassion. It is not possible to see people everywhere suffering and feel: "I don't care. I'm working for my liberation." This attitude demonstrates a lack of development in Dhamma. If one is progressing, then it is possible to help and to serve others naturally, in any field, to one's own capacity and power.

But while you are serving others in different social fields, in a school or in a hospital or in some other institution, you might develop this erroneous belief: "Now that I've really purified my mind and I'm offering all my time to help people, the process of purification will continue by itself. I should give up my daily morning and evening practice because I am so busy now. I am offering such a great social service." This is a great mistake. With real purity of mind, whatever service you give will truly be strong, effective full of good results.

Continue to purify your mind, continue to examine whether your mind is really purifying, and continue to serve people without expecting anything in return. Healthy and harmonious individuals are the foundation of every healthy and harmonious society. Only if every individual has a pure and peaceful mind can we expect peace and harmony in society. Vipassana is a unique way for the individual to obtain peace and harmony, and it is therefore an ideal means to attaining peace and harmony in society.

Q: How do you recommend that people use this technique in their daily lives?

SNG: The first thing is to strengthen and perfect *sīla*, morality. The five precepts we teach—no killing, no stealing, no sexual misconduct, no lying, not becoming intoxicated—are the base. Once one starts slipping in any of these, *samādhi* becomes weak, and *paññā* becomes shallow. You can't work at the level of your sensations; you just end up playing intellectual games at the surface of the mind. But if *sīla* is strong, you can start going to the depths of the mind. And then, when you've gone to the depths and eradicated even some of the impurities, *sīla* and *samādhi* are both strengthened. All three help each other.

The next thing is this: while you're working, give all your attention to your work. This is your meditation at that time. But when you're free, even for five mintues, be aware of your sensations with open eyes. Whenever you have nothing else to do, observe your sensations. This will give you strength while you are going about your tasks. This is how people can use this technique in their daily lives.

Q: Can't there be wholesome cravings and aversion—for example, hating injustice, desiring freedom, fearing physical harm?

SNG: Aversions and cravings can never be wholesome. They will always make you tense and unhappy. If you act with craving or aversion in the mind, you may have a worthwhile goal, but you use an unhealthy means to reach it. Of course you have to act to protect yourself from danger. You can do it overpowered by fear, but by doing so you develop a fear complex which will harm you in the long run. Or with hatred in the mind, you may be successful in fighting injustice, but that hatred will become a harmful mental complex. You must fight injustice, you must protect yourself from danger, but you should do so with a balanced mind, without tension. And in a balanced way, you can work to achieve something good, out of love for others. Balance of mind is always helpful and will give the best results.

Q: What is wrong with wanting material things to make life more comfortable?

SNG: If it is a real requirement, there is nothing wrong, provided you do not become attached to it. For example, you are thirsty, and you want water; there is nothing unhealthy in that. You need water—so you work, get it, and quench your thirst. But if it becomes an obsession, that does not help at all; it harms you. Whatever necessities you require, work to get them. If you fail to get something, then smile and try again in a different way. If you succeed, then enjoy what you get, but without attachment.

Q: How about planning for the future? Would you call that craving?

SNG: Again, the criterion is whether you are attached to your plan. Everyone must provide for the future. If your plan does not succeed and you start crying, then you know that you were attached to it. But if you are unsuccessful and can still smile, thinking, "Well, I did my best. So what if I failed? I'll try again!"—then you are working in a detached way, and you remain happy.

PART THREE

The Practice of Meditation

Chapter Eight

A Ten-day Course in the Tradition of Sayagyi U Ba Khin

The Buddha is the Teacher who shows the way. I am an individual who continues to show the way, having received the inheritance of Dhamma from the Buddha. The Buddha is not a person who can give nibbāna but only one who shows the way. Do not come and ask me to get the results for you; I cannot do that. How can U Ba Khin do what even the Buddha cannot? You have to practice yourself.

—Sayagyi U Ba Khin

Vipassana meditation, as emphasized numerous times in the preceding chapters, is the personal purification of the mind. It is the highest form of consciousness—total perception of phenomena in their true nature as experienced within the framework of the body. The practice is an art of living which produces profound benefits and deep value in our own lives. It diminishes and ultimately eliminates the craving, aversion and ignorance that are at the base of all our intolerant and painful relationships with others, from the personal level to the level of international political relations.

Every person, no matter of what race, caste, system of beliefs or social conditioning, can finally eradicate those mental tendencies, those conditionings, that have continually created and fed passion, rage, fear and anxiety in our lives. During a ten-day course a student focuses on one battle only—the battle against his own ignorance. There is no dependence on the teacher or competition among students. The teacher is there only to point out the way that he has followed in his own practical experience. With perseverance in the practice, the meditation will finally succeed in quieting the mind, increasing concentration, sharpening awareness, and opening the mind to the detached observation of reality as it is. Simply by deeply observing the reality within the framework of the body, the student disintegrates the apparent reality, penetrating to the depths of mind and matter and, eventually, beyond the conditioned world. There is no dependence upon books, theories or intellectual games in Vipassana. It is directly experiencing the truth of impermanence (*anicca*), of suffering (*dukkha*) and of the absence of a self (*anattā*).

The Ten-Day Course in Vipassana Meditation

Students who want to learn Vipassana meditation must undertake at least a course of ten days, during which they must remain for the entire time at the site where the course is taking place. These intensive courses—developed in detail by U Ba Khin and directed mainly to householders who have little time and must return immediately to their professional and familial occupations—are open to whomever wishes to participate. Although Vipassana meditation was developed as a technique by the Buddha, its practice is not limited to Buddhists. There is no question of conversion. The technique works on the simple basis that all human beings share the same problems, so a technique which can eradicate these problems will have universal application and value. In fact, these courses, now offered under the guidance of S.N. Goenka in the tradition of his teacher U Ba Khin, have attracted religious people from every creed, not only Buddhists but also Catholics, Jews, Hindus, Moslems, etc. Since the death of U Ba Khin, in 1971, S.N. Goenka has become the principal lay exponent of the teaching of Vipassana through these intensive ten-day courses.

There is no charge to participate in these courses, neither for the teaching nor for food and lodging. All expenses are covered by the donations of previous students. Donations are accepted only from students who have completed a course of ten days. In this way, each meditator who comes benefits directly from the gratitude of other students and is allowed to live completely on charity for ten days.

A ten-day course is challenging; it requires strong determination to complete it. For this reason a commitment is required from each student to respect the code of discipline and adhere to it scrupulously throughout the ten days.

Before applying for a course each person is asked to read an explanatory booklet (summarized here) to introduce them to the real seriousness of these courses. Strong effort, mental openness, and willingness to accept the rules and discipline are required. Naturally the benefits are proportional to the effort made.

Introduction and Code of Discipline
for a Ten-day Course
in the Tradition of Sayagyi U Ba Khin,
as taught by S.N. Goenka

Vipassana is one of India's most ancient meditation techniques. Long lost to humanity, it was rediscovered by Gotama the Buddha more than 2500 years ago. *Vipassanā* means seeing things as they really are. It is the process of self-purification by self-observation. The entire path (Dhamma or the law of nature) is a universal remedy for universal problems.

What Vipassana is not:

- It is not a rite or ritual based on blind faith.

- It is neither an intellectual nor a philosophical entertainment.

- It is not a rest cure, a holiday, or an opportunity for socializing.

- It is not an escape from the trials and tribulations of everyday life.

What Vipassana is:

- It is a technique that will eradicate suffering.

- It is an art of living that one can use to make positive contributions to society.

- It is a method of mental purification which allows one to face life's tensions and problems in a calm, balanced way.

Vipassana meditation aims at the highest spiritual goals of total liberation and full enlightenment; its purpose is never simply to cure physical disease. However, as a by-product of mental purification, many psychosomatic diseases are eradicated. In fact, Vipassana eliminates the three causes of *all* unhappiness: craving, aversion and ignorance. With continued practice, meditation releases the tensions developed in everyday life, opening the knots tied by habitually reacting in an unbalanced way to pleasant and unpleasant situations.

The process of self-purification by introspection is certainly never easy—students have to work very hard at it. By their own efforts students arrive at their own realizations; no one else can do this for them. Therefore, the meditation will suit only those willing to work seriously and observe the discipline, which is there for the benefit and protection of the meditators and is an integral part of the meditation practice.

The Code of Discipline

Ten days is certainly a very short time in which to penetrate the deepest levels of the unconscious mind and learn how to eradicate the complexes lying there. Continuity of the practice in seclusion is the secret of this technique's success. Rules and regulations have been developed keeping this practical aspect in mind. They are not primarily for the benefit of the teacher or the course management, nor are they negative expressions of tradition, orthodoxy or blind faith in some organized religion. Rather, they are based on the experience of thousands of meditators over the years, and are both practical and rational. Abiding by the rules creates a very conducive atmosphere for meditation; breaking them pollutes it.

The foundation of the practice is *sīla*—moral conduct. *Sīla* provides a basis for the development of *samādhi*—concentration of mind; and purification of the mind is achieved through *paññā*—the wisdom of insight. All who attend a Vipassana course must conscientiously undertake the following Five Precepts for the duration of the course:

1. to abstain from killing any being

2. to abstain from stealing

3. to abstain from all sexual activity

4. to abstain from telling lies

5. to abstain from all intoxicants.

Acceptance of the Teacher and the Technique

Students must declare themselves willing to comply fully for the duration of the course with the teacher's guidance and instructions; that is, to observe the discipline and to meditate exactly as the teacher asks, without ignoring any part of the instructions, nor adding anything to them. This acceptance should be based on discrimination and understanding, not blind submission. Only with an attitude of trust can a student work diligently and thoroughly. Such confidence in the teacher and the technique is essential for success in meditation.

Other Techniques, Rites, and Forms of Worship

During the course it is absolutely essential that all forms of prayer, worship, or religious ceremony—fasting, burning incense, counting beads, reciting mantras, singing and dancing, etc.—be discontinued. All other meditation techniques and healing or spiritual practices should also be suspended. This is not to condemn any other technique or practice, but to give a fair trial to the technique of Vipassana in its purity. Despite repeated warnings by the teacher, there have been cases in the past where students have intentionally mixed this technique with a ritual or another practice, and have done themselves a great disservice. Students are expected to work exactly as they are instructed by the teacher, without missing any steps or adding anything else. Any doubts or confusion which may arise should always be clarified by meeting with the teacher.

Outside Contacts

Students must remain within the course boundaries throughout the course. They may leave only with the specific consent of the teacher. No outside communication is allowed before the course ends. This includes letters, phone calls, and visitors. In case of an emergency, a friend or relative may contact the management.

Music, Reading and Writing

The playing of musical instruments, radios, etc., is not permitted. No reading or writing materials should be brought to the course. Students should not distract themselves by taking notes. The restriction on reading and writing is to emphasize the strictly practical nature of this meditation.

Noble Silence

All students must observe Noble Silence from the beginning of the course until the morning of the last full day. Noble Silence means silence of body, speech and mind. Any form of communication with fellow students, whether by gestures, sign language, written notes, etc., is prohibited.

Students may, however, speak with the teacher whenever necessary, and they may approach the management with any problems related to food, accommodation, health, etc. But even these contacts should be kept to a minimum. Students should cultivate the feeling that they are working in isolation.

Course Finances

According to the tradition of pure Vipassana, courses are run solely on a donation basis. Donations are accepted only from old students, that is, those who have completed at least one course with S.N. Goenka or an assistant teacher.

In this way, courses are supported by those who have realized for themselves the benefits of the practice. Wishing to share these benefits with others, one gives a donation according to one's means and volition. Someone taking a course for the first time may give a donation at the end of the course or at any time thereafter.

Such donations are the only source of funding for courses in this tradition around the world. There is no wealthy foundation or individual sponsoring them. Neither the teachers nor the organizers receive any kind of payment for their services. Thus, the spread of Vipassana is carried out with purity of purpose, free from any commercialism.

Whether a donation is large or small, it should be given with the wish to help others: "The course I have taken has been paid for through the generosity of past students; now let me give something towards the cost of a future course, so that others may also benefit by this technique."

There are several other rules that one may find in the pamphlets of regulations for students. But in brief the spirit behind the discipline and rules may be summarized as follows:

Take great care that your actions do not disturb anyone. Take no notice of distractions caused by others.

Program

The meditation day begins at 4:00 a.m. and ends at 9:00 p.m. It consists of about eleven hours of meditation with a few breaks throughout the day. Hours of individual meditation are alternated with hours of group meditation where, always in silence, one meditates in the presence of the teacher. Each evening a video-taped discourse by the principal teacher, S.N. Goenka, is played for about one hour or so. The discourse explains various aspects of the teaching and practice, and elaborates on the instructions as they are given each day. Students may request individual interviews with the instructor during times arranged for that purpose. From the first day on, the teaching emphasizes the practical aspect of the meditation and its usefulness in daily life.

As Mr. Goenka says:

> For us meditation is an art of living. We must train our minds not to escape problems but to go to their depths, to find the cause and eradicate it. The mind has accumulated so much negativity—anger, hatred, aversion, fear, jealousy, passion. We must liberate ourselves from these impurities.

The First Three Days

The course begins with the first instructions on the day of arrival. The students start by declaring their commitment to observe the five moral precepts listed above and to work under the guidance of the present teacher. The first two days are dedicated to developing awareness of the breath. Continuity of practice is attained through continuous observation of the breath. One observes the normal, natural breath as it comes in and as it goes out. This practice concentrates the mind and initiates a process which is a deep operation of the mind. Goenkaji explains it in this way:

> For us concentration serves to eliminate the instability of the mind and its tendency to distract itself continuously, in order to penetrate to its depths, eradicate the negativities stored there, and achieve total purification of the mind. We must learn to observe the truth, the reality of our minds and bodies. We must discover why, due to ignorance, we continue to create these knots of tension within ourselves.

Our breath is the bridge that connects the known part of the mind to the unknown part of ourselves. In fact, we don't have direct knowledge of all the electromagnetic and biochemical functions and processes that take place within our bodies. The breath connects the intentional part with everything that happens beyond our control. The breath, in fact, has a strong connection with mental impurities, because they make the breath heavy, agitated, light, etc.

During these days entirely dedicated to the awareness of the breath, students sit in a comfortable position, preferably with crossed legs but not necessarily so. Whatever position taken, the point is to be able to maintain it for a reasonable length of time. During the first three days the position may be changed if it becomes too uncomfortable, because priority is given to continuity of the practice of observation.

The area of observation is restricted, and includes the nostrils, the inside of the nostrils and the area above the upper lip. While seated tranquilly, student sustains attention on this limited area, observing vigilantly and attentively every inhalation and every exhalation. He or she must be aware of every variation in the breath, whether it is regular or irregular, strong or weak, short or long, letting it flow freely without forcing or interfering with it. Naturally, at times the old habit of getting distracted will prevail; then with patience, leaving aside every distracting thought or mental noise, we return immediately to awareness of the breath. To reinforce and sharpen concentration, on the third day the area of awareness is narrowed down even further, focusing only on the area below the nostrils and above the upper lip with attentive, continous awareness of the breath coming in and going out.

As preparation for the practice of Vipassana, the students begin observing whatever physical sensations may naturally appear in that area. We begin in this way to move from mere observation of the breath to observation of the body and the natural, physical sensations manifesting in it. If concentration is adequate, we begin to perceive the spontaneous sensations as they arise. From the findings of science we know that in our organism countless biological, physical, chemical and electrical processes are taking place; these are also happening at the molecular, atomic and subatomic levels. What we must begin to do is to become aware of these processes not only intellectually but also through direct experience. At the beginning we perceive only the most gross phenomena, the sensations that are most apparent, such as itching, pain, pressure, vibration, or whatever they might be. We must observe them with clarity and equanimity without letting the mind judge them or speculate about them. We must simply observe. With this initial training, the student is ready to observe the entire body methodically.

The Fourth Day

The student is ready to learn Vipassana. Meditators are directed to move their attention from the area below the nostrils to a small area on the top of the head, and to observe whatever sensations manifest themselves there—natural physical sensations, such as pressure, itching, tingling, pain, heat, cold, whatever sensations may arise. Gradually then the meditator begins to observe every part of the body—the head, the arms, the trunk, the neck, the legs, etc. They are continually reminded to regard with the most equanimity possible every sensation observed, whether pleasant or unpleasant. "Simply observing, remaining vigilant and attentive."

The entire universe is nothing but a mass of vibrations, of oscillations. The mind is nothing but vibrations. If the mind is attentive, sharp, more and more concentrated, it becomes possible to perceive the body as phenomena in continuous change —vibrations, molecules, electrical currents. The apparent solidity of our body begins to dissolve.

The second part of the meditation, the most important, is to develop wisdom through this experience. The measure of success is not how subtle and and pleasant are the sensations we perceive, but, rather, how free we are from reacting to them. The entire practice of Vipassana is about maintaining the balance of the mind, knowing thoroughly that every experience is continually changing. Like scientists we must dispassionately observe the chemistry and the physics that manifest in our bodies, all the biochemical reactions that take place every moment, without identifying with them, without identifying them with a personal self. This equanimity is the key to purifying the mind. Moreover, if we continue to develop vibrations of purity together with equanimity, these will counteract the flux of past conditioning and continue to destroy negativity.

One should never try to imagine or create sensations, because it is not possible; one must only observe what manifests naturally. This is an excellent opportunity to contemplate with attention and equanimity the sensations that arise in the body. At times, when some pleasant or painful sensation arises, the student is instructed to observe it without identifying with it, to observe it for what it is, a phenomenon in continuous change. One will come to understand through direct experience that all pain or suffering—even when it initially seems intense and unbearable—has the tendency, as with all other sensations observed in the body, to change, diminish, disappear. Observing everything that manifests, without attachment to pleasant sensations and without resistance or attempts to avoid pain or unpleasant thoughts, one has the direct experience of accepting reality as it is, a reality in constant change. This is the essence of Vipassana.

From the Fifth to the Ninth Day

From then on, from the fifth to the ninth day, the student continues the practice, persevering in the observation of the body, perfecting and refining the perception of phenomena that arise. The method basically consists of the detailed exploration of every part of the body, moving one's attention in different ways, depending upon the intensity and the quality of the sensations. For this purpose the teaching gradually introduces different ways of observing the body, increasingly deeper and more complete, along with constant continuity of practice. The uninterrupted observation of sensations allows one to directly experience that the organism is made up of phenomena in continual transformation, phenomena interacting at very high velocity and frequency and lasting but a brief period of time. This directly experienced knowledge of impermanence leads to realization of the absence of the identity of phenomena and, consequently, of their unsatisfactory character.

The entire practice is a path of purification. The purification does not permit new conditioning to begin, thereby letting old conditioning go. This gradual elimination of old conditioning, of reactions, offers the possibility of facing the various situations of our daily lives and our life in the world in a balanced and harmonious way.

In the *Maṅgala Sutta* the Buddha was asked what, according to him, was the best state to attain. He replied that the best state to achieve is the stage at which one can maintain balance of the mind in spite of all the vicissitudes, in every difficulty of life, through pleasant and unpleasant situations, victories or defeats, gains or losses, good or bad fortune.

The Tenth Day

On the last day, after so many days of hard work, after having faced numerous hardships in learning to control the mind and purify it from negative conditioning, the student is taught the final part of the technique. It is the practice of loving kindness, in Pāli called *mettā*. The mind, purified through the exercise of Vipassana, turns toward all beings with benevolence. Students are encouraged to share with all other beings the calm and balance they have attained.

As a glowing ember radiates heat, let the feeling of peace and goodwill flow from your whole body in all directions. Think of all beings—those near and dear to you, those that are indifferent and those that may be unfriendly; those you know and those you don't know; near and far; human and non-human, great and small; make no distinctions. Your fellow feeling, your loving kindness, goes to them all.

In the closing session of the retreat, in the early morning of the eleventh day, instructions are given on how to maintain the continuity of practice and how to apply the technique in daily life.

The Ten Soldiers of Māra

The following is condensed from a translation of a discourse by Sayagyi U Ba Khin. The discourse, in Burmese, was addressed to Vipassana students during a course.

You have to be very careful. You have to stand firm and face many difficulties, so that you can know true *anicca* (impermanence) with your own experience. You must work very hard—that is why we repeatedly remind you. Difficulties come at this stage of the course. During the time of our great benefactor, Saya Thetgyi, students would experience various difficulties in meditation, such as not being able to feel the object of meditation at all. When asked to focus their attention on the top of their heads, they couldn't feel anything. During Ānāpāna they couldn't feel the area around the nostrils. Some could not feel their breath while they were breathing. Some said that they could not feel their bodies. While you are here, you too will find these things happening. Sometimes you will not be able to feel sensations and you won't be able to maintain your attention.

Some think that they have attained *nibbāna* (the ultimate reality) when they cannot feel their bodies. If you cannot feel the presence of your body, just hit it with your hand, or punch yourself and see. There is no need to ask the Teacher. You will know if your body is there or not. These uncertainties are rather disconcerting, aren't they?

The nature of *vipallāsa* (mental distortion, corruption) makes fools of you. These are undesirable defilements hidden inside people. They are present in every one of us. When there is understanding of *anicca* the defilements have to leave; but they don't want to—

they want this understanding to leave instead. The *nibbāna* nature of *anicca* is very potent, so Māra (the negative forces) fights against it. The *Padhāna Sutta* describes the ten soldiers of Māra. We have to be careful of these ten soldiers, as they are the destroyers of meditation.

The first soldier of Māra is the desire to enjoy sense pleasures. Some people have come to meditate but not to attain *nibbāna* at all. They come with ulterior motives such as, "If I become close to Sayagyi, who knows so many people in high positions, I may get a promotion in my job." There are some persons like that. They come with greed in their hearts. They cannot be successful in their meditation. There must be no greed. When you asked for the technique of Vipassana you said, "*Nibbānassa sacchikaraṇatthāya*"—in order to realize *nibbāna*.... I will teach you to understand the Four Noble Truths, but if you are not interested, and intend to take your time about it, what can I do?

The second soldier of Māra is unwillingness to reside or be happy in a quiet place such as a forest dwelling.

Yesterday somebody planned to run away. He got up early and packed his belongings. He planned to sit at half past seven with you all, and then leave while I was checking the students at eight. He was planning to run like mad, catch a bus, and get home. He thought he would collect his bags at some later date. Luckily, I don't know why, I gave the one hour *adhiṭṭhāna* (strong determination) sitting earlier, and he had to sit that one hour. There he was—trapped! After the *adhiṭṭhāna* sitting, Māra left him, and he doesn't want to leave anymore.

When unwillingness to reside in a quiet place arises, the person wants to leave and run away. He may inform us that he wishes to leave, or he may just quietly leave. The second soldier does not want to stay in a quiet secluded place because of the turmoil inside.

The third soldier of Māra is hunger—not being satisfied with food. Are you all hungry now? Sao Shwe Theik was one of the very hungry ones. He came with boxes full of food. He said that he could not stay without eating, so I said, "In that case you may eat, but try one, two or three days and see for yourself." I had to go easy and cajole him; however, he was not hungry at all during the ten days.

Myanma Alin U Tin said that after about three days of eating only twice a day, he would become shaky, and that in all his life, he had never done that for more than three days at a time. He asked for permission to eat and I said, "Of course, if needed." When he got here, he meditated the first day, the second day, and so on, and was not hungry at all. One does not feel hungry if the meditation is progressing, but only when the meditation is not going well. Something inside is making one hungry. One cannot control the hunger then. Once the meditator is established in meditation, he does not feel hunger anymore.

The fourth soldier of Māra is the craving for various tastes and foods. You haven't eaten chicken curry for some time, you want to eat a kebab? Can't stay! Chicken is not served here, but we provide the best food we can. That is why they work so hard to prepare the food here, so that everyone will enjoy it and eat well.

What happens when very tasty, delicious food is eaten? Doesn't this stimulate more craving for food? Is it possible to eat without any appreciation of the taste of the food?... Only the *arahant* (fully liberated person) can do this. Wasn't the purpose of your coming here for this course to get rid of the *kilesa* (mental impurities), to get rid of the *taṇhā* (craving)? If you keep your eyes closed nothing can be seen, so you will not be craving and clinging for visual objects. The same goes for hearing. There is no one here with a tape recorder or radio playing songs by May Shin. You don't have to listen to them. It is the same with smell. Nobody here goes around wearing perfume, so there need not be any craving and clinging for any sense of smell. There is nothing here for you to feel that will give you pleasant bodily sensations. But the tongue—can it avoid taste? Only if you don't eat, and in that case a doctor would have to give you glucose injections for sustenance. Taste will occur when food comes in contact with the tongue. If you eat less tasty food, then craving and clinging for taste will be reduced.

Since you have come here to get rid of your defilements of craving, we should help you by providing the best environment so that they don't increase, shouldn't we? You are trying to annihilate them. We don't want to eradicate craving on the one hand, and increase it by food on the other. We do not provide an evening meal. By not providing it we have so much less to do. It is better for us and better for you too, because you are sure to become drowsy if you eat an evening meal. So you can do without it. If you eat well in the morning and at lunchtime the two meals will provide enough for your body's requirements.

The fifth soldier of Māra is drowsiness, sloth and torpor. You can understand this. Even Mahā Moggallāna (one of Buddha's chief disciples) suffered from it. Some of you can fall asleep while sitting. When I used to go for my meditation retreats, there was an old man who accompanied me. We sat in Saya Thetgyi's meditation center in the meditation room and he sat behind me wearing a big yogi shawl. A little while later, he started snoring aloud. Normally there are not many people who can sit and snore, but there are many meditators who can do this—sit and snore, then wake up! This is called *thīna-middha* (sloth and torpor). *Thīna-middha* cannot be avoided. When insight and wisdom become sharpened, the peaceful nature of *nibbāna* is felt; and when the wholesome and unwholesome natures clash, a reaction occurs and produces heat. Then the person becomes drowsy and sleepy.

If you feel drowsy at times, just breathe a bit harder; you've lost your *samādhi* (concentration). This is a kick from within. Your *samādhi* has gone. If you lose your *samādhi*, focus your attention on the nostrils again, breathe harder and try to calm down. Sometimes when the *aniccavijjā* (the wisdom of impermanence) becomes stronger, you experience the meeting of physical and mental experience in your body and your insight-intuition becomes very sharp and very strong. Then there's a very strong kick from within and you lose your understanding of *anicca* and become disoriented. You can't understand what happened and you ask the Teacher. If such a thing happens suddenly, there are two ways to cope with it. One method is to try and work to get re-established in *samādhi*, as I have told you. Or, you can go outside and wake yourself up and the reaction will pass away. Do not go and sleep when this reaction happens. I am giving you methods to cope. They are important from the practical aspect. Drowsiness always occurs when *saṅkhāras* (impurities) come up. Then we have to apply *anicca* firmly. It should not be just paying lip service to *anicca*, not just from the mouth. It should be the actual knowledge of the changing nature of the body with the awareness of sensations. If you practice in this way, you will overcome and win.

The sixth soldier of Māra is not wishing to be alone and being afraid of solitude. Some cannot sit in one room but keep changing rooms, looking for company and feel frightened when alone. Win Min Tham was among those who were afraid of solitude. Her house is very big but she dared not stay by herself in any room; she needed a companion at all times. She came here to meditate and brought a maid with her. She asked my permission to keep the lights on when she meditated in her room, so I allowed her to do so. Not only that, but somebody had to sit quite close to her when she meditated. She did not dare to stay alone. When she was by herself she felt flushed all over her body. After staying for a course, she got a little better. After the next course she was in the little cell by herself in the dark. She came regularly for ten days every month and benefited quite well from it. She was first class in being afraid but her fear is gone now. Isn't that nice?

The seventh soldier of Māra is doubt about whether one can be successful in meditation. I suppose this is true of everybody—wondering if his or her meditation will be successful or not. (That girl is laughing.) You can succeed. The important thing is to wash away the *akusala* (unwholesome conditioning), and *kilesa* (mental defilements) embedded in us. That is important.

The eighth soldier of Māra is becoming proud and arrogant when the meditation is successful. When the meditation improves, one can feel it inside. The defilements become lighter and one tends to get conceited and arrogant, and think, "That fellow does not seem to be doing too well. I'd better help him." I am saying this from my personal experience. A long time ago when I started this meditation center, for instance, we did not have a Dhamma hall then. There was a ten-foot square hut that was here when we bought the land. We used to sit in there and talk. One day U Hla Maung came out after the morning sitting and said, "Look." He hitched up his *longyi* and there were little lumps all over his thighs and legs just like the skin of a plucked duck. The kick from within was so strong that all those lumps appeared. He hitched his *longyi* up and showed us saying, "Please look. See how strong the kick from within was. You too, please try hard, please try hard."

This is why I'm telling you all not to preach. If there is anything that you want to ask, ask me. If there is anything that you want to say, tell me. When he preached, there was ego in it, the "I" was in it, "I am doing well. These people don't seem to be getting anywhere." He played very good soccer, was very short-tempered, ready to hit, strike and punch. When a very bad-tempered person with a lot of heat has a kick from inside, it shows up on the body surface. The next day U Hla Maung could not meditate. He could not feel any sensations and had to approach Sayagyi for guidance.

I am talking about others because I want to talk about the nature of things. If you progress in your practice, just stay quiet and proceed with your own meditation.

The ninth soldier of Māra refers to the Teacher and concerns becoming well known, receiving many offerings, gaining much respect and homage. I receive a lot of homage and offerings. I have to control myself to not get conceited. Look here, isn't it likely to cause conceit? I have to guard myself. We started this work here for the people of the Accountant General's office so they could meditate in their free time, but there are so few of them here now. We started this not on the basis of money, but on the basis of Dhamma. Any office worker who meditates for ten days becomes a member. The admission fee is ten days of meditation. Isn't it good? No need to pay a cent of subscription. Just meditate steadily, guard your practice, do not lose it. We started from that and have come to this.

Money can't do it. It was Dhamma that did it. We believe in this, and we do not have any money either.

This center does not belong to me. U Ba Khin should not get conceited, saying, "This is U Ba Khin's center." I do not own it. It belongs to the Vipassana Association of the Accountant General's office. I will have to leave if they drive me out. See, how nice! I do not own it. I have to be re-elected each year. Only if they re-elect me will I be here. If they say that they have found someone better than me, and elect that person, it's over for me. Or some members from the committee may not like me, they may say I talk too much and elect someone else. Then I would have to leave. I do not own the place.

The tenth soldier of Mára is following a false Dhamma, creating a new and special Dhamma, in order to acquire abundant offerings, praising oneself and looking down on others. This is why I do not want to say too much about others. Let others speak as they like about us, isn't that right? Some teachers get attached to receiving offerings. So as to get more students, they teach what the students would like—false teachings, teachings that are not Buddha's teachings—simply because they want the homage and offerings. They stop working with true Dhamma. That is the tenth soldier of Mára.

Dhamma dissolves sorrows and miseries and gives happiness. Who gives this happiness? The Buddha does not give it, it is the *aniccavijjā* (wisdom of impermanence) inside you that gives it. We should practice Vipassana so that the *aniccavijjā* will neither stop nor disappear. How do we practice? Focus your attention on the four elements, be calm, cultivate *samādhi* and do not let *sīla* (moral precepts) be broken. Telling lies is the one that I am afraid of among the precepts—I am not afraid of the others—because by lying, the basis of *sīla* is weakened. When *sīla* is weakened, *samādhi* will get weakened and *paññā* (wisdom) will also get weakened. Speak truthfully, work regularly, build up *samādhi* and pay attention to what is happening in your body; then the nature of *anicca* will come up naturally.

Our benefactor Saya Thetgyi said, "Very fast, vibrating incessantly, helter-skelter, broken up, burnt down, the destruction of
the body—these are the signs of impermanence." It is the body
that is changing. The thought that knows that the *rūpa* (matter) is
changing is the *nāma* (mind). When the *rūpa* changes and has gone,
the *nāma* which knew about the changed-and-gone *rūpa* also is
changed and goes. Both *rūpa* and *nāma* are *anicca*. Keep this in
your mind, be aware of it.

Focus your attention on the top of your head, and move down
through the whole body—from the top of the head to the forehead
and then the face, from the face to the neck, the neck to the shoulders, from the shoulders along to the hands. Wherever the mind
goes it may be like touching with a small torch and feeling the heat
wherever the torch touches, wherever the mind goes. Why? Because there is burning and annihilation taking place inside; it is the
innate nature of combustion of atomic units within. This is certainly present. Learn to be sensitive to it so that you can feel it. Try
it with an attentive mind and you will know.

Once the meditation is practiced and once one becomes aware
and observes with Vipassana knowledge, the defilements, the evil
samudaya akusala (arisen unwholesomeness) cannot remain much
longer. They have to leave gradually and when they are all gone,
the person becomes controlled and stable, and able to live well.

How long will one have to work? Until all the immeasurable,
uncountable old *akusala kamma* (unwholesome actions) accumulated along one's journey through the *saṃsāra* (cycle of rebirth)
are eradicated by observing the nature of *anicca*. Then one becomes
sotāpanna (one who has reached the first stage of saintliness, has
experienced *nibbāna*), and *ariyapuggala* (noble person). This cannot be achieved easily.

To reach the final *nibbāna* where all the *saṅkhāras* are abolished
is very far off, but wouldn't you like to try and see for yourself the
minor *nibbāna*? If it could be tasted only after death, these foreigners would never practice this meditation. They have tasted a

bit, liked it and have kept coming back from near and far. They send their friends and acquaintances who also come from afar. Why is this? Because they have experienced the taste of Dhamma.

It is important that there is a Teacher to help students to have a taste of Dhamma. But students have to work to experience the taste. What is this taste called? It is called the *dhamma rasa*. *"Sabba rasaṃ dhamma rasaṃ jināti"*—of all the tastes, the taste of Dhamma is the most noble, the best.

You have to try to work hard to get that taste. Just as the human monarch enjoys human pleasures, the *deva* (celestial being) monarch enjoys the *deva* pleasures and *brahmā* (a higher celestial being) enjoys *brahmā* pleasures; the noble *ariyas* (saintly persons) such as the Buddha and *arahants* can also enjoy the taste of the Dhamma that they have obtained. You must try hard until you too can enjoy this taste, but please do not work to the extreme, without moderation. Try to work according to the schedule we have given, work at the right time, to the fullest, with great care and effort.

Questions and Answers

Q: In a few words, what is learned from a meditation course?

S.N. Goenka: It teaches a way of life, a code of conduct, an art of living. The goal is to learn how to live peacefully and harmoniously, how to live in morality, how to live with control over the mind, and how to live with the spirit of the mind full of good qualities like love, compassion, goodwill.

Q: How do students learn Vipassana?

SNG: They have to join a meditation course. They have to live with the teacher, cut themselves off from all the connections with the outside world—at least for ten days. During this period they must abstain from all immoral activities of the body and the speech. Students train themselves to control their minds with the help of respiration. They start Vipassana by observing the reality pertaining to their own physical and mental structure, and by observing this they come out of their impurities.

Q: You say "control their minds with the aid of respiration." Are they doing breathing exercises?

SNG: No, it is not a breathing exercise. Actually, it is an exercise to develop the faculty of awareness. One starts observing the respiration as it is—not controlled respiration but natural respiration as it comes in, as it goes out. If a breath is long, it is long; if a breath is short, it is short—but natural.

Q: Doing this exercise for two or three days of a meditation course, when discomfort or agitation is experienced, how does one deal with it?

SNG: The meditators are free to change their position. This is not a physical exercise; one is not required to sit in a particular posture for a long time. They can sit in any posture that suits them, but, of course, they try to keep the back and neck straight.

Q: How does this technique differ from other meditation techniques, such as the use of mantras? Don't they also concentrate the mind?

SNG: With the help of visualization of any shape or form, one can easily get the mind concentrated, no doubt. But here the aim is to purify the mind, so this goes in a different direction. And mantras generate a particular type of artificial vibration. Every word, every mantra will generate a vibration, and if one keeps working with this mantra for long hours, one gets engulfed in the created vibration, whereas Vipassana wants you to observe the natural vibration that you have—vibrations when you become angry, or when you are full of passion, or fear, or hatred—so that you can observe them and come out of them.

Q: How do you actually observe this natural vibration?

SNG: Through sensations on the body, because every thought simultaneously generates a sensation on the body.

Q: Why does that happen?

SNG: Mind and matter are so interrelated that you can't separate them. When something arises in the mind, say anger, simultaneously there is bound to be some heat or tension in the body. This is a law of nature. You can't observe anger as abstract anger, but when you start observing the sensation on the body, which you experience at the time when you are generating anger in the mind, you can easily come out of anger.

Q: And by observing, do you control it?

SNG: No, controlling is a suppression. So far as Vipassana is concerned, there is neither suppression nor giving of free license. If you just observe, you will find that layer after layer of these impurities get eradicated.

Q: What are the practical benefits? I can see people sitting and meditating and coming out at the end of the course looking so wonderfully peaceful and happy, but how can someone apply this in everyday life with all the confusion that goes on?

SNG: People who come to a course like this for ten days are not supposed to come as an escape from the miseries of the worldly life. Actually, they come here to learn this technique so that they can apply it in their daily life. If Vipassana cannot be applied in daily life, then it is meaningless; it will become just another rite or ritual, and it won't help. So whoever learns the technique of Vipassana meditation tries to apply it to daily life.

Q: Could you be specific? How would someone in business, a factory worker, a housewife, or a doctor apply it?

SNG: Every person has some problem or other in life. There are tensions because of this problem and that problem. When tension arises, the mind gets confused and every decision is a wrong decision, and one generates negativities which are harmful to oneself and also to others. In the face of difficulties the good meditator of Vipassana will remain calm, even for a few moments, and then make a healthy decision, followed by positive action.

Q: Is this part of Buddhist religion? Can people of other religions practice it, or does it interfere with other kinds of religious practices? Why would Christians, for instance, want to do this?

SNG: One thing should be clear—this definitely is not Buddhist religion. At the same time it is definitely the teaching of Buddha. One should understand that Buddha means an enlightened person, a liberated person. Enlightened, liberated persons will never teach a religion, they will teach an art of life which is universal. They will never establish a sect or religion. So there is no such thing as "Buddhist religion"; it is an art of life. So anybody belonging to any community, to any sect, to any religious group can easily practice it because it is an art.

Peace of mind is sought by everyone; purity of mind is sought by everyone. Christ was a wonderful person who taught not only peace and harmony but also purity of mind, love, compassion. So those who follow the teachings of Christ certainly like to develop this good quality of purity, love, compassion. When they come to courses, they don't feel that they are coming to any foreign religion. A number of times very senior priests and nuns have told me that we are teaching Christianity in the name of Buddha.

Q: Is the diligent practice of Vipassana sufficient for progress, or must the general conduct and style of life change as a consequence of practice?

SNG: If the technique is practiced properly and continuously, automatically and unavoidably it will produce changes in the daily life. After all, this is the goal of practicing Vipassana. Naturally, mental purification will give rise to purification at the vocal and physical levels. However, to facilitate this process we need to make conscious effort to regulate our own conduct, that is, to abstain from actions that hurt or harm others and do actions that help others. Such behavior will help in the progress of Vipassana. As you increasingly progress, moral conduct will no longer be an imposed discipline but a normal, natural outcome of practice.

Q: What is the importance of nourishment, sexuality and livelihood in helping or hindering progress in meditation?

SNG: During an intensive meditation course it is essential that the meditator eat vegetarian food. Outside of that, it is sufficient that the meditator become moderate in nourishment, naturally taking care to eat healthy food. Many students become vegetarians naturally.

In the same way, during a course one is requested to abstain from any sexual activities, but in daily life you can continue to have sexual relations with your wife or husband. We have to also understand that the practice of Vipassana meditation leads you naturally to eliminate sexual desire. Gradually the meditator will become full of love for others without expecting anything in return. Passion is replaced by compassion. At this stage sexual activity becomes inadequate to express such pure love. Without any repression or suppression, the meditator enters into a stage of natural celibacy.

Regarding livelihood, a meditator can do any profession, but it should be a profession that does not harm other beings and that contributes to the welfare of others. In this regard, the most important thing is mental volition. Whatever job you are doing, you should do it with the feeling of serving society, in exchange for which you receive remuneration to maintain yourself and your family.

Q: Can people who have not taken a ten-day course observe the sensations on the body and be successful?

SNG: The ten-day course is not a rite or ritual. The ten-day course is to train people how to observe the sensations. Simply telling people will not work. They have to learn how to observe through actual practice, otherwise they will accept it on the intellectual level only; and at the actual level it becomes more difficult, because when an impurity arises it overpowers and you can't observe the sensations properly. Therefore, a ten-day meditation course is essential.

Q: So could anyone just cut themselves off for ten days and observe the sensations on the body, or do they need a teacher?

SNG: Because the technique is an operation of the mind and you go to the deeper levels of the mind and impurities come out on the surface, it is always advisable that the first lesson in the technique should be taken with somebody who is experienced. After ten days it is not necessary that all the time one should depend on a teacher. There is no "gurudom" in this technique. Nature is the guru and then you have the path and you can walk upon the path. Initially, when you make the operation, there must be a guide to tell you what is happening. A deep fear complex may come out, a deep passion complex may come out and one may lose the balance of the mind, so a guide is required to help youwork properly.

Q: So Vipassana actually is observing the sensations in the body while remaining equanimous?

SNG: Quite. It is observing the body and whatever arises in the body—the sensation. It is observing the mind and whatever arises in the mind. But the mind and whatever arises in the mind also manifest themselves as sensation on the body. Therefore, the basic principle is: observe the sensation on the body. Anything that arises in the mind will manifest itself as a sensation on the body; if you observe this sensation you are observing both the mind as well as matter.

Q: If we're not reacting to life situations are we really alive?

SNG: This is a very good question; it keeps coming up in many of the courses. People do not understand what the meaning of an equanimous or balanced mind is. Sometimes a misunderstanding arises, and they think that by developing an equanimous mind or detached mind they will be leading a life of inaction, that they will live like vegetables, letting anybody come and cut them because they are Vipassana meditators and they are equanimous. Actually this is not so; it is totally different. Vipassana will make the life full of action, but free from reaction. As it is, people are living the life of reaction; every moment they keep on reacting. And when you react with negativity, with craving or with aversion, your mind becomes unbalanced, you harm yourself, you harm others. But in a given situation, if somebody remains balanced and equanimous, even for a few moments, and then makes a decision, that decision is always the right decision—whatever action it takes is always positive. So then one's life becomes a life of positive action; it is not inaction, neither is it reaction.

Q: Some people would say that to sit and meditate all day is very selfish. What is your response? Is it better to isolate yourself or to be in the world as a student of Vipassana?

SNG: Certainly it would be very selfish if somebody wanted to live their whole life in a meditation center, only meditating and forgetting all about the world outside. Dhamma does not teach that. I keep saying to my students: "Go to the hospital to gain health, but not to live in the hospital for your whole life. Gain health and make use of this health in your daily life." You come to the meditation center to gain good mental health so that you can see this mental health in your daily life.

Q: So can people be involved in social issues and still devote time to doing Vipassana?

SNG: "Devoting time to Vipassana" is only when you join a course like this for ten days. Thereafter, it is a part of your life. You may lead a very good life as a social worker—you are serving people— but you will serve people much better if you serve yourself. If you keep your mind pure and full of peace and harmony, then you will find that your service is so positive, so effective. But deep inside, if you remain agitated, there is no peace in you, and then any service that you give will not be that effective.

Q: Do you need any special preparation to do this course?

SNG: The ten-day course *is* the preparation. Actually, you start from where you are and these ten days are your preparation for the whole life.

Conclusion

The following is an excerpt from the discourse S.N. Goenka gives at the end of a ten-day course. The guidance he offers to those who have just completed the intensive period of self-exploration also seems an appropriate conclusion to this book.

Covering one day after the other, one day after the other, we have come to the closing of this ten-day Dhamma seminar. When you started your work, you surrendered yourself, surrendered yourself to this technique. This was essential. Otherwise one does not give a fair trial to the technique. You all surrendered. Now ten days are over, and you are your own masters.

Having given a trial to the technique, going back home, you should review very calmly what you have learned here during these ten days. If you find that what you have learned here is logical, pragmatic, reasonable—only then accept it. A human being is a rational being. A human being should not accept things which are not acceptable even to normal intelligence. If you find that it is pragmatic, then only accept it. But this is not the only yardstick to measure the quality of the technique.

There are so many things in the world which look very pragmatic, very rational, but don't give any benefit. So, another yardstick is: "If I practice this is it going to give me any benefit—real benefit, tangible benefit?" Only then should one accept it. This is not something for intellectual entertainment. One must get real benefits in life by practicing it.

And not only these two, but there is one more yardstick to measure the quality of this technique of meditation. The third yardstick: "It looks very logical. If I practice, certainly it will give me benefit. But by my practicing it, will any being be harmed? Will it prove harmful to others? If so, it is not good. By my practicing it, will it also be beneficial to other beings? If so, it is acceptable."

If something is acceptable by using all these three yardsticks: that what I have learned here is rational, acceptable by the intellect, and good for me and for others without causing harm to anyone, then an intelligent person, a wise person, should have no hesitation in accepting it.

When a really wise person accepts, it will not be an acceptance merely at the devotional level, the emotional level. It should not be an acceptance merely at the intellectual level. The acceptance should be at the *actual* level, at the level of practice. Then only will it benefit you throughout your life. The life of a human being is a real life of a human being if one applies Dhamma in life, if one practices Dhamma. So one surrenders, and tries to live the life of Dhamma: the life of *sīla*, morality; the life of *samādhi*, developing mastery over the mind; the life of *paññā*, developing one's own wisdom to purify the mind; the life of *mettā, karuṇa*—love, compassion, goodwill for all others. One must *live* this life.

Of course, during the course, every evening we had a discourse, a Dhamma talk, for about an hour or so. This was not for intellectual entertainment. This was not to prove the superiority of this particular sect or that particular belief—nothing doing. The purpose of the Dhamma talk was to explain the technique: how you should practice, and why you should practice in this particular way— just to allow you to understand this.

When Dhamma talks are given, they are meant to explain the practical aspect of Dhamma. But at times, intentionally or unintentionally, the theoretical aspect of Dhamma comes to light in these Dhamma talks. And at times someone may have difficulty in accepting certain parts of the theoretical aspect of Dhamma. People coming from different backgrounds, different religions, in their first ten-day course—sometimes they have some hesitation in accepting certain parts of the theoretical aspect of Dhamma. So far as the practical aspect of Dhamma is concerned, I have not come across a single person coming from any community, any country, any tradition, who has any objection.

Any religion worth the name cannot have anything against *sīla*. Every religion asks us to live the life of *sīla*, the life of morality. This is what one is doing here. Any religion worth the name cannot have anything against a practice which makes us master of our own minds. To remain a slave of the mind is so dangerous, so harmful. The practice develops *samādhi* (mastery over the mind), and this too, with an object which is universal. The object is respiration, which is not limited to a particular sect, a particular religion, a particular belief or a particular dogma. The object is the truth pertaining to one's own self—the breath coming in, the breath going out. Nobody ever objects to this.

And the practice of *paññā* (developing your own wisdom). You see how you are generating negativities and becoming miserable. You stop generating negativities. You come out of your misery. Your mind becomes purer and purer. Nobody ever objects to this. Because, again, the object is truth—the truth pertaining to your own mind and matter; the contact between the two resulting in this sensation or that sensation. It is natural, universal; it is not limited to a particular sect, particular community, or particular religion. So the practical aspect of Dhamma is always acceptable to everyone. But about the theory—at times some difficulties arise.

If you find some difficulty in the theory: take it out; you won't miss much. Later on if it becomes understandable you can accept it then. Of course, one who has given the theoretical part of Dhamma has also given it with love and compassion so that the practical aspect becomes clearer.

There is a story from our country. A mother, with all the love and compassion and goodwill, prepared a very delicious dish for her child. We call it *khir*, a milk pudding made from very good quality milk, very good quality rice, with dried fruits, etc. A very delicious dish. It was offered to the child. But he said:

"No, I won't take it."

"Hey, what's wrong?"

"I won't take it. It is not in my plate. My plate is more important."

The mother had to give the dish again: "All right, your plate. Take it in your plate. Be happy now."

Again he said, "No, I won't take it."

"Why not? Now it is in your plate."

"There is a small black stone in it. I can't take it."

"That is not a black stone. It is cardamom. It has its own taste. Try it; it is so good."

"No, I won't take it. There is a black stone in it, there is black stone in it!"

The poor mother, what will she say? She says: "All right, if you think this is a black stone, then take it out. Enjoy the rest. Later on when you realize that this is also tasty, then enjoy it. But for now, take it out and enjoy the rest."

A mad child will throw away the whole plate: "There was a black stone in it, there was a black stone in it!"

So don't throw away the entire theoretical aspect of Dhamma. Whatever you find to be a "black stone," take it out; enjoy the rest. And have it in your plate." The terminology doesn't matter, as long as you understand the essence of Dhamma. But from the practical aspect, nothing can be taken out. *Sīla, samādhi, paññā:* nothing has to be taken out.

As long as you are practicing *sīla* (morality), *samādhi* (mastery of your own mind), and *paññā* (the wisdom that purifies the mind), you are practicing Dhamma and you will get benefits from it. It is the practical aspect of Dhamma which is of utmost importance.

If we accept the theoretical aspect without doing anything to practice Dhamma, it is useless, it will not help us. Again, there is a story. Once a professor was travelling in a ship. He was a young professor, not mature in life but very highly educated, with a number of alphabets after his name—a long tail of alphabets. And in the ship there was also a sailor, a worker—a very old, illiterate man. Sometimes he would come to the cabin of the professor, to listen to his words of wisdom: "What an intelligent person!" he thought, "What a learned person, wonderful person!"

One day after one of the talks, as the old man was leaving, the professor asked him: "Old man, have you studied geology?"

"What is geology, sir? I don't know. I have never been to any school, I have never been to any college. Please tell me, what is geology?"

"Geology is the science of the earth. Have you studied it?"

"No, sir. As I said, I have not studied anything."

"Oh, old man. You are so unfortunate. You have not studied geology. You have wasted one quarter of your life."

The old man was very sad. With a long face, he went out: "Such a learned person says I have wasted a quarter of my life. Certainly I must have wasted a quarter of my life."

The next day he came again. After a long talk, when he was leaving, again the professor asked him: "Old man, have you studied oceanology?"

"What is that, sir?"

"The science of the ocean, the sea."

"Oh no, sir. I have not studied anything."

"What an unfortunate person! You have wasted half of your life."

The old man felt very sorry: "I have wasted half of my life."

And the third day, again he was questioned: "Old man, have you studied meteorology?"

"What is this, sir? I have never heard this name."

"The science of the wind, the rain, the weather."

"No, sir. As I said, I have never been to any school or college. I have not studied anything."

"Old man, you are so unfortunate. You have not studied geology, the science of the earth on which you are living. You have not studied oceanology, the science of the sea on which you travel every day. You have not studied meteorology, the science of the wind, the rain, the weather which you encounter every day. You are very unfortunate. You have wasted three quarters of your life."

The old man, very sorry: "I have wasted three quarters of my life."

The next day it was the turn of the old man. He came running: "Professor sir, professor sir! Have you studied swimology?"

"What is swimology?"

"Can you swim, sir?"

"Oh, no, old man. I can't swim."

"I am so sorry, professor sir. You have wasted your whole life. There is a shipwreck now. This ship is going to sink. Those who can swim, they will reach the shore there. Those who can't swim... I am so sorry for you."

We may learn all the "-logies" of the world. But if we don't learn "swim-ology," then what is the use of all of these "-logies"? And even swimology: if we keep reading books on swimmology and keep discussing about swimmology without touching the water, then what is the use of this swimology? One has to learn how to actually swim because one has to swim the ocean of misery and reach the other shore, free from misery. And this is Dhamma. This is the practical aspect of Dhamma. This alone gives benefit. Mere intellectualization does not help. Mere devotionalism does not help. The actual experience is what helps; and this is what you were doing these ten days. It is what you can use for your life, to come out of all the suffering, the conditioning, the illusions and delusions, to enjoy real peace and harmony, real happiness.

Glossary of Pāli Terms

This glossary presents only those Pāli terms that are directly related to to the practice of Vipassana. For other words that may have appeared in the book the explanation was given in the context of the text, or in a footnote.

Adhiṭṭhāna   strong determination. One of the ten *pāramī*

Ānāpāna   respiration. *Ānāpāna-sati:* awareness of respiration.

Anattā   non-self, egoless, without essence, without substance. One of the three basic characteristics. See *lakkhaṇa.*

Anicca   impermanent, ephemeral, changing. One of the three basic characteristics. See *lakkhaṇa.*

Arahant / arahat   liberated being; one who has destroyed all his mental impurities. See *Buddha.*

Ariya   noble; saintly person. One who has purified his mind to the point that he has experienced the ultimate reality *(nibbāna).* There are four levels of *ariya,* from *sotāpanna* ('stream-enterer'), who will be reborn a maximum of seven times, up to *arahat,* who will undergo no further rebirth after his present existence.

Ariya aṭṭhaṅgika magga   the Noble Eightfold Path. See *magga.*

Ariya sacca   Noble Truth. See *sacca.*

Avijjā   ignorance, illusion. The first link in the chain of Conditioned Arising *(paṭicca samuppāda).* Together with *rāga* and *dosa,* one of the three principal mental defilements. These three are the root causes of all other mental impurities and hence of suffering. Synonym of *moha.*

Āyatana   sphere, region, esp. the six spheres of perception *(saḷāyatana),* i.e. the five physical senses plus the mind, and their corresponding objects, namely:
eye *(cakkhu)* and visual objects *(rūpa),*
ear *(sota)* and sound *(sadda),*
nose *(ghāna)* and odor *(gandha),*
tongue *(jivhā)* and taste *(rasa),*

body *(kāya)* and touch *(phoṭṭhabba),* mind *(mano)* and objects of mind, i.e., thoughts of all kinds *(dhamma).* These are also called the six faculties.

Bhaṅga dissolution. An important stage in the practice of Vipassana, the experience of the dissolution of the apparent solidity of the body into subtle vibrations which are constantly arising and passing away.

Bhāvanā mental development, meditation. The two divisions of *bhāvanā* are the development of calm *(samatha-bhāvanā),* corresponding to concentration of mind *(samādhi),* and the development of insight *(vipassanā-bhāvanā),* corresponding to wisdom *(paññā).* Development of *samatha* will lead to the states of *jhāna;* development of *vipassanā* will lead to liberation. See *jhāna, paññā, samādhi, vipassanā.*

Bhāvanā-mayā paññā wisdom developing from personal, direct experience. See *paññā.*

Bhikkhu (Buddhist) monk; meditator. Feminine form *bhikkhunī:* nun.

Bodhisatta literally, 'enlightenment-being.' One who is working to become a Buddha. Used to designate Siddhattha Gotama in the time before he achieved full enlightenment. Sanskrit *bodhisattva.*

Bojjhaṅga factor of enlightenment, i.e. quality that helps one to attain enlightenment. The seven such factors are awareness *(sati),* penetrating investigation of Dhamma *(Dhamma-vicaya),* effort *(viriya),* bliss *(pīti),* tranquillity *(passaddhi),* concentration *(samādhi),* equanimity *(upekkhā).*

Buddha enlightened person; one who has discovered the way to liberation, has practiced it, and has reached the goal by his own efforts. There are two types of Buddha:
1) *pacceka-buddha,* 'lone' or 'silent' Buddha, who is unable to teach the way he has found to others;
2) *sammā-sambuddha,* 'full' or 'perfect' Buddha, who is able to teach others.

Cakka wheel, *bhava-cakka,* wheel of continuing existence (i.e., process of suffering), equivalent to *saṃsāra. Dhamma-cakka,* the wheel of Dhamma (i.e., the teaching or process of liberation). *Bhava-cakka* corresponds to the Chain of Conditioned Arising in its usual order. *Dhamma-cakka* corresponds to the chain in reverse order, leading not to the multiplication but to the eradication of suffering.

Cintā-mayā-paññā wisdom gained by intellectual analysis. See *paññā.*

Citta mind. *Cittānupassanā,* observation of the mind. See *satipaṭṭhāna.*

Dhamma   phenomenon; object of mind; nature; natural law; law of liberation, i.e. teaching of an enlightened person. *Dhammānupassanā,*
observation of the contents of the mind. See *satipaṭṭhāna.* (Sanskrit
dharma.)

Dosa   aversion. Together with *rāga* and *moha,* one of the three principal
mental defilements.

Dukkha   suffering, unsatisfactoriness. One of the three basic characteristics (see *lakkhaṇa).* The first Noble truth (see *sacca).*

Jhāna   state of mental absorption or trance. There are eight such states
which may be attained by the practice of *samādhi,* or *samatha-bhāvanā*
(see *bhāvanā).* Cultivation of them brings tranquillity and bliss, but does
not eradicate the deepest-rooted mental defilements.

Kalāpa / aṭṭha-kalāpa   smallest indivisible unit of matter, composed of the
four elements and their characteristics.

Kamma   action, specifically an action performed by oneself that will have
an effect on one's future. See *saṅkhāra.* (Sanskrit *karma.*)

Kāya   body. *Kāyānupassanā,* observation of body. See *satipaṭṭhāna.*

Khandha   mass, group, aggregate. A human being is composed of five
aggregates: matter *(rūpa),* consciousness *(viññāṇa),* perception *(saññā),*
feeling / sensation *(vedanā),* reaction *(saṅkhāra).*

Lakkhaṇa   sign, distinguishing mark, characteristic. The three characteristics *(ti-lakkhaṇa)* are *anicca, dukkha, anattā.* The first two are common
to all conditioned phenomena. The third is common to all phenomena,
conditioned and unconditioned.

Loka   1. the macrocosm, i.e. universe, world, plane of existence; 2. the
microcosm, i.e. the mental-physical structure. *Loka-dhammā,* worldly
vicissitudes, the ups and downs of life that all must encounter, that is,
gain or loss, victory or defeat, praise or blame, pleasure or pain.

Magga   path. *Ariya aṭṭhaṅgika magga,* the Noble Eightfold Path leading to
liberation from suffering. It is divided into three stages or trainings:

I. *sīla,* morality, purity of vocal and physical actions:
  i. *sammā-vācā,* right speech;
  ii. *sammā-kammanta,* right actions;
  iii *sammā-ājīva,* right livelihood;

II. *samādhi,* concentration, control of one's own mind:
  iv. *sammā-vāyāma,* right effort;

v. *sammā-sati*, right awareness;

iv. *sammā-samādhi*, right concentration;

III. *paññā*, wisdom, insight which totally purifies the mind:

vii. *sammā-saṅkappa*, right thought;

viii *sammā-diṭṭhi*, right understanding.

Magga is the fourth of the Four Noble Truths. See *sacca.*

Māra   death; negative force, evil one.

Mettā   selfless love and good will. One of the qualities of a pure mind, one of the *pāramī. Mettā-bhāvanā*, the systematic cultivation of *mettā* by a technique of meditation.

Nibbāna   extinction; freedom from suffering; the ultimate reality; the unconditioned. (Sanskrit *nirvāṇa.)*

Pāli   line; text; the texts recording the teaching of the Buddha; hence language of these texts. Historical, linguistic, and archaeological evidence indicates that this was a language actually spoken in northern India at or near the time of the Buddha. At a later date the texts were translated into Sanskrit, which was exclusively a literary language.

Paññā   wisdom. The third of the three trainings by which the Noble Eightfold Path is practiced (see *magga*). There are three kinds of wisdom: received wisdom *(suta-mayā paññā)*, intellectual wisdom *(cintā-mayā paññā)*, and experiential wisdom *(bhāvanā-mayā paññā)*. Of these, only the last can totally purify the mind; it is cultivated by the practice of *vipassanā-bhāvanā.* Wisdom is one of the five mental strengths, of the seven factors of enlightenment (see *bojjhaṅga*), and of the ten *pāramī.*

Pāramī / pāramitā   perfection, virtue; wholesome mental quality that helps to dissolve egoism and thus leads one to liberation. The ten *pāramī* are: charity *(dāna)*, morality *(sīla)*, renunciation *(nekkhamma)*, wisdom *(paññā)*, effort *(viriya)*, tolerance *(khanti)*, truthfulness *(sacca)*, strong determination *(adhiṭṭhāna)*, selfless love *(mettā)*, equanimity *(upekkhā)*

Paṭicca samuppāda   the chain of Conditioned Arising; causal genesis. The process, beginning in ignorance, by which one keeps making life after life of suffering for oneself.

Rūpa   1. matter; 2. visual object. See *āyatana, khandha.*

Sacca   truth. The Four Noble truths *(ariya-sacca)* are:

1. the truth of suffering *(dukkha-sacca);*

2. the truth of the origin of suffering *(samudaya-sacca);*

3. the truth of the cessation of suffering *(nirodha-sacca);*
4. the truth of the path leading to the cessation of suffering *(magga-sacca).*

Samādhi   concentration, control of one's own mind. The second of the three trainings by which the Noble Eightfold Path is practiced (see *magga*). When cultivated as an end in itself, it leads to the attainment of the states of mental absorption *(jhāna),* but not to total liberation of the mind. Three types of *samādhi* are:

1. *khaṇika samādhi,* momentary concentration, concentration sustained from moment to moment;
2. *upacāra samādhi,* 'neighborhood' concentration, of a level approaching a state of absorption;
3. *appanā samādhi,* attainment concentration, a state of mental absorption *(jhāna).*

Of these, *khaṇika samādhi* is sufficient preparation in order to be able to begin the practice of *vipassanā.*

Samatha   calm, tranquillity. *Samatha-bhāvanā,* the development of calm; synonymous with *samādhi.* See *bhāvanā.*

Sampajañña   understanding of the totality of the mind-matter phenomenon, i.e. insight into its impermanent nature at the level of sensation.

Saṅgha   congregation; community of *ariyā,* i.e. those who have experienced *nibbāna;* community of Buddhist monks or nuns; a member of the *ariya-saṅgha, bhikkhu-saṅgha* or *bhikkhnī-saṅgha.*

Saṅkhāra   (mental) formation; volitional activity; mental reaction; mental conditioning. One of the five aggregates *(khandhā),* as well as the second link in the Chain of Conditioned Arising *(paṭicca samuppāda). Saṅkhāra* is the *kamma,* the action that gives future results and that thus is actually responsible for shaping one's future life. (Sanskrit *saṃskāra).*

Saṅkhārupekkhā   literally, equanimity towards *saṅkhārā.* A stage in the practice of Vipassana, subsequent to the experience of *bhaṅga,* in which old impurities lying dormant in the unconscious rise to the surface level of the mind and manifest as physical sensations. By maintaining equanimity *(upekkhā)* towards these sensations, the meditator creates no new *saṅkhārā* and allows the old ones to pass away. Thus the process leads gradually to the eradication of all *saṅkhārā.*

Saññā   (from *saṃyutta-ñāṇā,* conditioned knowledge) perception, recognition. One of the five aggregates *(khandhā).* It is ordinarily conditioned by one's past *saṅkhārā,* and therefore conveys a colored image of reality.

In the practice of Vipassana, *saññā* is changed into *paññā*, the understanding of reality as it is. It becomes *anicca-saññā, dukkha-saññā, anattā-saññā, asubha-saññā*—that is, the perception of impermanence, suffering, egolessness, and of the illusory nature of physical beauty.

Sati awareness. A constituent of the Noble Eightfold Path (see *magga*), as well as one of the five mental strengths and the seven factors of enlightenment (see *bojjhaṅga*). *Ānāpāna-sati*, awareness of respiration.

Satipaṭṭhāna the establishing of awareness. There are four interconnected aspects of *satipaṭṭhāna:*
1. observation of body *(kāyānupassanā);*
2. observation of sensations arising within the body *(vedanānupassanā);*
3. observation of mind *(cittānupassanā);*
4. observation of the contents of the mind *(dhammānupassanā)*
All four are included in the observation of sensations, since sensations are directly related to body as well as to mind. The *Mahā-Satipaṭṭhāna Suttanta (Dīgha Nikāya, 22)* is the main primary source in which the theoretical basis for the practice of *vipassanā-bhāvanā* is explained.

Sīla morality; abstaining from physical and vocal actions that cause harm to oneself and others. The first of the three trainings by which the Noble Eightfold Path is practiced (see *magga*). For a lay person, *sīla* is practiced in daily life by following the Five precepts.

Sotāpanna one who has reached the first stage of saintliness, and has experienced *nibbāna*. See *ariya*.

Suta-mayā paññā literally, wisdom gained from listening to others. Received wisdom. See *paññā*.

Sutta discourse of the Buddha or one of his leading disciples. (Sanskrit *sutra*.)

Taṇhā literally, 'thirst.' Includes both craving and its reverse image of aversion. The Buddha identified *taṇhā* as the cause of suffering *(samudaya-sacca)* in his first sermon, the "Discourse Setting in Motion the Wheel of Dhamma" *(Dhammacakkappavattana Sutta)*. In the Chain of Conditioned Arising *(paṭicca samuppāda)* he explained that *taṇhā* originates as a reaction to bodily sensations.

Theravāda literally, 'teaching of the elders.' The teachings of the Buddha, in the form in which they have been preserved in the countries of south Asia (Burma, Sri Lanka, Thailand, Laos, Cambodia). Generally recognized as the oldest form of the teachings.

Tipiṭaka (Sanskrit *Tripiṭaka.*) The three collections of the teachings of the Buddha namely:
1. *Vinaya-piṭaka,* the collection of monastic discipline;
2. *Sutta-piṭaka,* the collection of discourses;
3. *Abhidhamma-piṭaka,* the collection of the higher teaching, i.e. systematic philosophical exegesis of the Dhamma.

Upekkhā equanimity; the state of mind free from craving, aversion, ignorance. One of the four pure states of mind, the seven factors of enlightenment (see *bojjhaṅga*), and the ten *pāramī.*

Vedanā feeling / sensation. One of the five aggregates *(khandhā).* Described by the Buddha as having both mental and physical aspects; therefore *vedanā* offers a means to examine the totality of the mental-physical phenomenon. In the Chain of Conditioned Arising *(paṭicca samuppāda),* the Buddha explained that *taṇhā,* the cause of suffering, arises as a reaction to *vedanā.* By learning to observe *vedanā* objectively one can avoid any new reactions, and can experience directly within oneself the reality of impermanence *(anicca).* This experience is essential for the development of detachment, leading to liberation of the mind.

Vedanānupassanā observation of sensations within the body. See *satipaṭṭhāna.*

Viññāṇa consciousness, cognition. One of the five aggregates *(khandhā).*

Vipassanā introspection, insight which purifies the mind; specifically insight into the impermanent, suffering, and egoless nature of the mental-physical structure. *Vipassanā-bhāvanā,* the systematic development of insight through the meditation technique of observing the reality of oneself by observing sensations within the body.

Yathā-bhūta literally, 'as it is.' The existing reality. *Yathā-bhūta-ñāna-dassana,* knowledge-realization of truth as it is.

Bibliography

The following works are by teachers, assistant teachers, and students of Vi-passana meditation in the tradition of Sayagyi U Ba Khin. They deal directly with the practice or with closely related subjects. All are available from Pariyatti Book Service: www.pariyatti.com; 800-829-2748.

The Essentials of Buddha-Dhamma in Meditative Practice
by Sayagyi U Ba Khin
A brief essay of extraordinary concision, clarity, and power, in which the teacher of S.N. Goenka sums up the technique of Vipassana.
Vipassana Research Publications, Seattle, 1995; 25 pages
The Essentials of Buddha-Dhamma in Meditative Practice is also available as an audio tape, with an interview with S.N. Goenka on the B side.

Sayagyi U Ba Khin Journal
A varied selection of articles by Sayagyi U Ba Khin, S.N. Goenka, assistant teachers and other meditators.
Vipassana Research Institute, Bombay, 1994; 320 pages

S.N. Goenka: The Discourse Summaries
A condensation of each of the eleven discourses given by S.N. Goenka in a ten-day Vipassana meditation course. Also includes Pāli passages quoted in the discourses with their translation, and a glossary of Pāli terms.
Vipassana Research Institute, Bombay,1995; 95 pages

Satipaṭṭhāna Sutta Discourses of S.N. Goenka
by S.N. Goenka, condensed by Patrick Given-Wilson
A condensed version of S.N. Goenka's discourses from a seven-day meditation course on the *Mahāsatipaṭṭhāna Sutta*. Mr. Goenka reads and interprets the *sutta* in these discourses, giving life and inspiring relevance to the primary text from the Buddha's teaching about meditation practice.
(Available singly or paired with the annotated translation of the *Mahāsatipaṭṭhāna Sutta*, below.)
Vipassana Research Publications, Seattle,1999; 138 pages

Mahāsatipaṭṭhāna Sutta
The principal discourse in which the Buddha explains the technique of
Vipassana. The original Pāli and English translation, reflecting the
approach of S.N. Goenka, on opposing pages.
Vipassana Research Publications, Seattle, 1996; 94 pages

The Gracious Flow of Dharma
by S.N. Goenka
A three-day series of public talks given in Hyderabad, India. The Sanskrit word *Dharma* (spelled *Dhamma* in the Pāli language) originally
meant "the law of nature" or "the truth." In today's India, unfortunately,
the word has lost its original meaning, and is mistakenly used to refer to
"sect" or "sectarianism." Using this theme as an introduction, Goenkaji
explains that Vipassana meditation teaches how to live a life of pure
Dharma—a life full of peace, harmony and goodwill for others.
Vipassana Research Institute, Bombay,1994; 70 pages

Dhamma Verses (book and audio tape)
by S.N. Goenka
A collection of inspiring Hindi *dohas* (couplets) composed and chanted
by S.N. Goenka in the tradition of the poet-sages of India. The book
contains Hindi and English translation.
Vipassana Research Publications, Seattle, 1999; 78 pages; tape: 92 minutes

Come, People of the World
by S.N. Goenka
An inspirational collection of Hindi verses of S.N. Goenka from a Vipassana course. These are transliterated into Roman script and appear
together with their English rendering.
Vipassana Research Institute, Bombay, 1992; 35 pages

The Art of Living: Vipassana Meditation as Taught by S.N. Goenka
by William Hart
A full-length study of the teaching of S.N. Goenka, prepared under his
guidance and with his approval. Useful for meditators and non-meditators alike.
Harper San Francisco, 1987; 170 pages

The Art of Living Audiobook
The definitive guide to the teaching of S.N. Goenka, prepared with his
approval by William Hart, who also narrates this audio book. The practice of Vipassana is accurately described for a general audience and

vividly conveys Goenkaji's inspiring teaching style, with original stories
from the ten-day discourses by Goenkaji himself.
Pariyatti Audio Editions, 1999; 4 cassettes / 5 hours

The Noble Eightfold Path and Its Factors Explained
by Ledi Sayadaw, tr. U Saw Tun Teik
This and the three following works are presentations of the teachings of
the Buddha aimed particularly at Westerners. They are by one of the
modern predecessors of S.N. Goneka, renowned in his time as a scholar
and master meditation teacher.
Buddhist Publication Society, Kandy, Sri Lanka,1977 (Wheel Publication
No. 245/247); 92 pages

The Requisites of Enlightenment
by Ledi Sayadaw, tr. U Sein Nyo Tun
Buddhist Publication Society, Kandy, Sri Lanka, 1971 (Wheel Publication
No. 171-174); 127 pages

A Manual of Insight
by Ledi Sayadaw, tr. Sayadaw U Nyana
Buddhist Publication Society, Kandy, Sri Lanka, 1961 (Wheel Publication
No. 31/32); 87 pages

The Buddhist Philosophy of Relations
by Ledi Sayadaw, tr. Sayadaw U Nyana
Buddhist Publication Society, Kandy, Sri Lanka, 1986 (Wheel Publication
No. 331/333); 82 pages

Essence of Tipitaka
compiled by U Ko Lay
An overview of the collection of Pāli texts that contain the teaching of
the Buddha, with a brief summary of the contents, prepared by a leading
student of Sayagyi U Ba Khin.
Vipassana Research Institute, Bombay,1995; 221 pages

Tranquility and Insight,
by Amadeo Sole-Leris
This work covers the entire range of meditation approaches described in
the Visuddhimagga, in the two divisions of *samatha* (concentration or
tranquility) and *vipassanā* (insight). It also examines the two major contemporary forms of the traditional teaching, one of these being
Vipassana meditation as taught by S.N. Goenka.
Buddhist Publication Society, Kandy, Sri Lanka, 1992; 176 pages

Karma and Chaos
by Paul R. Fleischman, M.D.
Collected essays on Vipassana meditation by an eminent psychiatrist
who practices and teaches Vipassana. Dr Fleischman explores the inter-
face between psychiatry, science and the timeless teaching of the
Buddha.
Vipassana Research Publications, Seattle, 1999; 160 pages

Cultivating Inner Peace
by Paul R. Fleischman, M.D.
Examines the factors involved in cultivating that elusive human quality:
inner peace.
U.S.A.: Tarcher/Putnam, 1997; 300 pages

A Re-appraisal of Patanjali's Yoga-sutras in the light of the Buddha's Teaching
by S.N. Tandon
"Siddhārtha Gotama the Buddha, who lived in the 6th century B.C.,
preceded Patanjali by a few centuries… While Patanjali, the author of the
Yoga-Sutras, could draw upon the oral as well as the living tradition of
the Buddha's teaching, which were extant in his time, his commentators
and sub-commentators remained ignorant of both. This fact itself seems
to have resulted in inadequate—and, at times, uncalled for—interpretations being offered by these commentators when explaining the *Yoga-Sutras.*
The flaw can be rectified by attempting a reappraisal of the *Yoga-Sutras*
in the light of the Buddha's teaching as enshrined in the Pāli Canon."
— *from the Preface, by S.N Tandon*
Vipassana Research Institute, Bombay, 1995; 142 pages

Vipassana, Its Relevance to the Present World
A collection of reports presented at an international seminar sponsored
by the Vipassana Research Institute, held at the Indian Institute of Technology in New Delhi in April, 1994. The papers focus on Vipassana's
impact in the fields of education, prison reform, improved management
in business and government, physical and mental health, and the Pāli
Tipiṭaka research and publication project.
Vipassana Research Institute, Bombay, 1995; 141 pages

Dharma — Its True Nature
A report on the proceedings of an international conference held at
Dhamma Giri, Igatpuri, India in May, 1995. The papers and discussion
focus on the meaning of the word "*Dharma*" which in India is synonymous with "religion." Papers are interspersed with lively discussion

extracts about the definition of the term Dharma and focus on the role of Dharma in relation to current social issues, science, and the rapidly changing nature of society today.
Vipassana Research Institute, Bombay, 1995; 75 pages

Vipassana Pagoda
A Souvenir from the Groundbreaking Ceremony, October 26, 1997. In 1998 construction began on the Grand Pagoda Project outside Bombay, India. A huge pagoda 325 feet tall will be built to spread awareness of the Buddha's teaching and the meditation technique of Vipassana. The pagoda will be able to accommodate nearly 10,000 meditators in its central hall and will house genuine Buddha relics. This book is a souvenir commemorating this awe-inspiring project and includes articles about the current growth of Vipassana written by S.N. Goenka and many others.
Global Vipassana Foundation, Bombay,1997; 127 pages

The Wheel of Dhamma Rotates Around the World
Full color photographs and descriptions of Vipassana meditation centers around the world.
Vipassana Research Institute, Bombay, 1996; 37 pages

Contact Information for Vipassana Centers

Courses of Vipassana meditation in the tradition of Sayagyi U Ba Khin as taught by S.N. Goenka are held regularly in many countries around the world. Worldwide schedules, information and application forms are available from the Vipassana website: www.dhamma.org. *Information may also be obtained from the following primary centers:*

Australia

Vipassana Meditation Centre　　　　　　　　*Dhamma Bhūmi*
　P.O. Box 103, Blackheath, NSW 2785
　☎　[61] (2)4787-7436; Fax: [61] (2) 47877-7 221
　Email: info@bhumi.dhamma.org

Vipassana Centre Queensland　　　　　　　　*Dhamma Rasmi*
　P.O. Box 119, Rules Road, Pomona, Qld 4568
　☎　[61] (7) 5485-2452; Fax: [61] (7) 5485-2907

Vipassana Meditation Tasmania　　　　　　　*Dhamma Pabhā*
　GPO Box 6A, Hobart, Tas 7001
　☎　[61] (3) 6263-6785
　Email: mjr@southcom.com.au

Canada

Quebec Vipassana Meditation Center　　　　　*Dhamma Suttama*
　(1738 Scenic Road; Sutton, Quebec)
　c/o P.O. Box 32083, Les Atriums, Montreal, QC H2L 4Y5
　☎　[1] (514) 481-3507; Fax: [1] (514) 879-3437
　Email: info@suttama.dhamma.org

Vipassana Meditation Center of B.C.　　　　　*Dhamma Surabhi*
　Box 529, 3495 Cambie St., Vancouver, BC V5Z 4R3
　☎　[1] (604) 730-9877
　Email: info@surabhi.dhamma.org

France

European Vipassana Centre　　　　　　　　　*Dhamma Mahī*
　"Le Bois Planté," 89350 Louesme, Champignelles
　☎　[33] (386) 45-75-14; Fax: [33] (386) 45-76-20
　Email: info@mahi.dhamma.org

Germany

Vipassana Meditationshaus　　　　　　　　　*Dhamma Geha*
　Kirchenweg 2; 76332 Bad Herrenalb
　Tel: [49](7083) 51169; Fax: [49](7083) 51328
　Email: dhammageha@aol.com

India

Vipassana International Academy   *Dhamma Giri*
P.O. Box No. 6, Igatpuri 422 403 (Dist. Nasik), Maharashtra
☎ [91] (2553) 84076, 84086; Fax: [91] (2553) 84176

Vipassana International Meditation Centre   *Dhamma Khetta*
12.6km. Nagarjun Sagar Road, Kusum Nagar, Vanasthali Puram
Hyderabad, 500 070 A.P.
☎ [91] (40)402- 0290, 402- 1746
City off. [91] (40) 473-2569; Fax: [91] (40) 241-005
Email: bprabhat@hd1.vsnl.net.in

Vipassana Centre   *Dhamma Thalī*
P.O. Box 208, Jaipur 302 001, Rajasthan
☎ [91] (141) 641-520

KutchVipassana Centre   *Dhamma Sindhu*
Gram Bada, Dist. Mandvi, Kutch 370 475, Gujarat
☎ [91](283) 420-076; Fax:[91](283) 420-997

Vipassana Centre   *Dhamma Gaṅgā*
Baro Temple, Sodpur, Panihati (Calcutta) 743 176, West Bengal
☎ [91] (33) 553-2855
City off.: 9 Bonfield Lane, Calcutta 700 001
☎ [91] (33) 251 767, 258 063; Fax: [91] (33) 275 174

Himachal Vipassana Centre   *Dhamma Sikhara*
above Elysium House, Macleod Ganj, Dharamsala 176 219
Dist. Kangra, H.P.
☎ [91](189) 221-309; Fax: [91](189) 221-578

Japan

Japan Vipassana Centre   *Dhamma Bhānu*
Iwakamioku Hatta, Mizuho-Cho, Funai-Gun, Kyoto-Fu 622-0324
☎ & Fax: [81] (771) 860- 765
Email: info@bhanu.dhamma.org

Myanmar

Vipassana Centre   *Dhamma Joti*
Nga Htat Gyi Pagoda Road, Bahan Township, Yangon
☎ [95] (01) 549-290; Fax: [95](01) 289-965

Nepal

Nepal Vipassana Centre   *Dharmashriṅga*
Budhanilkantha, Muhan Pokhari, Kathmandu
☎ [977] (1) 371-655, 371-007
City off.:Jyoti Bhawan, Kantipath, P.O. Box 133, Kathmandu
☎ [977](1) 225-490; Fax: [977] (1) 224-720, 226-314

New Zealand

Vipassana Centre   *Dhamma Medinī*
  Burnside Road, RD3 Kaukapakapa
  ☎ [64] (9) 420-5319

Sri Lanka

Vipassana Meditation Centre   *Dhamma Kūṭa*
  Mowbray Galaha Road, Hindagala, Peradeniya
  c/o: Mr Brindley Ratwatte, 262 Katugastota Road, Kandy
  ☎ [94] (8) 34649; Fax: [94](01) 573-054

Thailand

Thailand Vipassana Centre   *Dhamma Kamala*
  200 Baan Nerrupasuk, Tambon Dongkheelek,
  Amphur Muang, Prachinburi 25000
  For registration contact: c/o Mrs Pornphen Leenutaphong
  929 Rama I Road, Patumwan, Bangkok
  ☎ [66] (2) 216-4772; Fax: [66] (037) 403-515
  Email: pornphen@bkk.a-net.net.th

United Kingdom

Vipassana Centre   *Dhamma Dīpa*
  Harewood End, Hereford, HR2 8JS, England.
  ☎ [44] (1989) 730 234, Fax: [44] (1989) 730 450
  Email: info@dipa.dhamma.org

U. S. A.

Vipassana Meditation Center   *Dhamma Dharā*
  P.O. Box 24, Shelburne Falls, MA 01370
  ☎ [1] (413) 625-2160; Fax: [1] (413) 625 2170
  Email: info@dhara.dhamma.org

California Vipassana Center   *Dhamma Mahāvana*
  P.O. Box 1167, North Fork, CA 93643
  ☎ [1] (559) 877 4386, Fax: [1] (559) 877 4387
  Email: info@mahavana.dhamma.org

Northwest Vipassana Center   *Dhamma Kuñja*
  P.O. Box 345, Ethel, WA 98542
  ☎ [1] (360) 978-5434; Fax: [1] (360) 978-5433
  Email: info@kunja.dhamma.org

Southwest Vipassana Meditation Center *Dhamma Sirī*
  P.O. Box 190248, Dallas, TX 75219
  ☎ [1] (214) 521-5258, 932-7868; Fax: [1] (214) 522-5973
  Email: info@siri.dhamma.org